ADVANCE PRAISE FOR

TRUSTING SCHOOLS AND TEACHERS

"This is an extremely important and groundbreaking work of scholarship. The authors adopt a low-key, dispassionate tone, recognizing the validity of different positions on what they refer to as a spectrum of approaches to school evaluation. Yet the values of the work are clearly located in a concept of enhanced teacher professionalism. Perhaps most important, the book provides a blueprint for development that can facilitate both professional autonomy and public accountability. This book is an important contribution to the international literature on evaluation. It uses the Irish context not just as a case study but as an exemplar of how a serious engagement with educational politics can provide professionally satisfying outcomes. In doing so, it elevates educational evaluation from the realm of fraught political tensions to a site of teacher empowerment and professional fulfillment."

Gary Granville, Head of Faculty of Education,
National College of Art and Design, Dublin

"*Trusting Schools and Teachers* offers informative insights into the complexities of developing and implementing meaningful school evaluation in the European Union but more specifically in Ireland. For an experienced U.S. evaluator and aspiring evaluation scholar, this book echoes similarly noted challenges to establish school-based evaluation communities led by school principals and teachers. Gerry McNamara and Joe O'Hara do not attempt to disguise the blemishes that were evident in the critically important educational evaluation efforts undertaken in Ireland via its Whole School Evaluation and Looking at Our Schools initiatives. Rather, they present these blemishes as opportunities for increasing their understanding of this new phenomenon of school-based evaluation in Ireland for the purpose of refining their future efforts."

Stafford Hood, Associate Dean for Research, Professor of Psychology of Education,
Mary Lou Fulton College of Education, Arizona State University

TRUSTING SCHOOLS AND TEACHERS

Irish Studies

Robert Mahony
General Editor

Vol. 8

PETER LANG
New York • Washington, D.C./Baltimore • Bern
Frankfurt am Main • Berlin • Brussels • Vienna • Oxford

Gerry McNamara and Joe O'Hara

TRUSTING
SCHOOLS AND
TEACHERS

Developing Educational
Professionalism
Through
Self-Evaluation

PETER LANG
New York • Washington, D.C./Baltimore • Bern
Frankfurt am Main • Berlin • Brussels • Vienna • Oxford

MT

Library of Congress Cataloging-in-Publication Data

McNamara, Gerry.
Trusting schools and teachers: developing educational professionalism
through self-evaluation / Gerry McNamara, Joe O'Hara.
p. cm.—(Irish studies; v. 8)
Includes bibliographical references and index.
1. Teachers—Self-rating of—Ireland. 2. Educational
evaluation—Ireland. I. O'Hara, Joe. II. Title.
LB2838.M388   371.14'4—dc22   2007023365
ISBN 978-0-8204-8638-3
ISSN 1043-5743

Bibliographic information published by **Die Deutsche Bibliothek**.
Die Deutsche Bibliothek lists this publication in the "Deutsche
Nationalbibliografie"; detailed bibliographic data is available
on the Internet at http://dnb.ddb.de/.

The paper in this book meets the guidelines for permanence and durability
of the Committee on Production Guidelines for Book Longevity
of the Council of Library Resources.

Printed in Germany

10/13/09

To our respective wives,
Linda and Rachel,
for their help, support and patience.

CONTENTS

Part 3: Developing the Self-Evaluating Teacher

INTRODUCTION

The primary purpose of this book is to describe an experimental approach to the empowerment of teachers and schools, enabling them to become self-evaluating entities. Part one of the book describes how the evaluation and inspection of many public services, including education, has become increasingly common in most countries in the developed world. There are various reasons why this may be the case. It can be argued that it is, on the one hand, part of the movement towards low-trust policies derived from the ideology of neoliberalism which seeks to apply the values of the market to the public sector. On the other hand, it can be argued that increased evaluation is a necessary and defensible component of democratic accountability, responsibility and transparency.

What cannot be denied is that this process of evaluation and inspection, both at the level of nation states and through the policies of influential organisations such as the OECD, the EU and the World Bank, continues to gather pace. However, there is also a growing debate regarding the appropriate extent of such evaluation, particularly as research increasingly shows that external monitoring of an intrusive kind can seriously damage the autonomy and morale of professionals and organisations. In consequence, in many areas of professional regulation and in relation to the public sector in particular, a worldwide debate continues as to the balance to be achieved between accountability and professional autonomy, between professional development and external judgement.

As part of this debate a relatively new concept has begun to gain sway. This suggests that professionals should be empowered to systematically analyse their own practice and thus generate the data and evidence necessary both to empower their own development and also to justify their professional judgements to external audiences. Education is perhaps the best of all exemplars of this emerging focus on what has become known as self-evaluation. It has become understood that there are serious drawbacks to monitoring systems which are primarily concerned with making judgements from an external perspective. In consequence, across many education systems, there are increasing efforts being made to develop models of evaluation which can reconcile the competing goals of autonomy and accountability. Much of this developmental effort encourages teachers and schools to internally evaluate performance through the use of data and evidence and present the outcomes to justify their actions to external agencies such as inspectorates. However the success of such an undertaking depends to a huge extent on the capacity of individual professionals and schools to undertake self-evaluative research. To date there is a paucity of evidence to demonstrate that significant progress has been made in developing the necessary attitudes and skills to achieve this goal. The heart of this work, therefore, is about experimenting with new and innovative approaches to empowering teachers and schools to develop self-evaluation capacity.

Part one of this work contains three chapters. Chapter one deals with the emergence of evaluation as a central element in public sector governance in the late twentieth and twenty-first centuries. The political background to this development is analysed and competing theories and practices of evaluation are discussed. Chapter two looks more specifically at evaluation, self-evaluation and inspection as these concepts are being applied to education, teachers and schools. Here it is suggested that the simplistic notions which seem to underpin a good deal of the agenda in this area are naïve and that this realisation is now beginning to influence policy. Chapter three analyses the type of school and teacher evaluation systems which are emerging in many countries and jurisdictions. It is argued that there is clear evidence of a convergence in educational evaluation towards a compromise between internal self-evaluation and external inspection and monitoring. It is further argued that this compromise is gradually but steadily moving in the direction of greater reliance on professional self-evaluation with light touch external monitoring.

In the context of part one, chapters four, five and six, which make up part two of the work, chart the emergence of a new school and teacher evaluation/inspection regime in Ireland. Chapter four analyses the pilot project on which the new evaluation process is based. Chapter five investigates the key documents which underpin school evaluation Irish style. Chapter six reports on research in twenty four schools concerning the perception of school leaders and teachers with regard to the new evaluation system. What emerges from these chapters is that whole school evaluation in Ireland exemplifies vividly the type of school evaluation systems emerging in many other countries. For example, it is a compromise between self-evaluation and external inspection which has been developed through elaborate consultative processes designed to allay the fears of the various partners involved. On the other hand because it is such a compromise it contains serious flaws including a very underdeveloped focus on data and evidence, a very limited role for key stakeholders such as parents and pupils and an extremely cautious approach to the content and use of the final evaluation reports. In common with many similar systems a key failure is the unacknowledged but very clear lack of capacity in schools to collect evidence to support the evaluation of their professional activities.

In order to contribute to the long and complex task of assisting schools to develop a self-evaluative capacity part three of this work describes an extensive project undertaken with trainee teachers and experienced practitioners in Dublin City University. The goal of the project was to enable teachers firstly to develop a theoretical understanding of and sympathy for self-evaluation. Secondly it was designed to equip the participants with the methodological skills necessary to undertake self-evaluation. Finally it experimented with the use of Virtual Learning Environments (VLEs) to support and sustain practitioner self-evaluation. This final part of the work contains three chapters. Chapter seven analyses initiatives and projects in other parts of the world designed to develop professional self-evaluation capacities. Chapter eight describes the experimental programme created to empower the trainee and experienced professionals to understand and undertake self-evaluation. Chapter nine evaluates the outcomes of the project under three key headings. These are the response of the practitioners to developing and using research methodologies and instruments, the extent to which the participants demonstrated an understanding of and enthusiasm for the process of self-evaluation and an analysis of the extent to which the participants took ownership of the process and began to use it in their professional practice.

Finally, chapter ten draws together the strands of the three parts of the work and links the key findings in each. It elaborates a coherent framework through which self-evaluation can become the underpinning foundation of an effective system of whole school evaluation.

Introduction

In part one of this study the rise of school and teacher evaluation as a world-wide phenomenon is charted. It is argued that this process has been driven by influential political ideologies characterised by their opponents as neo-liberalism and managerialism and by their proponents as 'new public management' and much needed reform. These ideologies and an associated 'reform agenda' have been systematically encouraged by governments, sections of the media and perhaps most influentially by key trans-national agencies such as the OECD, the World Bank and the European Union. Key words and concepts have come to characterise this agenda. These include choice, accountability, transparency, value-for-money and decentralisation of responsibility for performance to individual institutions such as schools. These goals are to be achieved through privatisation or marketisation of public services followed by increased surveillance in the form of quality assurance, quality control, audit, benchmarking, evaluation and inspection.

The impacts of these policies on public services have been felt in many countries. In education they have been manifested in the prioritisation by many governments of two key goals. The first is that of transferring primary responsibility for pupil achievement from central authority to individual schools and teachers. To achieve this it is envisaged that schools and teachers will become more autonomous, taking greater responsibility for budgets, planning, teaching and learning, self-evaluation and professional development. Somewhat paradoxically, however, to ensure the maintenance and indeed constant improvement of standards these same schools and teachers are to be the subject of sophisticated surveillance procedures including teacher-proof curricula, increased student testing, benchmarking, inspection and external evaluation. One result of these policies has been that virtually every education system in the developed world and indeed many others has been busy creating or, where they existed before, reforming their school evaluation policies and procedures.

However it is gradually becoming apparent that as the two key policy goals of greater school and teacher autonomy and increased accountability are difficult to reconcile in practise it follows that the design and implementation of evaluative systems that can encompass both is problematic. In consequence, it is argued in this study, a kind of hybrid system of school evaluation is gradually emerging in very many education systems. This hybrid involves a varying mixture of self-evaluation by schools and teachers, which encourages autonomy and professionalism, combined with external inspection to ensure accountability. The balance in these hybrid systems between internal responsibility for evaluation and external monitoring is largely, it will be argued, a function of very complex factors specific to each jurisdiction. Part one will explore these emerging theories and practices in detail.

THE AGE OF EVALUATION

Evaluation, Neo-liberalism and the New Public Management

In an article entitled 'I audit, therefore I am' in The Times Higher Education Supplement (THES, October 18, 1996, quoted in Simons 2002: 17) Michael Power, Professor of Accounting at the London School of Economics, defined our era as 'the age of inspection, the evaluative state and the audit society'. He went on, 'whatever term one prefers, there can be little doubt that something systematic has occurred since nineteen seventy one. In every area of social and economic life, there is more formalised checking, assessment, scrutiny, verification and evaluation'. Thrupp and Willmott (2003: 14), suggest that the 'something systematic' that happened was the perceived failure of Keynesian social democracy around the time of the first oil crisis in the nineteen seventies. This has subsequently underpinned what they describe as 'the neoliberal project whose aim is to inject the competitive nature of the market into what is perceived as a stifling, inefficient and expensive public sector'. Bottery (2004: 62) postulates that these policies are impacting on the provision of public services in several contradictory ways, of which the following are the most relevant to this study:

1. Satisfying the greater demands of clients will be hindered by the need to reduce expenditures and increase efficiency.
2. The pressure to use private sector concepts and practices such as efficiency and profit will conflict with traditional, contrasting public sector values such as care and equity.
3. There will be tension in terms of trust as governments see the need to allow enhanced autonomy and creativity but yet are unwilling to abandon low-trust policies of targets, performativity and compliance.

Imposing these low-trust policies (O'Neill, 2002) has, in the view of Schwartz and Struhkamp (2004), brought evaluation to the centre of the stage. They suggest that in the current mode of transformed governance called new public management evaluation often plays a crucial role as an instrument to maintain bureaucratic control.

Johannesson *et. al.* (2002: 335–337) agree that these developments represent 'the new liberal agenda and the new public management', both characterised by 'buzzwords' such as 'decentralisation, choice, goal setting, accountability, transparency, managerialism, evaluation, competition and privatisation'. They go on to argue that the 'marketisation' of every sphere of public life is an international trend that represents a radical move away from the concerns around equity and inclusion that dominated public policy discourse in the nineteen seventies and the nineteen eighties. In the new 'discourse of progress' or 'system of reasoning', as they define it, 'science' is relied upon to rationalise social systems, preferably 'packaged as easy to install techniques to secure and measure social and economic progress'. This process, they suggest, gradually norms both institutions and professionals to accept what Foucault describes as 'governmentality', by which he means, according to Johannesson *et. al.*, the acceptance and internalising of language and techniques (such as, for example, appraisal, inspection and so on) which ultimately undermines their freedom and professional status.

Not all commentators take such a negative view of the new public management or accept that the underpinning theory is neoliberalism. For example, Dan O'Brien, senior editor of the Economist Intelligence Unit, suggests that it is the 'end of ideology' by which he means the left / right divide that has brought 'the rise and rise of evidence–based policy making'. He goes on to argue that since policy is no longer driven by ideology it now responds to 'evidence about what works' and that this has also contributed to the 'internationalisation of thinking on policy' (O'Brien, 2006: 12). What is problematic about

O'Brien's interpretation is the implicit view that relying principally on empirical evidence to drive school policy is somehow 'non-ideological'. In fact it involves an ideology of faith in positivist and technical rationalist approaches to social science research which is open to question. Moreover, as Chevalier *et. al.*, (2004) point out, such an ideology tends to be strongly linked to theories of choice, competition and the role of the free and quasi-free market in driving school efficiency. This of course can only work in practice if the information on which consumer decisions are based is founded on valid and reliable evidence and of course if the consumers have the economic independence and resources to make real choices. The latter point is perhaps beyond the scope of this work, but the former, the validity and reliability of much positivist educational research, is a dubious proposition as we shall see in due course.

New public management theory of course has been applied in education as much or arguably more than in any other area. Anthony Giddins (2004: 510) remarks that 'the commercialisation and marketisation of education reflects the cost cutting pressures of globalisation as schools are being reengineered in much the same way as business corporations'. Guy Neave (1998: 265), speaking of the European Union as a whole, and specifically of schooling, also uses the term, 'the evaluative state' and remarks on the paradoxical blend of devolution and centralisation being experienced by schools in most European countries. Neave goes on to spell out this paradox: while it appears that schools are being given more autonomy to manage their own affairs, they are at the same time being subjected to greater government regulation and scrutiny, mostly by way of the setting and monitoring of performance targets and through increased inspection and evaluation. Meuret and Morlaix (2003: 53) regard this process as 'a logical consequence' of what they perceive to be a genuine effort to decentralise power to schools and report that the OECD sees evaluation as 'a key way to enhance the responsiveness of schools to the needs of their intake as well as to allow them to improve'. Moos (2003) perceives a wide international movement to shift decision making down to school level while simultaneously increasing the pressure on schools to render a value for money account in both financial and achievement terms. In the US, work by Elmore and Fuhrman (2001:4–5) argues that 'the theory that measuring performance and coupling it to rewards and sanctions will cause schools and the individuals who work in them to perform at higher levels underpins performance based accountability systems operating in most states and thousands of districts'. These systems, Elmore and Fuhrman (2001:5–6) suggest, represent a significant change from traditional approaches to accountability in that, the new approaches focus primarily on schools, while in the past school districts were held primarily responsible. The new approaches focus on performance and other outputs while in the past districts were held responsible for offering sufficient inputs and complying with regulations. Significant concessions such as bonuses are now offered as are threats of school closure.

In Australia, Banks describes education as one of the many services now 'measured' by government. He explains the process as follows:

◻ Equality indicators measure how special needs groups compare in terms of participation and retention rates
◻ Effectiveness is measured in terms of learning outcomes- currently limited to reading, writing and numeracy in specified year levels- and estimated completions. Such outcomes can, of course, be affected by factors outside the school system
◻ Efficiency is measured in terms of government expenditure per student, staff expenditure per student and staff to student ratios. (Banks 2005 : 11)

Of course, inspection of itself is not new, nor indeed is educational research concerned with identifying effective teaching methods, assessment models and so on. As Nevo (2002: 4) points out,

even before the terms accountability, standards or benchmarking were in use, there was a clear demand by politicians, administrators and the public at large that schools be evaluated externally to find out if they were fulfilling their duties . . . This demand has never ceased, even when external evaluation was highly criticised by innovative educators and when internal evaluation was encouraged by way of an alternative.

Similarly, educational research directed to finding ways of improving schools has also been highly visible and influential for at least the past three decades. Importantly, in the context of this work, this research increasingly suggests that formal school and teacher self-evaluation as opposed to external inspection represents an important component in making schools more effective. Zepeda (2003) brings together from the school improvement literature the factors that are found in improving schools. Firmly embedded in this list is the capacity of the school to engage in self-evaluation, and internal monitoring of progress. Schmoker (1999) stresses the need to use data to inform school improvement and includes this along with effective teamwork and the establishment of common and measurable goals as key factors in effective school improvement. Joyce and Showers (2002) provide evidence of the importance of using a range of data including student achievement to inform the provision of professional development for teachers and organisational improvement for schools. Leithwood et al (2001) argue that internal monitoring systems and frameworks in schools are vital in informing strategic direction and should include data on areas such as policies and procedures, planning processes, instruction, assessment and management and leadership. In short, research on growth oriented teacher and school evaluation, though limited, strongly suggests that schools and teachers can benefit greatly from evaluation processes that provide data and evidence to feed into awareness building, goal setting and professional development. Hargreaves (2006) argues that the collection, analysis and use of evidence by teachers and schools as part of their own continuous improvement is a key and inescapable element of professionalism. In essence, therefore, the idea of schools and teachers being involved in formal evaluation and self-evaluation is not new and is strongly endorsed by the research evidence.

What appears to be a relatively new phenomenon, however, is the attempt to limit or certainly change the nature of professional autonomy in teaching by, as Judith Sachs (2003: 22) puts it, 'placing teachers in a long line of authority in terms of their accountability for reaching measurable outcomes . . . a line that stretches through the principal to the district or region and then to the central administration'. This corporate or managerial model of educational control perceives the teacher to be, in the words of Brennan (1996: 22),

> a professional who clearly meets corporate goals set out elsewhere, manages a range of students well and documents their achievements and problems for accountability purposes. The criteria of the successful professional in this corporate model is one who works efficiently and effectively in meeting the standardised targets set for the accomplishment of both students and teachers as well as contributing to the school's formal accountability processes.

Kincheloe (2004: 9) describes this process as 'the deskilling of teachers which involves breaking down their tasks and delegating them to low skill workers', something he urges teachers to resist, by becoming 'empowered'.

As a result of these trends, teachers throughout Europe, North America, the Far East and in Australia and New Zealand are today working in conditions characterised by increased public scrutiny, more sophisticated techniques ensuring accountability and a myriad of strategies measuring student learning outcomes. Research by Hargreaves (reported in Wolf and Craig, 2004) in New York

State and Ontario, Canada reports that as a result of these developments many teachers feel 'demeaned and degraded', 'unfairly criticised' and 'sick and tired of being asked to justify their existence' and of 'constant government put downs'. De Lissovoy and McLaren (2003: 131) suggest that 'the growth of these policies, rules and regulations seem to be crowding out all else as they come to constitute a new industry, bureaucracy and language'.

This pressurised atmosphere is further heightened by a general distrust of teachers at political level and an instrumentalist attitude to education, or at least schooling in society at large (Thrupp and Wilmot, 2003). This is evidenced by the demand for the publication of league tables of results and the 'naming and shaming' of under-performing schools and teachers. As Whitty *et. al.* observe (1998: 5),

> whether or not what we are witnessing here is a struggle between a professionalising project and a deprofessionalising one, it is certainly a struggle among different stake-holders over the definition of teacher professionalism and professionality for the twenty-first century.

Examples of this push to itemise, define and control every aspect of teaching and learning can be found across the entire curriculum spectrum. These include ever more detailed definition of course content and required learning outcomes, foolproof teaching methods for every occasion, standardised attainment measures and assessment models, and of course teacher and school appraisal and evaluation (Cochrane-Smith, 2005 b; Coolahan, 2005).

In each of these areas one could make a case similar to that which emerges in the rest of this study, namely, that policies and practices which impinge upon the professional autonomy of teachers are ultimately likely to be anti-educational, philosophically speaking, and self-defeating from a practical point of view. In making this argument, the researchers have chosen to concentrate on evaluation, firstly because they are experienced educational evaluators, and have seen at first hand the damage superficial and ill thought out approaches to evaluation can cause; but secondly, and more importantly, because within the theory and practice of educational evaluation, there exists a strong tradition which stresses the importance of professional development, collegiality and respect for practitioner autonomy and independence. This tradition, although very much on the defensive in the age of evaluation, remains a viable alternative to narrow, behaviourist and empiricist conceptions of evaluation. However, before turning to conceptualisations of evaluation specifically, it is necessary to consider the broader issue of the nature of educational evaluation research and its relationship to teacher autonomy and professionalism.

Evaluation and Teacher Professional Autonomy

Ángel Diaz Barriga (2003: 454) remarks in an essay entitled 'Curriculum Research: Evaluation and Outlook in Mexico' that 'evaluation has become one of the central subjects in the educational debate at the beginning of this century'. A glance through many of the other essays in the *International Handbook of Curriculum Research* (Pinar, 2003) in which Diaz Barriga's essay appears, confirms this view. For those of us who, as it were, overlap the fields of curriculum development and curriculum evaluation it is clear that increasingly and overwhelmingly in recent years the latter has become the main driver of the former. For example launching a recent collection of essays which he had edited on the National Curriculum in England and Wales, John White (2004) rather wryly suggested that as the work was largely theoretical and philosophical in nature it would lack the impact on decision makers of curriculum work grounded in evaluation research. Likewise it has been widely noted around the world that President Bush's educational legislation No Child Left Behind contains 110 references to the role of scientific research in curriculum reform and evaluation. Similarly in the European Union curriculum issues are being increasingly determined at continental, national and local levels by evaluations, a process which will undoubtedly be accelerated by the adoption of specific 'benchmarks and quality indicators for the improvement of education' by the European Commission in 2003. Yet another example of the dominance of curriculum evaluation in determining reform is the intense public interest generated by comparative evaluations of education systems such as the International School Effectiveness Project (ISEP), The Third Mathematics and Science Study (Timms) and most recently and influentially the Programme on Student Assessment Project (PISA). In summary, Christie (2003) suggests that concerns with evaluating standards in education and the associated ever-closer scrutiny of the performance of teachers has become a global obsession.

In Ireland it has been largely the influence of European Union policy that has led to continuous programme and institutional evaluations. Boyle (1997:51) points out that EU evaluation requirements in relation to the spending of monies given to Ireland for various purposes has resulted in 'consistent and systematic evaluation procedures in many areas of the public service'. A similar point is made by Lenihan *et. al.* (2005:72) who argue that 'the increased impetus for evaluation in Ireland during the nineteen nineties was largely driven by the EU which emphasised the need to assure accountability and measure the impact of significant EU transfers'. Importantly, for our purposes, even where EU evaluation requirements do not as yet impinge directly as, for example, in mainstream (as opposed to vocational) education, evaluation concepts, policies, systems and processes have tended to migrate.

Interestingly, Boyle (1997:52–53), the most influential chronicler of the rise of evaluation in the Irish context, suggests that the phenomenon in Ireland has rather different roots or at least is strongly influenced by factors other than neoliberalism and the new public management. While Boyle acknowledges the influence of the OECD and the EU in the form of 'a more results orientated approach to public service management, performance indicators and evaluation', he nonetheless goes on to suggest that the,

> new public management is not a monolith . . . and the Irish experience is very different from Britain or New Zealand. There is little or any evidence, for example, of any great theoretical underpinning to the Irish public service reform programme. It does not draw significantly from public choice or agency theories . . . neither is there any significant ideological drive to recast the public sector.

Be that as it may, the evaluation and quality assurance culture now firmly embedded within the EU (Lion and Martini, 2006) has been gradually incorporated as a key element of the national social partnership agreements which have determined economic and social policy in Ireland for nearly two decades. For example, in national partnership programmes such as *Work and Competitiveness 1998*, *Prosperity and Fairness 01*, *Sustaining Progress 03–05* and the current national agreement, *Towards 2016*, the terms 'efficiency', 'effective', 'performance', 'quality', 'flexibility', 'rationalisation' and 'evaluation' are mentioned throughout. This represents what has been called the institutionalisation of evaluation. In consequence, recent legislation, including the 1997 Universities Act, the Education Act, 1998 and the Qualifications (Education and Training) Act, 1999, all have specific sections requiring evaluations of programmes and institutions. As a result, right across the education and training sector, new evaluation systems have been designed and rolled out in the past decade. This is the context within which the subject of this study, whole school evaluation in primary and post primary schools, has emerged. An important point to note is that all these social partnership agreements and subsequent actions, including the setting up of evaluation structures, have been negotiated and agreed with the social partners, including trade unions, and have been effectively paid for in the form of higher salaries.

The present authors argue, therefore, that the corporatist approach adopted in Ireland, in the form of 'partnership' between the state and the 'social partners' such as the trade unions, has undoubtedly limited in practice the extent to which managerialist notions such as performance related pay or stringent appraisal of work quality can be employed. Paradoxically, therefore, while all these concepts, ideas and processes appear in the various agreements mentioned above, their implementation on the ground is highly constrained by the partnership context and niceties. As Boyle (1997) goes on to argue, the Irish reform programme might better be conceptualised as more akin to that pursued in other small European countries such as the Netherlands and Denmark. As in these countries, a corporatist type democracy exists which ensures that multi-party coalition and consensus rather than majority rule is the norm. Accommodation, compromise and consensus are key words in the political lexicon.

A good example of this culture of compromise with regard to evaluation is provided by the emerging school evaluation process in Ireland. The Education Act describes the task of school inspection and whole school evaluation as being 'to monitor and assess the quality, economy, efficiency and effectiveness of the education system' (Section 7(2)(b)). This terminology is closely aligned with neoliberalist philosophy and EU/OECD policy, but as we shall see what has emerged in practice is considerably diluted. Flynn (2006) captures this dichotomy well when describing the new system of school evaluation in Ireland as 'answering the challenges of accountability in an Irish way rather than a European way'.

However, while Boyle's analysis is largely correct, it is important perhaps not to overstate the case. Even if the context and politics are different, nonetheless a good deal of the neo-liberal agenda has found an echo in Ireland. Across the public sector and very strongly in education, the language of the new public management is in vogue, as are its outward and visible signs in the form of targets, standards, benchmarks, accountability, evaluation and so on. For example, the website of the Department of Education and Science now refers to parents and pupils as 'clients' and 'consumers'. Now schools must engage in 'evidence- based quality assurance', 'school development planning' and 'whole school evaluation', and most educational programmes, projects and interventions are subject to regular evaluation. In fact in educational circles where the talk used to be of 'change fatigue' we now have complaints of 'evaluation fatigue'. Yet it is important to note that on the whole, in the area of educational evaluation, emerging policies and practices are characterised by moderation and consensus. It is hard to envisage the application of the type of 'robust' school evaluation system introduced in England (now considerably diluted) being a practical proposition in the Irish context, at least for the moment. In fact, supporters of a more robust evaluation culture implicitly agree with this view. For example, Lenihan *et. al.*, (2005:72) argue that there 'continues to be a poor evaluation culture in Ireland' while Ruane (2004) agrees and suggests that this is so because of 'a weak history of planning, inclusive negotiated agreements which may lead to compromise solutions and a political tradition of client focus which may bias against economic rationality'.

The key point here however, is that commentators such as Boyle and Ruane see the current situation regarding evaluation as being in flux and highly contested. While there may be little ideological impetus driving low trust accountability policies in Ireland, nonetheless the influence of this agenda is steadily gaining ground under the impetus of EU and OECD pressure. How this contest will play out in the medium and longer term is at this stage unclear.

Given then, the increasing role of evaluation in influencing educational decision making abroad and slowly but increasingly at home, one has to ask what challenges are posed for the teaching profession. The answer may be a dramatic one—influencing the philosophy of evaluation may become the key battleground for the future of teaching in the broadest sense. In essence, if school and teacher evaluation were to become ever more dominated by external monitoring and control and increasingly narrow concepts of what can be measured and therefore of what counts as being of educational value, the curriculum space so desperately needed for the consideration of issues of citizenship, globalisation, culture and spirituality may dwindle further. In tandem, the space for teachers to exercise their professional prerogative of autonomous judgement and decision-making will also further narrow. On the other hand the defence of generously conceived concepts and traditions of educational evaluation may be the strongest weapon still available to progressive education since, as noted above by John White, the power of theory to influence policy and practice seems in decline. The importance of these battles around evaluation to the future of education is emphasised by C. T. Fitz-Gibbon: 'fear does not promote quality, wherever there is fear we get the wrong figures . . . the system which introduces fear as in the publication of everything, is a system which corrupts . . . eastern Europe was full of development plans and targets' (1995: 100).

The next chapter will attempt to develop these arguments by analysing the currently competing evaluation philosophies and practices at work in education. It will be argued that both in the US and Europe, among a minority (but an increasingly vocal one) of educational evaluators, the efficacy and ethical justification of applying positivist research principles to the evaluation of social processes such as education is being strongly challenged (Heywood Metz and Page, 2002; MacBeath, 1999; McNamara and O'Hara, 2004; McNiff, 2002 a). Recent work in educational evaluation has tried to develop this challenge by moving the evaluation focus away from external judgement and towards understanding the impact of curricula on recipients (Kushner, 2000). However the dominant form of curriculum evaluation still involves judgements made through the eyes of external agencies and the connotation of curriculum evaluation as the external monitoring of professional performance and practice remains strong.

The next chapter suggests that hopes for genuine educational improvement are closely bound to a reversal of this trend and towards the empowerment of autonomous self-evaluating teachers and schools capable of resisting 'academic researchers who use research to develop market scripted curricula that result in the de-skilling of practitioners' (Anderson, 2002: 24). This imperative was well understood in the past as the work of Lawrence Stenhouse (1975) and John Elliot (1991; 1998), to name but two curriculum scholars, testifies. In more recent times it seems clear that the dominance of centralising political forces obsessed with control, standards and accountability achieved through measurable objectives and instrumental evaluation has gained sway. As a result what is at stake is the locus of power in curricular decision-making.

Livingston and McCall (2005), in an interesting paper on the ever widening influence of evaluation in education, suggest that only local level school and practitioner self- evaluation can hold up the seemingly inevitable impetus towards one size fits all solutions based on internationally and nationally formulated benchmarks and standards. In the Irish context, Boyle (2006: 37) makes a similar point calling for 'organisation based and bottom up initiatives to assess performance in public services'. Johannesson et al (2002:335), in an otherwise gloomy section of their paper entitled 'An Incurable Progress?' also argue that although school self-evaluation has become emphasised - 'mandated by law and as a discourse' - as an intrinsic component of neo-liberal governance, 'this term is one of the magic terms of restructuring'. What they are suggesting is that school self-evaluation may provide, paradoxically, a real if rare opportunity for practitioners and schools to, as MacBeath et al (1996) put it, 'speak for themselves'. This is because self-evaluation may be mandated as part of the process of 'improvement', and schools and teachers required to internalise the norms expected of them and oversee their own implementation of them without the costly external intervention of the state. Yet at the same time the knowledge and skills acquired through self-evaluation might well have the unintended side effect of empowering professionals and organisations to protect their autonomy and responsibility. This is a similar concept to the empowerment possibilities often suggested by the theorists of emancipatory action research (Carr and Kemmis, 1983). The difference though is that as increasingly schools and teachers are mandated to conduct self-evaluation, the sheer volume and depth of this activity will almost certainly move far beyond the rather small scale and individualistic nature of action research as it has developed in practice.

It will be suggested in later chapters that precisely as described above, the possibilities inherent in self-evaluation which rather surprisingly has become a central plank of the 'new management' of schools should and can be exploited by schools and teachers to inform their own decision making and enhance their professional autonomy. First, however, it is necessary to show why the drive to use externally imposed solutions to problems of practice derived from large scale quantitative systems-wide evaluative research is a misconceived and futile endeavour, and it is to this we now turn.

TRUSTING THE TEACHER

The Case for Professional Self-Evaluation

The Limits of Evaluative Research in Education

In recent years, the authors' experiences in their role as educational evaluators has led them increasingly to question both the wisdom and practicality of what Heywood Metz and Page (2002: 26–27) call the 'tendency to impose abstract findings on schools and teachers with little discussion of local variations and necessary adaptations'. The same authors go on to remind us that 'researchers may all too easily dismiss or ignore the non-linear character of schools' reality, while practitioners must find a viable professional practice within it'.

Much of this 'tendency', it is alleged by the critics, emanates from those who wish to limit or eliminate the professional autonomy of teachers (Darling-Hammond and Youngs, 2002). It is argued (Clarke et al, 2000: 9) that a central tenet of the now dominant managerialism has been a concentrated effort to displace or subordinate the claims of professionalism, 'managerialism refutes the idea that professionals know best, rather we are invited to accept that managers do the right thing and this legitimises and seeks to extend the right to manage'. Similarly, Power (1997: 97) suggests that the main objective of highly organised audits or evaluations is to 'challenge the organisational power or discretion' of relatively autonomous groups such as doctors and teachers by making these groups more publicly accountable for their performance. These developments, it is further argued, are leading to the de-skilling and disempowerment of teachers who are being increasingly cast in the role of technicians implementing 'teacher proof' curricula. These curricula are developed through self-styled rigorous experimental designs (Slavin, 2002) and are concerned increasingly with preset and supposedly easily measured attainment standards.

The strength of this obsession with uniformity, conformity, accountability and standards is evidenced in relation to the United States by Slavin (2002). Slavin points out that in President Bush's Education Act 'No Child Left Behind' there are 110 references to the centrality of 'scientifically based research' in formulating successful curricula. It is clear that Slavin strongly approves of this approach. He confidently writes about 'transforming educational practice and research' and refers with almost messianic fervour to the value of 'experimental–control comparisons on standards-based measures'. These methods will, he assures us, produce, 'valid knowledge, through rigourous systematic and objective procedures, using experimental or quasi experimental designs, preferably with random assignments'. (2002: 16)

Equally, in the UK Geoff Whitty (2002) points out that while in theory the policy is one of decentralisation of power in many areas to schools, the reality is an increasing obsession with central control, measurable standards and diminution of teacher autonomy. A key figure in this movement in England was influential former advisor to the Government, David Hargreaves. Hargreaves suggests (1997: 413) that 'educational research should provide conclusive evidence that if teachers do x rather than y in their professional practice that there will be a significant and enduring improvement in outcomes'. He goes on to suggest (1999: 247) that the future of educational research is more experimental studies and randomised controlled trials in search of what works in practice, 'actionable knowledge' to improve the 'performativity' of teachers with respect to the measurable outcomes of their teaching.

At one level it is hard to believe that this type of overstatement is still regarded as credible let alone that it has effectively become the driver of educational policy in much of the English-speaking world. As long ago as 1975 Cronbach (1975: 72) described experimental research in the social sciences as 'a hall of mirrors that extends to infinity'. More recently, in one of the seminal works of our time, *After Virtue*, Alistair MacIntyre describes the predicament of the empiricist social scientist as follows,

if his predictions do not derive from a knowledge of law like generalisations the status of the social scientist as a predictor becomes endangered–as it turns out it ought
to be for the record of social scientists as predictors is very bad indeed. (1981: 22)

In a similarly devastating critique of the 'arrogance and presumption of the pro-
ducers of certainties' in her own field of special needs education Deborah J
Gallagher, concludes that,

social science research at least in its present state of development does not appear to
allow for the scientific findings that will lead to a robust technology of teaching and
learning much less rival the technological advances that have occurred in many areas
of the physical sciences–if the sciences that contribute to civil engineering were
equally ambiguous, crossing the Severn Bridge or riding the lift to the top of the
Sears Tower would be an exciting experience indeed. (2004: 6)

Helen Simons remarks that three decades have passed since 'quantitative
methodology was found to be inadequate as the sole provider of knowledge for
action in the sphere of public services', yet 'despite the rather obvious limitations we are now faced with a politically driven restoration of the numbers
game' (2004:410). Shadish *et al* (2005:97) make a similar argument, suggesting that behind the rhetoric of efficiency these policies signal a return to the
oft criticised positivistic ideal of objective social knowledge. In the Swedish
context, Bjorklund *et al* (2005) demonstrate that despite the fact that the
relationship between family background and school performance has hardly
budged since before the 'reforms' were enacted, pressure for further market oriented reforms in education remains intense.

Given these and any number of similar demolitions one can only wonder
at the naivety of the empiricists in education still seeking unbiased certainty
and scientific truth. But perhaps naivety has little to do with it? With his
usual acuity Michael Apple suggests an alternative motive. Speaking specifically of external evaluation based on empiricist and behaviourist principles
Apple notes that,

it is also of no help whatsoever in determining the difficult issue of whose knowledge
should be taught and who should decide. It focuses instead on the methodological steps
one should go through in selecting, organising and evaluating the curriculum–the ultimate effect is the elimination of political and cultural debate. (2001:83)

As Apple implies here what may seem simplistic notions of 'what works' or
'actionable knowledge' may not be so simplistic at all. In emphasising the

'performativity' of teachers and thereby implying blame for the failures of the system politicians gain two useful advantages, namely an excuse to limit the role and autonomy of teachers while reducing curriculum debate to experiments about means rather than arguments about ends.

All this is not to argue that there is no place for 'scientific research' (in the sense meant by its proponents, namely quantitative experimental studies) in education but only that the role accorded to it and indeed claimed by it should be, in the words of David Nevo, more modest (Nevo, 1995). Undoubtedly Simons (2004) is correct to suggest that while this type of research is relevant for many intervention studies, it falls far short of providing an adequate basis for professional practice, since it lacks the conceptualisation and understanding of personal experience that is required in explaining educative practice. Such research of itself alone provides no credible basis on which to build, in the words of John Elliot, 'an unprecedented extension of the operation of political and bureaucratic power to regulate the pedagogical activities teachers engage their students in within classrooms' (2004b:169). MacIntyre goes further when he argues that it amounts to 'an amazing misuse of power to impose such unreliable notions on schools and teachers' (1981:12). Richard Pring (2004: 212) as always strikes a sensible balance when arguing that the real danger lies 'in the imperialism of any one form of discourse together with its distinctive notion of evidence . . . leading to the false dualism between the quantitative and qualitative approaches to research'.

One symptom of the malaise of the dominance of scientific research in education (and indeed in other fields—healthcare being a good example (Caufield, 2004))is that it entertains only certain types of evidence, largely quantitative, while qualitative evidence is marginalised. Moreover, quantitative research evidence is also privileged as against that from other sources such as teacher knowledge, experience and intuition, or indeed ideas from the history and philosophy of education. Another problem is the unjustified expectation that such research can or does in any significant way impinge directly on practice or that certain research applications such as empirical external evaluation can make practice transparently accountable. Such 'knowledge' even if it were in any real sense valid and reliable is invariably far divorced from practice, overly theoretical and very difficult to disseminate.

A final and increasingly widely stated concern with the dominance of high stakes evaluation, testing and so forth, is that, as Ball (2001) and Thrupp and Willmott (2003: 41) put it, 'the pressure to perform leads to fabrication'. Ball (2001: 202) illustrates many of the forms of fabrication that occur in 'the performing school' including 'the manipulation of statistics and indicators, the stage management of events, hiding and sidelining underperforming children and the kind of accounts that schools and individuals construct around themselves'. Moreover, recent research indicates that fabrication and cheating are highly symptomatic of the effects of low trust policies on professional practice. Brunsson and Jacobsson (2002) show that the implementation of a set of standardised procedures in professional organisations often results in unwanted and destructive consequences in relation to existing professional norms and values.

It should be clear, therefore, that the value of empirical educational research should not be overplayed. It is one, but only one, of the influences that should inform the professional judgements and decisions of teachers. In the words of Martyn Hammersly:

> The search for one size fits all solutions to complex questions around teachers and teaching is a futile enterprise–it offers a false hope of dramatic improvement in quality, while at the same time undermining the conditions necessary for professionalism to flourish. (2004: 134)

It is to this last key point–the relationship between educational research and teacher professionalism–that we now turn our attention.

Trusting the Teacher: Practitioner Professionalism and Teacher Education

Against this very powerful anti-teacher tide voices are being raised which stress the centrality of the autonomous professional teacher to any generously conceived notion of what counts as education. For example John Elliot, as always a beacon of reason, argues that since,

> human life is accompanied by a high degree of unpredictability as a condition . . . limiting the predictive power of social science generalisation . . . trusting teachers in their capacities to exercise wisdom and judgement . . . is the wise policy. (2004 b:170)

Research on teacher autonomy seems to confirm this view. Pearson and Moomaw (2005: 45) suggest that the evidence demonstrates that as 'general teacher autonomy increased, so did empowerment and professionalism'. They go on to argue that 'empowering teachers is an appropriate place to begin in solving the problems of today's schools'. They define the teacher empowerment process as, 'like other professionals, teachers must have the freedom to prescribe the best treatment for their students, as doctors and lawyers do for their patients and clients'.

Chief among the voices of resistance is the practitioner research movement seeking to empower teachers to develop and implement their own theories and practices of education through researching their own professional practice (McNiff, 2002 (a); Black and Delong, 2002). Anderson (2002: 24) well represents this view when arguing that through their own research teachers can refute politicians and corporate leaders who have made them the scapegoats for failed policies and practices:

> Through research school practitioners can begin to talk back to those current school reform efforts. Practitioners can also use research to provide an analysis that runs counter to that of academic researchers who use research to develop market scripted curricula that result in the de-skilling of practitioners.

For similar reasons it is equally important that practitioners should also be at the heart of the evaluation of educational innovations. It is the making of educational judgements and curricular interpretations that should be at the core of teacher professionalism.

The notion of the primacy of the teacher in evaluating education would, however, find little favour with many in the world of evaluation. Despite the warnings of Denzin and Lincoln (2000:13) about 'the fallacy of objectivism' in social science research, antiquated but still dominant modes of evaluation remain strong. In practice the dominant strand in educational evaluation continues to be the instrumental one where the prime purpose is judgement 'to prove rather than improve' in the terms of the evaluation dichotomy described by Elliot Stern (2002). The fact that as Stern shows, very few evaluations in reality have a direct or immediate impact on policy does not appear to deter this approach.

However, in contrast there has been and continues to be a distinct strand of evaluation theory and practice which values incremental and professional development outcomes over short term instrumentalism. Currently fashionable but essentially simplistic notions of evaluation as being about generalisations and 'what works' hark back to early conceptualisations concerned with measuring behavioural objectives. Theoretically, this approach has been long superseded by more sophisticated models. These more recent conceptualisations of evaluation conceive of it as being about people working collaboratively towards a common understanding of personal and interpersonal processes. In theory at least, evaluation has evolved in the social sciences from a method of legitimating the imposition of external frameworks of control to being about enabling collaborative change and improvement–in short the purpose of evaluation has developed 'from social control to participative social evolution' (McNiff, 2002b: 3).

Evaluators in this tradition described by Stern as the 'processual' tradition (Weiss, 1998; McDonald, 1998; Kushner, 2000) are aware that the implementation of change and improvement has more to do with mobilising the interest and support of those involved and contributing to the professional development and autonomy of practitioners then it has to do with rigorous experimental research designs. In consequence, since the 1970s, educational evaluation has shifted steadily away from experimental and objectives focussed, pre- and post-test research towards case study and participatory democratic methods concerned with situational understanding, context and professional learning. Stern (2002) completes his comparison of the instrumental and processual traditions in evaluation by concluding that the latter 'may be more appropriate in educational and other social interactive discourses'.

Recent approaches to educational evaluation have sought to build on this 'processual' tradition (Stern, 2002) but take it a step further. The processual tradition may be more concerned with processes than products, with consensus building than judgement but is still driven by the figure of the external evaluator. Kushner (2000) for example seeks to personalise evaluation by concentrating on understanding the impact of programmes or innovations on their recipients, but this understanding is still to be achieved through the lens of the evaluator / researcher. McNiff (2002 b) in contrast suggests moving the practitioner to the centre of the evaluation process and in so doing emphasise teacher development and autonomy and recognise the responsibility and right of the teacher to make judgements about the value of educational innovations.

Inviting teachers to become the key evaluators of educational innovation as opposed to measuring the outcomes in some 'external' and 'objective' way is of course controversial. For example it can be argued that teachers cannot be objective evaluators as at one level it is their own work and effectiveness that is being evaluated. On this account evaluation must be primarily external.

However, herein lies the dilemma not just of evaluation but also of perceptions of teaching and learning and indeed curriculum. On the one hand, as has been argued, there is increasing pressure to reduce teaching to merely implementing a 'proven' programme of instruction. On the other hand the literature of school improvement has come increasingly to emphasise that the quality of pupil learning has to be seen in relation to the quality of teachers' learning (MacBeath, 1999; Special Edition of the British Educational Research Journal, Sept 2001; Sachs, 2003). This view of the teacher's professional learning emphasises that the quality of teaching is closely bound up with the capacity of teachers to make professional research based judgements on their own practice and on the programmes and methodologies they are being required to implement. This approach is coming to fruition in initiatives such as self-evaluation, peer review and peer observation of teaching, action research, reflective practice, practitioner-led research and whole school development planning. These developments although dating from the nineteen seventies have all become increasingly influential in pre-service teacher education and ongoing teacher professional development in the nineteen nineties.

This generous conceptualisation of teachers and teaching is fundamentally at odds with the perception of the teacher as a piece of technology or a device for achieving pre–determined levels of outcomes. It is also at odds with a concept of evaluation as merely a test of effectiveness entirely related to reaching these outcomes. Few would deny that pupil achievement in this sense is a justifiable goal of teaching but it is not the only goal and in any genuinely educational practice it cannot even be the most important goal. Genuinely educational practices, as Richard Pring (2004) reminds us, are or should be concerned with the intrinsic value of the pursuit in question, engaging with texts, becoming an autonomous and critical thinker, in short an educated person - in the words of Richard Peters, 'coming to care about an activity for what there is in it as distinct from what it may lead to' (1973:42). Standards, targets and benchmarks, narrow and mechanistic objectives, however amenable to easy measurement, have little to do with education in this sense, since they are extrinsic to it, a by-product as it were.

Recapturing this broader conceptualisation of education immediately challenges the notion of limiting teacher professional roles and autonomy. While a trainer or technician may well enable students to reach specified standards and targets, only a teacher can facilitate education understood in this way. Inevitably, therefore, reducing teacher autonomy is likely to impoverish education and narrow the curriculum as experienced by students in schools. This is well understood by many influential curriculum theorists who movingly evoke the nature of teaching. For example, Slattery suggests that as education is 'a contested terrain that challenges singular hermeneutic interpretations or methodologies, educators must enter the cultural and political debates with a commitment to justice, solidarity, compassion, liberation and ecological sustainability'. He goes on, in a fine passage, to describe the uncertainty and challenges facing the educator:

> An unexpected question triggers an exciting or provocative tangent, the changing moods and emotions of individuals create a unique and often perplexing life within the classroom, the same methodology is not always successful with every group of students. Teachers cannot predict the ambiguous and ironic nature of life in the classroom . . . all educational discourses reflect interpretative and hermeneutic endeavours. (2003:657)

In similar vein, Judith Sachs (2003:92) remarks that in the new world of accountability, 'what is often left out is a clear sense of the social and moral visions and missions which should underpin professional teaching'. David Geoffrey Smith suggests that 'the teacher must be possessed of true hermeneutic skill to show the essential openness of life and its conversational character' (2003:43). Matus and McCarthy argue that 'the great task confronting teachers and educators as we move into the twenty-first century is to address the radical reconfiguration and cultural re-articulation taking place in educational and social life' (2003:73). The centrality of the skilled autonomous teacher to a genuinely educational practice appears therefore to be clearly understood. However, it may well be that the threat posed to this conceptualisation of teaching by managerialist bureaucracies wielding ill founded theories and generalisations is perhaps less so.

What is at stake here then is fundamentally the locus of power in educational decision-making. The currently dominant instrumental practices of educational research and particularly of evaluation are a factor in maintaining this locus as it is. Evaluation even where concerned primarily with social and educative processes still carries the connotation that an external observer is best placed to make judgements about the professional practice of practitioners. Some recent evaluation work (Kushner, 2000) promotes a shift in the locus of evaluation power to the 'recipients, end users, or victims' of new programmes and innovations but as has been argued elsewhere the trend in educational evaluation is largely in the other direction (O'Hara and McNamara, 1999). The 'professionalisation' of evaluation, the dominance of the contract and terms of reference and the increasing use of consultants with little knowledge of the field in which they are trying to apply generic research methods are all likely to contribute to the legitimisation of market driven innovations which deskill and disenfranchise practitioners.

Educational evaluation is not therefore an objective, external, value free process but rather is deeply influential in shaping educational philosophy and policy. The conceptual and ethical stance it adopts is influencing the educational environment and educational debates to a significant degree.

Of course empowering practitioners to self-evaluate professional practice raises other issues. Among these is the status of practitioner-research in relation to other forms of 'scientific' inquiry, concerns relating to quality, rigour and legitimacy and of course arguments around the purpose and value of evaluative research. In relation to the status of practitioner and self-evaluation research, the argument has recently featured in the pages of *Educational Researcher*, the journal of the American Educational Research Association (see for example Vol. 31, No.7 and Vol. 31, No. 8). Despite a clear shift in the US in recent years back to systems wide experimental research programmes many educationalists are willing to argue for the legitimacy of practitioner research. This is in itself significant. Without revisiting all the arguments some key elements are summarised by Heywood Metz and Page (2002: 27) as follows:

> Although research carries honorific status it has a questionable record in shaping practice, public understanding and policy. Developing diverse genres of educational inquiry, including practitioner inquiry, may be critically useful at a time when the complexity of schools is not well understood by outside decision makers who are increasingly making the decisions.

Specifically in relation to external evaluative research, issues regarding both the purpose and ultimate value of such research have become deeply contentious. The authors' experience of whole-school evaluation has led them to wonder whether any such externally mandated exercise however benignly meant or conducted can yield significant positive outcomes.

Speaking of the UK Cullingford (1999: 13) has no doubt,

> there are certain factors which raise standards and others which do not. . . . Those factors that impede improvement are constant outside interference and detailed external control and inspection. Factors which help improve standards include teachers' feelings of ownership and responsibility over change, the sense of the school as a centre of change and changes that happen over time rather than at once.

W Norton Grubb (1999:84) in the same volume remarks that inspection, appraisal and evaluation has become 'stressful and punitive, its benefits only grudgingly admitted by teachers and administrators, are hardly worth the costs'. Carol Taylor Fitz-Gibbon, one of the leading figures in educational evaluation research commenting on the English Office for Standards in Education (Ofsted), remarks that 'it was predictable before any Ofsted inspector set foot in a school that their so called judgements would be inaccurate due to, among other things, inadequacy in sampling and the lack of established reliability in research methods used' (1999:14). Christopher Winch also suggests that 'Ofsted is unpopular because it is unfair' and describes why he believes this to be the case in a way that is relevant to the whole debate on school evaluation:

> The quite erroneous assumption made by such a system is that failures are, in the end, individual failures of staff and governors and possibly of local education authorities and no one else. Seen in this light inspection can be perceived as a cynical exercise of putting the blame for the failures of the national system not on those who are ultimately responsible but on their subordinates. (2001: 688)

Winch goes on to argue that unless an inspection system can intervene 'to improve school processes and disseminate principles underpinning best practices to the rest of the school system' then 'it will arouse fear without providing reassurance and support' (2001:690) This is a key point to which we will return in chapter six when the emerging school evaluation system in Ireland is analysed in some detail.

In contrast the value and effectiveness of internal or self-evaluation based approaches to improvement is emphasised by many educational theorists. Earley (1998: 74) suggests that 'evaluation is most effective when people internalise quality standards and apply them to themselves'. In the same vein MacBeath (1999: 153) argues for a model of evaluation in which 'external evaluation focuses primarily on the school's own approach to self evaluation'. He goes on to argue that external evaluation is unlikely to motivate teachers to achieve high standards and recommends 'a supportive, developmental, threat free approach to quality improvement' since 'self-evaluation is the crucial mechanism for achieving any kind of school improvement–underpinning everything are questions of ownership and empowerment'. Stoll and Fink (1996: 48) conclude similar lessons from their research:

> While opening mandated doors will certainly get people's attention there is little evidence that it engenders commitment on the part of the people who have to implement the change - it is through opening as many internal doors as possible that authentic change occurs.

Nonetheless it is reasonable to ask questions about the quality of practitioner research and the role (if any) for 'professional' evaluators and researchers in a practice-led research environment. John Elliott (1995) notes, in examining why the teacher self-evaluation movement which was much in vogue in the late nineteen seventies and nineteen eighties eventually fell on stony ground, that neither training, experience nor professional culture had allowed teachers to develop the discursive consciousness necessary to become reflexive, self aware and thus able to self-evaluate. Teachers, he argues, are methodologically adrift, unsure of what questions to ask, what kinds of data to collect, by what methods and how to analyse it when it had been collected. More recently, the growing influence of Schon's (1983, 1987, 1995) concept of the reflective practitioner has resulted in much greater emphasis in pre- and in-service teacher education on methodological competence. However, we are still quite a bit away from the goal of such competence being widespread among teachers. Progress both on the research skills side and more importantly in giving teachers a belief in self-evaluation and the confidence to engage in it is central to defending and enhancing the professional role of teachers. So far such progress has been slow and as we shall see failure in this regard emerges as the key issue limiting the effective implementation of the school evaluation system being developed in Ireland. Addressing this research skills and attitudes gap is the major concern of the work reported in part three of this study.

Self-Evaluation as a Professional Prerogative

In describing her approach to educational evaluation the influential action research theorist Jean McNiff (2002b) advocates an un-ashamedly teacher-centred approach. Urging that in the interests of the status of teaching and teachers what counts as evaluation needs to be urgently addressed in educational debates she proceeds to outline a perspective very different to the dominant positivistic paradigm now in vogue:

> I regard evaluation as a process of self-study in which people make claims, supported by evidence, to have improved the quality of their work in terms of their educative influence in the lives of others. (2002 b: 2)

McNiff goes on to develop her ideas of evaluation as follows,

> evaluation should be conducted participatively. Its epistemological base would be self-study and its methodology would be action research. In the school, teachers and principals would undertake their action research enquiry into their practice and produce accounts to show how they felt they were justified in claiming that they have

improved the quality of educational experience for themselves and for the children in their schools. (2002 b: 3)

McNiff, in espousing this view of evaluation, rejects external monitoring and control of teachers saying 'my own view is that people are capable of thinking, learning and acting for themselves' (2002b:4)

Perhaps surprisingly this conceptualisation of evaluation as being primarily concerned with self-evaluation for professional development has now become influential in project and school evaluation in Europe (including Scotland and Ireland, but less so yet increasingly in England and Wales). This owes much, as has been indicated, to the work of Jean McNiff and John Mac Beath and to American scholars such as Michael Quinn Patton, Carol Weiss and Robert Stake, although oddly, as Scheerens (2002) notes, the concept of self-evaluation by schools and teachers is not widely known or practised in the US. Particularly influential has been the work of Donald Schon, whose concept of the reflective practitioner immersed in the 'swampy lowlands' of practice, far away from the clean, neat high ground of most quantitative research has focussed attention on teaching as a possible arena for practitioner led research such as self-evaluation. Also influential was the work of Lawrence Stenhouse, who proposed more than thirty years ago that,

teachers can make use of evidence to inform their decisions, but to do this involves their adoption of a research stance towards their teaching, and the gathering of case study evidence about its effects. (1975: 45)

Sceptics of course argue (Woodhead, 2002) that such notions are largely a way of avoiding the conflict inherent in real evaluation which should lead to clear-cut judgements and firm interventions to bring about change. However, it is clear that even in England, where this type of tough evaluation of schools and teachers was most entrenched, that the very ambiguous outcomes and undeniable side effects have given pause for thought. It is now widely accepted that there is little evidence of external evaluation leading directly to clear unambiguous proof of improvement and considerable evidence of the damage that can be caused to professional autonomy and teacher morale (MacBeath, 2006). In consequence, the Office for Standards in Education (Ofsted), the body responsible for school evaluation in England, now places noticeably more emphasis on school and teacher self-evaluation, and while external monitoring remains a significant element of the system, the tone and substance has changed significantly. Throughout the rest of Europe there exists, what one might describe as a spectrum of approaches to school evaluation, which runs from little or no external monitoring at one end (e.g. Finland) to self-evaluation systems with a significant degree of external inspection (e.g. Holland). The largely externally driven inspection system of England and Wales is unusual in Europe and has only been adopted in other English speaking countries notably New Zealand (MacBeath, 2006). Moreover, the influential theorist Andy Hargreaves in a recent interview (Wolf and Craig, 2004: 137) goes so far as to say that,

> almost all English speaking countries are moving into what I call a post standardisation era. Putting paramount emphasis on measured achievement above anything else actually undermines learning, destroys creativity and reduces the likelihood of good people being attracted to and retained in the teaching profession. This over time depresses quality even further.

However an important caveat regarding the increasingly influential practice of self-evaluation is the extent to which it genuinely offers opportunity for practitioner empowerment or is simply imposed by outside authorities as a cheaper but fundamentally similar process to external evaluation. This point is well made by Hansson (2006: 163) who warns that the growing integration of evaluation into the process of management is 'a forceful demonstration of how evaluation is becoming an integrated part of the organisational environment under the new public management systems'. The point here is that despite rhetoric extolling the value of self-evaluation and practitioner empowerment, such systems may in practice simply require schools and teachers to research their own processes and practices according to externally imposed templates and methods. It is hard to argue that such systems constitute self-evaluation by any reasonable definition of the term—a point that will arise again in our examination of whole school evaluation in the Irish context.

Whether self-evaluation, properly understood as being related to professional autonomy and practitioner driven, will work any better than external inspection as a method of enabling improvement and empowering teachers remains to be seen, as its implementation on a systems wide basis is really only commencing in most countries. Evidence from particular projects and programmes where genuine practitioner-led evaluation with some support from external agencies has taken place is very positive. Helen Simons, who has facilitated several such self-evaluations, concludes as follows:

> When the motivation is intrinsic, schools respond . . . schools, teachers and administrators become their own best critics if they have control over the evaluation process, over the choice of issues to be evaluated, the methods and procedures to be employed

and the audience to whom the results will be disseminated. (2002: 33)

Simons goes on to summarise the case for self-evaluation for teachers and schools:

◻ Teachers are in the best position to evaluate curriculum change
◻ The quality of education can best be improved by supporting the professional autonomy of teachers and schools
◻ This is best done by creating a collaborative, non-threatening professional culture in which work can be publicly discussed and evaluated.

Carol Taylor Fitz-Gibbon, founder of the Centre for Curriculum Evaluation and Management (CEM) at Durham University, and a strong supporter of school self-evaluation based on good evidence, suggests that if schools have good self-evaluation systems, external evaluation should only need to be 'light touch'. She goes on as follows, 'UK schools currently lead the world in self-evaluation, demonstrating that teachers are quite willing to be accountable if the methods of assessment of their work are clear and believable' (1999: 8). Stevenson (2006) suggests that his work on the 'research engaged school' demonstrates the immense possibilities for development inherent in teacher enquiry, reflection and self-evaluation.

However, a somewhat less sanguine view of the perceived usefulness of self-evaluation to teachers themselves, let alone to policy makers and the public at large, is also to be found in the literature. For example, Meuret and Morlaix, speaking of France, remark that,

school self-evaluation is not common practice . . . the Ministry advises school to develop a culture of evaluation, and sends them indicators to assist them in that process, but these indicators are used by at best 5% of the schools. (2003:70)

In relation to the European pilot project on school self-evaluation involving 101 secondary schools throughout Europe, in which they were involved, Meuret and Morlaix note that 'school self-evaluation is not very popular among school staff . . . they were a little more inclined to appreciate self-evaluation as opposed to external evaluation, but only a third declared that it was 'liked by most staff' (and these schools were chosen for supposedly having positive attitudes to evaluation !) (2003 : 54). Speaking of Iceland, Lisi and Davidsottir (2005: 3) report that although schools have been mandated to conduct self-evaluation since 1996, few do so since 'all such ideas are met with distrust in the beginning, particularly as Icelanders are used to their independence and find it insulting that anyone would tinker with their freedom to do as they wish as teachers'.

A number of points are important here. One is that, as Fullan suggests, schools are hard to change,

> we have an educational system which is fundamentally conservative. The way in which teachers are trained, the way in which schools are organised, the way that the educational hierarchy operates and the way that education is treated by policy makers, all result in a system that is more likely to retain the status quo than to change. (2006:6)

Consequently, relatively new ideas must be strongly supported and be seen by teachers to be relevant to have a chance of becoming accepted and used. Understanding this, Carol Taylor Fitz-Gibbon founded the CEM centre to provide usable and easily understood data to schools undertaking self-evaluation and over a thousand schools now take part voluntarily in the system. Meuret and Morlaix concludes their comments on the European school self-evaluation project by suggesting that the evidence indicates that to get teachers and schools on board,

> the process of evaluation has to be a participatory one and not just a technical one, not only at the operational level but in its conception and monitoring. Data and indicators appear to be useful but they have to be user friendly in order to be actually employed in discussion among the stakeholders and not just by the technocrats. (2003:69)

In other words, it is clear enough that school and teacher self-evaluation systems which are just 'mandated' by bureaucrats but provide no convincing justification or rationale to schools and teachers and no support in providing either usable data or research training to enable schools to obtain and analyse their own evidence are most unlikely to have any impact. This, then, becomes one of the key indicators against which emerging school evaluation and self-evaluation schemes need to be judged. The point is emphasised by Barzano (2002: 84), who suggests that case studies undertaken in an EU funded school evaluation project, as well as analysis of the documentation from other projects, makes clear that the possibility of schools undertaking self-evaluation activities without support and training seems to be very limited. An approach to providing such support and training is the subject matter of part three of this study.

Conclusion

The central argument of this chapter is not that we should abandon large scale educational research, still less that we should ignore demands from the public, parents and politicians for schools to be evaluated in some way to ensure that they are fulfilling their responsibilities. The former has an important role to play in educational improvement while the latter are perfectly reasonable in a democratic society. However what is being argued is that these imperatives must be limited, balanced against the very important, central role of teachers in education. Anything that de-skills, de-professionalises and disempowers teachers will ultimately do a great deal of harm regardless of whatever short term gains it may be hoped to achieve. It is suggested that whether as deliberate policy or unintended side effect the current drive to apply entirely positivist notions of social science research to complex problems of curriculum, teaching and evaluation is having and will increasingly have these negative and regressive ramifications. This is both fundamentally anti-educational and in practice self-defeating since the effective implementation and mediation in the classroom of whatever new ideas emerge from research is entirely dependent on having the support and commitment of a teacher with the talent and skill to make it work.

In relation then to school evaluation, the point of this chapter is that the status and role of the teacher must be researched, conceptualised and defended as an absolutely integral component of the remit of the discipline. The chapter represents a suggestion, perhaps unjustified, that the defence of teacher professional autonomy is not perceived as the priority it ought to be by many in the field. Certainly, influential voices–Linda Darling-Hammond in the US and John MacBeath and Michael Schratz in Europe, for example–have laboured hard to resist encroachment on the role of the teacher. Similarly wise words have been quoted from, Patrick Slattery and David Geoffrey Smith extolling the importance of teachers and teaching. However in the school and teacher evaluation literature in general issues around the relationship between research, evaluation, teachers and teaching receive surprisingly little consideration.

It has been argued throughout this chapter that antiquated but still dominant conceptualisations of educational research in general and teacher and school evaluation in particular pose a significant threat to the professional independence and freedom of educators. It seems perhaps that the fundamental connection between empowered teachers and a progressive and challenging curriculum for learners may not be fully appreciated but this relationship is in fact crucial.

Impositions and limitations upon teacher autonomy not only de-professionalise the teaching role but inexorably impoverish education and the curriculum. Increasingly the pressure to conform to allegedly scientifically proven notions of 'what works' results in forms of teaching where genuinely educational practice can hardly take place at all. In this context genuinely educational practice refers to the sustained immersion of the learner in the traditions, practices and procedures of the many fields of knowledge and endeavour that make up the human experience. Without this immersion the learner has little chance to in the words of the philosopher Gerry Gaden, 'make his own of some aspect or part of this inheritance in the sense of coming to appreciate the intrinsic value of an activity or pursuit as opposed to using it to achieve some extrinsic goal' (1983:53). These conceptualisations of learning and curriculum depend fundamentally on a perception of teaching that is not about the delivery of a product but is rather a two way transaction from which both learner and educator can profit and grow.

It is arguable therefore that as the role of the teacher is crucial to the curriculum, the academic field of evaluation studies must be more active in defending and supporting the professional role of teachers and teaching and in resisting ill–considered and poorly founded interference in their reasonable autonomy. In fact, as the next chapter argues, there are signs of the emergence of an approach to school and teacher evaluation which attempts to reflect these concerns and to respect professional autonomy while seeking to ensure a reasonable degree of public accountability. We now turn to the emerging systems of school and teacher evaluation, particularly in Europe, but with some reference to the wider world.

· 3 ·

THE SCHOOL EVALUATION
SPECTRUM

An Emerging Consensus?

Changing Perceptions of School
and Teacher Evaluation

Some time ago in a paper at the conference of the European Evaluation Society (McNamara and O'Hara, 2001) the authors caused controversy by suggesting that an external yet collaborative and outwardly successful school evaluation process may have in fact caused more damage to the organisation than any benefit which accrued. The idea that a negotiated and largely sympathetic evaluation could be a bad thing seems absurd but in this case there was considerable evidence that it would have been better if it never had happened.

Subsequently therefore the suggestion by critics such Cullingford (1999) and Taylor Fitz-Gibbon, (1995, 1998, 1999, and 2001) that more intrusive evaluative interventions such as those of Ofsted in England may cause deep and lasting tensions came as no surprise to the authors given the impact that relatively benign evaluations can have.

These concerns about best practice in the area of school evaluation, quality assurance, inspection and so on are becoming increasingly pressing and polarising. The debate to date has largely centred on inspection and evaluation and whether these are best seen as an internal school driven process or alternatively in the interests of accountability and quality enforced and monitored from the outside. Earley (1998: 168) describes the issues in the following terms:

> The reality facing schools is that they must improve but the question is how? In simple terms the school improvement debate can be seen as being polarised between those who advocate either internal or external factors as the mechanism for change. The former stress the importance of school review, self- evaluation and school self- improvement all predominately internal mechanisms in which the school itself is seen as the main change agent. The latter point to the significance of external forces such as school inspection, appraisal or audit and see them as the main driving forces for school improvement.

This chapter will go on to suggest that for a variety of reasons and with considerable ambiguities and contradictions the emphasis in Europe in general has moved towards the former model described by Earley above, 'internal mechanisms' and away from the latter model, 'external control'. Not all specialists in the area would agree with this view. Johannesson et al (2002) , for example, in their study of developments in Iceland, Finland and Sweden, perceive a clear move towards the marketisation of education along the Anglo American / OECD line and away from the more school-centred traditions of those countries. This is also the view of Söderberg (2004), who in relation to developments in Sweden is of the view that an important trend throughout the nineties has been the successive introduction of market forces. As a result the number of independent schools has increased rapidly, a radical shift compared to the uniformity that was for a long time a distinguishing feature of Swedish educational policy.

MacBeath, on the other hand, suggests that his work, *Schools Must Speak for Themselves* (1999), has influenced many European countries in the direction of self-evaluation as the key mechanism in school evaluation (MacBeath 2004: 21–22). This view was echoed in a recent address to the Irish inspectorate by Andy Hargreaves (2006),

> for all sorts of reasons partly to do with resources but as much to with concerns about teacher recruitment, morale and retention there is a discernable move away from external monitoring and towards internal quality assurance mechanisms in school systems virtually everywhere.

MacBeath goes on to suggest that the EU funded school self-evaluation project which he jointly led and which was published as *Self Evaluation in European*

Schools (MacBeath *et. al.* 2000) has given rise to what he describes as the European model of school evaluation which 'continues to thrive. 'School inspectors from across Europe', he adds, 'have acknowledged the significant influence of the European model in shaping policy in their countries'. He further argues that these European countries have now been joined by Canada, although he acknowledges that recent North American legislation is still primarily concerned with accountability and that trends in some Canadian provinces are also towards, 'hard-edged accountability'. These developments MacBeath suggests, 'illustrate constraints which inhibit rather than promote school self-evaluation'.

MacBeath (2006 : 2) is at pains to deny that self-evaluation is an easy option or that it excludes an accountability component,

> inside the velvet glove of support and critical friendship is the fist of accountability, intolerant not only of low standards by also of self-delusion. Self-evaluation must be owned by a school staff and is manifestly not a soft option. Schools have to prove their ability to know themselves with appeal to authoritative and verifiable evidence.

This 'European model' of school and teacher evaluation/inspection as defined by MacBeath contains 'certain essential ingredients which make it engaging and empowering'. These are listed as:

- The central involvement of key stakeholders in the process
- Identifying what matters most to teachers and school leaders in evaluating school quality and effectiveness
- The support and challenge of "critical friends" chosen by, or in consultation with, the schools
- The dialogue which flowed from the different viewpoints and the press for supporting evidence
- The repertoire of tools for use by teachers
- The simplicity and accessibility of the framework
- The focus on learning and support for teaching. (2004: 21)

Despite what he sees as the growing influence of the 'European model', MacBeath accepts that since each country has 'different accountability contexts' significant differences in approach and emphasis remain. Thus, within the overall 'European model' MacBeath identifies three sub models of inspection / evaluation which he defines as follows:

- ▫ Proportional: inspection takes the school's own data as its starting point; a high standard of self-evaluation should lead to a less intensive inspection. The Netherlands, Scotland, Portugal, Flanders, The Czech Republic, Ireland and England fall into this category.
- ▫ Ideal: inspectors report on the quality of self-evaluation and identify areas where improvement is needed. Northern Ireland, Austria and France are in this category.
- ▫ Supporting: the inspectorate provides support for schools in carrying out self-evaluation more effectively. Denmark and some German Lander fall into this category. (2004:21)

From an Irish perspective, the inclusion of Ireland in the same category as England would be a cause of some surprise and this may well illustrate the extent of the differences within the common European model alleged to exist by MacBeath. The English system known colloquially as Ofsted would be regarded in Ireland (among teachers) as a dangerously threatening, intrusive and demoralising approach to evaluation and inspection, involving punitive levels of stress and potential naming and shaming of weak teachers and schools. Even in the context of the clear softening of the Ofsted approach since as far back as 1998 (as exemplified by the increasing emphasis on self evaluation and the recent policy of the 'new relationship with schools' (Milliband, 2004)) it seems reasonable to argue that there remains a significant gulf between the English approach and that emerging in Ireland. The English system is still primarily concerned with external inspection, is high stakes in that interventions very damaging to schools and teachers may follow a negative inspection and has developed very extensive tools for gathering data to monitor school performance. The system emerging in Ireland is, as we shall see, quite different with an emphasis on self-evaluation, light touch external inspection and very little emphasis on data or evidence to support findings.

This seems, perhaps, to somewhat invalidate the category structure proposed by MacBeath, since it demonstrates that systems placed in the same category are very different in practice. Part of the problem here is that the objectives and the language of different evaluation schemes may well look very similar on paper but their working out in practice is so constrained by national contexts that they become substantially different. For example, the significant difference in practice between the evaluation systems in Ireland and England has already been noted, although both are surprisingly similar on paper and much the same can be said in relation to England and Scotland.

A different conceptual framework for categorising school evaluation systems in Europe is proposed by Meuret and Morlaix (2003: 55). Building on the work of Saunders (1999) they propose a two-category theory which they describe as the technical model and the participative model. The technical model they suggest rests on quantitative indicators which, 'are often imposed or strongly suggested by the authorities' while the participative model 'rests on school stakeholders' judgements'. These models are similar to Saunders (1999) categories, the 'English model' and the 'alternative model', and are, suggest Meuret and Morlaix (2003: 56) 'opposite regarding their organisational and also political meaning'.

Importantly, however, Meuret and Morlaix go on to say that in fact ambiguities exist in these models, or at least in the way in which they are implemented, which makes the categorisation much looser in practice. For instance, they suggest that the participative model does not in fact rule out external authorities from having any role in the process since, in some self-evaluations the judgement is delivered by the school on itself but partly on the basis of criteria advised or data provided by outside agencies. Similarly, many participative evaluations tend to make use of external agents in the form of critical friends to guide and facilitate the process. It is arguable, therefore, that the level of overlap between these categories is so great that they are more or less meaningless as categories.

A third system for categorising school evaluation or accountability systems is proposed by Anderson (2005: 3–7). The categories she proposes are:

1. Compliance with regulations
2. Adherence to professional norms
3. Results driven.

The first category is described by Anderson as 'rooted in an industrial model of education' and involves compliance with a set of laws, criteria and regulations laid down by the authorities. The example she chooses of this model is Ofsted in England and she defines this category as follows: 'educators are accountable *for* adherence to rules and accountable *to* the bureaucracy'. Her second category is 'based on adherence to professional norms' which are usually neither 'mandated nor required' but often grew out of traditions or professional self-regulation. Anderson summarises this model as 'educators accountable *for* adherence to standards and accountable *to* their peers' and suggests that this model is common in much of Europe. The third of Anderson's categories speaks for itself–evaluation of school and teacher performance 'based upon results with results defined in terms of student learning'. Interestingly, Anderson sees this third category as one which is growing more widespread due to 'increasing political involvement in education'. She summarises this third category as, 'educators are accountable *for* student learning and accountable *to* the general public'. This approach is dominant in the US.

However, as in the case of the two previous models of school evaluation that have been described above, those of MacBeath and Meuret/Morlaix, Anderson's model is, arguably, too rigid. Indeed, she somewhat acknowledges this herself when she remarks that 'educators often find themselves responding to all three systems attempting to balance the requirements of each'. In fact, in our view, the borderlines between Anderson's categories are so fluid that they are hard to justify as separate categories. For example, Ofsted the compliance system Anderson (2005: 7) cites, has in fact a very heavy emphasis on hard data, particularly pupil results, and thus could as easily fit into her third category. Equally, most professional norms have grown over time out of compliance systems, such as, for example, the regulation of teacher training requirements or fitness to practice criteria laid down by state teacher registration authorities or professional associations and therefore the border between these categories is also fluid.

There is in fact a remarkable range of other school evaluation models suggested by various writers. For example, Scheerens (2002), in a summary paper on the area, places all the models of school evaluation into four broad categories which he describes as the human relations model, the internal process model, the open system model and the rational goal model. It would be pointless to attempt to analyse all these models in detail. Suffice it to say that they all suffer from a similar problem namely that of over-rigid theoretical categorisation which breaks down when the systems categorised are examined in their implementation.

In essence, therefore, the more these proposed models and categories of school evaluation were examined in the course of this study, the more convinced the researchers became that the best way of conceptualising the different approaches is as a spectrum rather than as distinct categories. Therefore in the following section, it is proposed that such a spectrum or perhaps a number of related parallel spectra of subtly graduated approaches is the best way of both conceptualising and visualising the field of school evaluation.

The Spectrum of School Evaluation

This conceptualisation of school evaluation is reinforced by the work of another highly influential theorist and practitioner in the area, David Nevo. Nevo's (2002) recent work brings together essays from ten countries (seven in Europe, Israel, the US and Canada) around the theme of approaches to school evaluation and self-evaluation in each. As Nevo (2002 : x) remarks in his introduction, 'these case studies . . . represent actual experience with school based evaluation in various educational and social contexts with a wide range of local constraints and reflecting multiple evaluation perspectives'. What emerges clearly is the very broad range of different approaches with varying degrees of similarity and difference. For example,in the essay on Canada (entitled 'School based evaluation and the neo-liberal agenda') (McLean 2002 :201) argues that there is, in effect, no school-based evaluation remaining in Canada, as it has been destroyed by budget cuts and more and more external testing. In contrast, at the other end of the scale lies Germany where systematic evaluation or self-evaluation of schools is only now being seriously considered (ironically in the aftermath of national recriminations over the country's poor performance in the PISA international comparative achievement tests). Even within the examples drawn from Europe, the range of evaluation and self-evaluation methodologies is remarkably broad. It extends from England with the imposition of formal external inspection (even if, as we have seen, increasingly tempered by an emphasis on systematic self-evaluation) to most of Scandinavia where there is even less tradition of systematic external or self-evaluation than in Germany (although, as Johannsson et al (2002: 12) argue, the 'mania of evaluation' is fast spreading in Scandinavia also, a point supported by recent publications of the Finnish National Board of Education (1999)).

Bringing together the substantial literature on the field, the authors propose, if somewhat tentatively, that the following trends can be discerned:

1. School evaluation mechanisms are being further refined or newly constituted in virtually every country
2. Up to the recent past these mechanisms ranged from very 'hard-edged' evaluations, largely based on a student results model (mostly in North America) to a norms based approach founded on teacher compliance with general regulations and the 'norms of teacher professionalism' (as laid down through teacher training requirements or state regulation). The latter mode involves little or no systematic conduct of evaluation

or self-evaluation and was common in many parts of Europe particularly Scandinavia until very recently.

3. It is suggested that both models are in fact in decline and are being replaced by a standards-based model. This involves the definition of standards or performance indicators or themes for evaluation and self-evaluation. These indicators are produced either by schools themselves or by an external authority or a combination of the two. The standards are then enforced through a mixture of external inspection and internal self-evaluation based on the systematic collection of a range of data including but not confined to student attainment. The main variation within this model as increasingly applied in different jurisdictions is the relationship between external monitoring and self-evaluation.

4. Because of variations in practice from jurisdiction to jurisdiction the emerging map of school and teacher evaluation may most usefully be envisaged as a spectrum.

The spectrum being proposed would look something like the following:

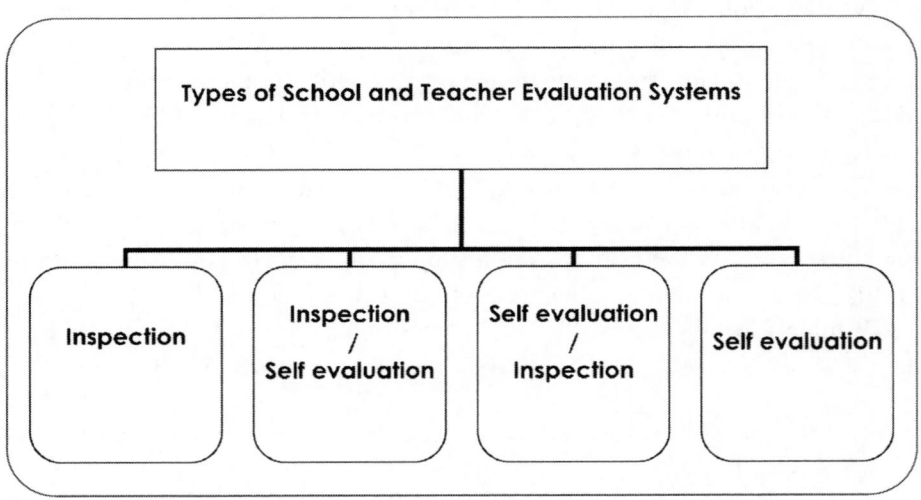

FIGURE 3: 1 : TYPES OF SCHOOL AND TEACHER EVALUATION SYSTEMS

It is argued that there is significant evidence that slowly and tentatively a convergence is emerging towards one area of the above spectrum namely around self-evaluation with a light-touch external inspection component.

To further understand the direction that school evaluation is taking, it is suggested that two further spectra parallel to the one above need to be explored and defined. Since it is the view of this study that the consensus emerging as described above is closely connected to the shifting purposes for which school evaluation is being utilised, the first of these parallel spectra is characterised as the accountability–teacher/school professional development spectrum. This ranges from the purpose of evaluation being perceived by the policymakers as primarily that of enforcing accountability at the one end to the encouragement of school and teacher professional development and autonomy at the other.

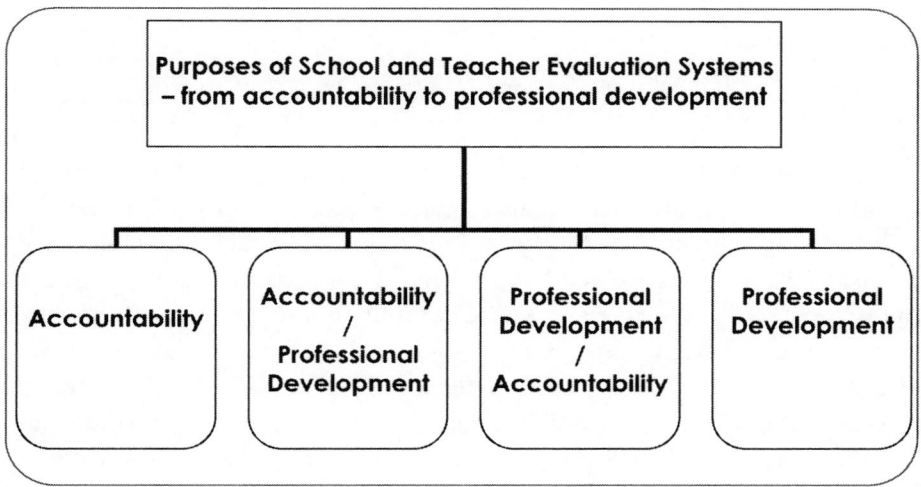

FIGURE 3: 2 : PURPOSES OF SCHOOL AND TEACHER EVALUATION SYSTEMS

Again it is argued that the evidence available suggests a clear convergence around an emphasis on professional and organisational development combined with a lesser concern for accountability.

The second parallel spectrum refers to the data and evidence required to support evaluation and ranges from systems where there is little or no systematic data collection for evaluation purposes to systems where the only data regarded as of value is pupil achievement scores and perhaps some other quantitive indicators. Once again it is argued that there is clear evidence of an increasing emphasis on a range of evidence beyond the merely quantitive.

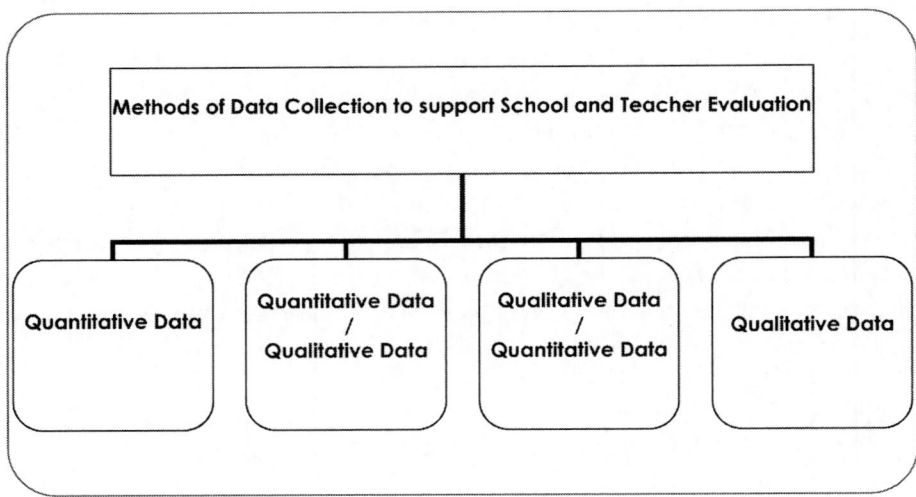

FIGURE 3: 3 METHODS OF DATA COLLECTION TO SUPPORT SCHOOL AND TEACHER EVALUATION

When we put these three spectra together, the range of options, as it were, for school evaluation systems becomes clearer. In practice, since it is argued that these three spectra are linked, it is not simply a matter of choice for policy makers to choose different elements from each spectrum and combine them into one system. In fact the evidence indicates that choosing an approach on the first spectrum above effectively implies a parallel position on the other two. Arguably as self-evaluation becomes increasingly dominant it follows that on the accountability–professional development spectrum, the emphasis increasingly lies on professional development with limited concerns around accountability. Equally it follows that in terms of data/evidence the emphasis will increasingly be on mixed methodologies including qualitative data and stressing internal collection and analysis of evidence. Thus combining the three spectra the following consensus emerges (see Figure 3.4).

Given that much of the recent concern with school and teacher evaluation is alleged to be an outcome of neoliberalism and the new public management, it may seem strange that such a consensual approach is emerging. However, it should be borne in mind that in countries where the neoliberal agenda is strongest, as in Bush era America, there are only limited, localised signs of this development. On the other hand, as Boyle (1997:52) points out, large swathes of Europe, including Ireland, have not been hugely influenced at all by neoliberalist theory. Moreover, the EU, a driving force in the direction of standardisation, competencies, evaluation and so on, and as such often

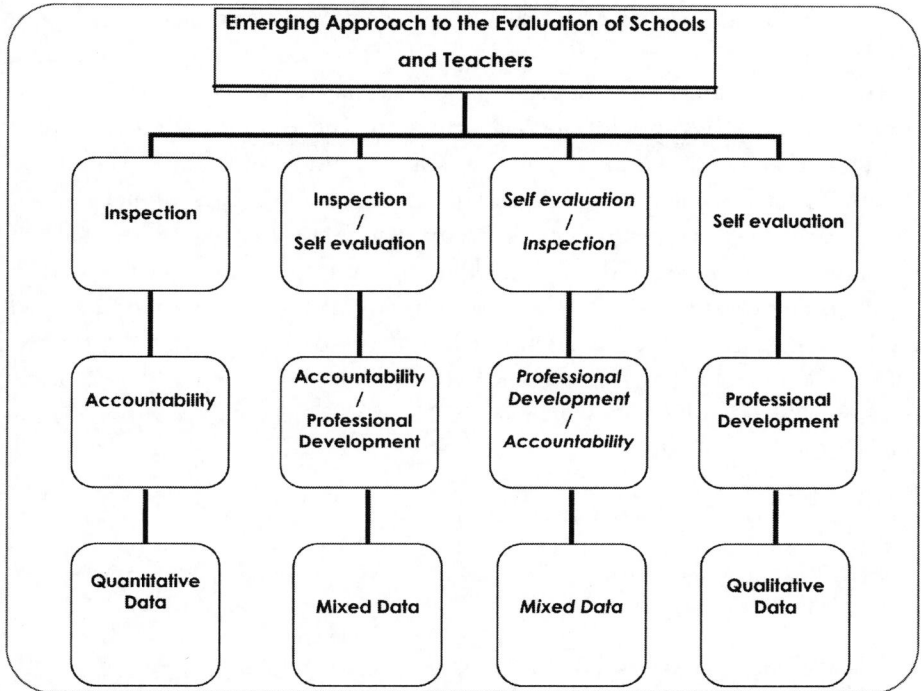

FIGURE 3: 4 EMERGING APPROACH TO THE EVALUATION OF SCHOOLS AND TEACHERS

accused of being focussed on the neoliberal agenda, has increasingly emphasised that its concern is essentially with compatibility of systems to facilitate the free market rather than with hard-nosed evaluation as such. In consequence, as we shall see, the theory and practice of quality assurance mechanisms including evaluation, which is emerging from developments in the EU, for example in the field of higher education, is very much in line with the moderate, cautious, consensus-driven self-evaluation model outlined above (McNamara and Kenny, 2006).

Even in England, where the neoliberal agenda was strong, a move towards the centre of our proposed school evaluation spectrum is evident. A number of factors are influencing this trend. Firstly, evidence has emerged that 'robust' school evaluation policies, whatever their merits, have major downsides in terms of school and teacher morale and are very costly to implement and maintain. Moreover, it has become clear that schools like pupils can be coached to the test and that therefore very widely spaced snapshots of school or teacher performance may in fact tell us little about the day to day reality (MacBeath, 2006). Undoubtedly the influence of seminal theorists of school and teacher evaluation, particularly John MacBeath, taken together with the apparently successful collaborative approach his work has bequeathed to Scotland, may have given pause for thought. At all events, and for whatever reasons, the Ofsted system in England has steadily inched across our spectrum, moving towards a greater concern with school and teacher self-evaluation and the associated elements of professional and organisational development and mixed methodology evaluative research techniques. A cursory glance at the school self-evaluation instruments developed and now widely used by Ofsted, confirms this trend.

The movement towards what one might call mixed theory and mixed method evaluation was predicted and even regarded as inevitable by Nevo (2002). Stating the dilemma that 'everyone seems to hate external evaluation but nobody trusts internal evaluation' (2002: 182), Nevo suggests that each is indispensable to the other:

> Educational officials ask me sometimes "we believe in external evaluation and are spending a lot of money on implementing our national school evaluation system. Why should we waste money on internal evaluation" and my answer is: "if you can overcome the resistance to external evaluation and if you think that it is useful and being used don't waste a penny on internal evaluation. But deep in your heart you know this is not the case". And schoolteachers often ask me "we know that you are a strong believer in teacher professionalisation, in school autonomy and in self evaluation and reflection, then why do you agree with external self evaluation", and my answer is "if you won't respect the responsibility and authority of the ministry of education, and the right of parents to know about the schools their children go to, don't expect them to respect your right for autonomy and reflection and to trust your judgement as a professional teacher." (ibid : 183)

Conclusion

In summary, then, it is argued in this chapter that as most school systems are in effect seeking a working compromise between external and internal evaluation and between school and teacher accountability and a reasonable degree of professional autonomy, a consensus around a particular approach to school evaluation is slowly but surely emerging, certainly in Europe. The framework of a model attempting to balance these seemingly irreconcilable objectives is becoming clearer. This model represents a series of compromises. Self-evaluation is prioritised but with a degree of external monitoring. School and teacher autonomy and professional development is emphasised but the system is also expected to provide a level of accountability. A wide range of data both quantitative and qualitative is to be used to generate evidence to support self-evaluation judgements and to justify these judgements to external stakeholders.

As a contribution to this development, part two of this study analyses the emerging model of school evaluation in Ireland. This is not to suggest that this model could or should be applied in its entirety anywhere else, indeed there is a strong counter argument to be made against any such attempt. The main reason that school evaluation systems are best represented as a spectrum is that contextual and cultural conditions are central to the evaluation of schools and teachers and thus are not the same in any two places. Rather it is to place the emerging system in Ireland within the theoretical framework outlined in this chapter and to suggest ways in which shortfalls both in theory and emerging practice might be made good. This it is hoped will contribute not only to the further improvement of the system in Ireland but also influence and improve the school evaluation model as it is developing in other systems.

PART 2

LOOKING AT OUR SCHOOLS

School and Teacher Evaluation in the Irish Context

Introduction

Schools and teachers in Ireland have a long history of being evaluated by a centralised inspectorate, a division of the Department of Education and Science. However, by the early nineteen nineties this system had broken down to a significant degree. The inspection of primary schools had become sporadic and rather idiosyncratic but still existed. In secondary schools inspection had nearly ceased entirely and in fact the largest teacher union supported its members in refusing to teach in front of an inspector.

The reasons for this decline in inspection are varied and need not detain us here. What is interesting is that the impetus for a new approach to inspection and school evaluation in the mid nineteen nineties came from external sources rather than from any pressing domestic demand. This is made clear in the evaluation report prepared by the Department of Education and Science (DES) after the first Whole-School Evaluation (WSE) pilot project form nineteen ninety six to nineteen ninety nine (DES 1999 a). For example, the introduction justifies the development of the WSE pilot scheme by noting that 'across the European Union a wide range of approaches is evident to the assessment and evaluation of schools' (DES 1999 a: 8). On page nine we read that 'there is now a growing tendency across Europe to see external and internal school evaluation processes as being inextricably linked'. Later on the same page it is suggested that 'there is an increasing effort to encourage schools to review their own progress in a formal way . . . to engage in their own development planning'.

The external influences made explicit in the above quotes show clearly that, as Boyle (1997) argues, EU policy in the direction of new public management systems such as strategic planning and systematic evaluation have been a key driver of change in the Irish context. As Boyle (1997, 2002) suggests, it was not so much any domestic policy or ideology that drove this process, but rather a migration of EU evaluation policy, together with a strong sense that, as these developments appeared to be happening everywhere else, it was potentially dangerous to lag behind. It is no coincidence that in other areas of education, particularly vocational, adult and higher education, in health and other social services, and indeed across the public sector as a whole, the late nineteen nineties and early years of this century have witnessed similar developments to those described in the following three chapters.

However, as Boyle (1997) also points out, the implementation of these initiatives in Ireland has been strongly governed by the corporatist tradition of political and social partnership on the one hand, and the lack of any significant ideological commitment on the other. These factors, combined with other contextual restraints, notably the strength of the trade unions, have strongly influenced the consensus approach to evaluation in general and particularly to school and teacher evaluation which has emerged in practice.

The following three chapters chart these developments and analyse the strengths and weaknesses of the system of evaluation now operational in all Irish schools. In chapter four, the earliest iterations of a school development planning and whole-school evaluation approach is described and analysed. This took the form of a pilot project which ran from nineteen ninety six to nineteen ninety nine and was thoroughly evaluated on completion. In chapter five, the eventual outcome of this experimental pilot project is described. A framework for school and teacher evaluation entitled *Looking At Our School (LAOS)* emerged, which now forms the basis of a national system of school evaluation. This framework is considered in detail. Finally, chapter six reports on research case studies conducted in two thousand and five and two thousand and six in twenty-four schools from among the first cohort to undergo whole school evaluation. The purpose of this research was to identify the strengths and weaknesses of the emerging school and teacher evaluation system.

A TOE IN THE WATER

The Whole-School Evaluation Project

Starting from Scratch–Developing a School Planning and Evaluation Framework

This chapter analyses important interrelated developments in school development planning (SDP) and whole-school evaluation (WSE) in Ireland in the
past decade. In particular, it examines the outcomes of a pilot project on
whole-school evaluation conducted by the Department of Education and
Science (DES). This project subsequently became the foundation for the
national system of school and teacher evaluation which has emerged in Ireland
since two thousand and three. The chapter also is concerned to an extent with
the school development planning framework which has emerged contemporaneously with WSE. This is because the DES sees both processes as closely
linked forming between them a system of quality assurance for schools and
teachers.

Traditionally, schools in the Irish education system and the teachers within them have not tended to engage in collaborative planning or evaluation
processes (Lynch and O'Riordan, 1996). Moreover the implementation of these
processes in other systems, particularly in England, or at least the way in which
these experiences are often characterised, resulted in considerable reluctance

to engage in anything that smacks of appraisal, planning, target-setting, bench-marking and so on (O'Hara and McNamara, 1999). In addition, as mentioned previously, by the mid nineteen nineties, inspection, for a variety of reasons, had become sporadic at best and at worst non-existent in the Irish school system.

In recent times, however, a number of factors have conspired to encourage or perhaps even coerce the DES to begin to revisit the issue of school and teacher evaluation. Chief among these factors was, as we have seen, education, and evaluation policies and initiatives at EU level and in many European coun-tries. The influence of this development is clearly indicated in the foreword to the WSE pilot project report (1999a: 8). Also influential, however, were less prag-matic, more education focussed factors such as the trend towards openness and accountability in all public institutions and the increasing acceptance among educationalists that whole-school planning and evaluation are purposeful means of promoting school effectiveness and development (Hargreaves, 1994).

In order to encourage these developments, the DES designed a WSE pilot project involving some thirty five schools, both primary and post primary, throughout Ireland. The project ran from nineteen ninety six to nineteen ninety nine. To evaluate this project, data of both a qualitative and quantita-tive nature were collected from each school in the project by the DES and used as the basis of a substantial government report (DES, 1999a).

At the same time, the DES has in recent years actively encouraged all schools to develop a school plan through a process of school development plan-ning. In fact, the Education Act of 1998 made the development of such a plan compulsory. The Education Act (section 21) (1998) requires the following:

21. (1) A board shall, as soon as may be after its appointment, make arrangements for the preparation of a plan (in this section referred to as 'the school plan') and shall ensure that the plan is regular-ly reviewed and updated.

(2) The school plan shall state the objectives of the school relating to equality of access to and participation in the school by students with disabilities or who have other special educational needs.

(3) The school plan shall be prepared in accordance with such direc-tions, including directions relating to consultation with the par-ents, the patron, staff and students of the school, as may be given from time to time by the Minister in relation to school plans.

(4) A board shall make arrangements for the circulation of copies of the school plan to the patrons, parents, teachers and other staff of the school.

Interestingly, all thirty five schools in the WSE project had a school plan or were developing one, although this was not a requirement for inclusion. The results of the WSE project therefore allow us to examine the relationship between the process of evaluation as conceived and conducted in this project and the process of school development planning. The DES expresses the view in the WSE Report (DES 1999a: 16) that the two processes are inseparable, 'two sides of the same coin, complementing each other'. Yet while there is evidence that in some ways the relationship is a positive one, some of the project data appear to indicate that pressures and tensions also exist.

To appreciate the complexity of the whole-school evaluation/school development planning relationship it is necessary to see how these processes have been conceptualised in the Irish education context. This is particularly the case with WSE since the approach adopted in Ireland has been defined as 'consultative evolutionary evaluation' (McNamara and O'Hara, 2001:101) and is, to put it mildly, less threatening and intrusive than approaches taken elsewhere. This chapter therefore continues with a brief description of the emergence of the policy and practice of school development planning in the Irish context. It proceeds to look in more detail at the WSE pilot project and, finally, it attempts to isolate the positive and negative elements of the relationship between the two processes. The overall purpose is to contextualise how policy has developed as WSE and SDP have subsequently been 'mainstreamed' in tandem.

School Development Planning: A Key Reform Policy

Isolationism in schools, the egg crate structure as described by Lortie (1975), has been particularly prevalent in Ireland (Lynch and O'Riordan, 1996). These authors suggest a number of possible reasons for this; the willingness (or determination, depending on your point of view) of the members of religious orders to take upon themselves the management of schools (including middle management roles) and the resultant lack of opportunity for teachers to manage, plan and collaborate being probably the most convincing.

At all events, rapid change in the Irish education system, and influential research at home and abroad, have moved school development planning and school and teacher evaluation from the periphery to the centre of education policy in a very short time. As indicated above, the Education Act of 1998 in effect makes SDP and WSE compulsory, and very detailed frameworks and guidelines for conducting both procedures in schools have been issued by the DES (DES, 1999b; DES, 1999a). The rationale underpinning SDP and WSE offered in these framework documents makes reference to the domestic and international research on the topic.

Particularly influential has been research in Ireland by Hannan et al. (1996), Devine and Swan (1997) and more recently by Smyth (1999), highlighting the importance of school climate in determining pupil outcomes including both academic and personal development. Key variables identified in this regard include:

- The creation of an orderly learning environment for pupils along with the clear and consistent application and enforcement of school rules
- The quality of teacher-pupil relationships
- High expectations of pupils and staff
- A positive, caring culture which values, challenges and supports pupils, teachers and the school community
- A commitment to developing pupils' personal and social development (in addition to their academic development) and providing the necessary supports for pupils with special learning needs
- A shared collaborative approach to school development.

Devine and Swan (1997) in their research, as part of a larger international school effectiveness research project, suggest that the care exhibited in the formulation of the school plan was a characteristic of effectiveness in the case-study schools.

Similarly the international literature on the subject suggests that a school climate which encourages discussion, review and evaluation is less likely to suffer the ravages of 'group think' (Fullan, 1993) or what MacBeath (1999) calls the ostrich mentality, seeing problems as out there and hiding in the hope that they go away! A positive climate is often cited as a major feature of effective schools (Mortimore et al., 1988; Teddie and Springfield, 1993).

Influenced by this research the framework documents stress that collaboration is the key to effective SDP and WSE and emphasise that the planning and evaluation process is of more importance than the product. The view of Hargreaves and Hopkins (1993: 57) that 'internal conditions' are paramount in enabling effective change management in schools is fully endorsed.

The research on effective schools, both in the UK (Mortimore *et al*, 1988) and in the USA (Purkey and Smith, 1983), has found that certain internal conditions are typical in schools that achieve higher levels of outcomes for their students.

The 'internal conditions' referred to revolve around the capacity of each school to harness its own resources in the effective management of change. This in turn requires the empowerment of the staff through shared ownership of change and innovation in a framework enabling each staff member to take a much fuller role in self-evaluation, strategic planning and professional decision-making. The goal is to improve schools from within by employing teachers as active agents of change within their own organisations.

The emphasis on SDP as an entirely internal process centring on the school community and its stakeholders is fully followed through in defining the nature of the plan which it is hoped will emerge. The SDP framework envisages that the school plan, as a written document (the 'product which emanates from a shared collaborative process' (DES, 1999b: 6)), will primarily aim to facilitate coordinated development within the entire school community. The school plan, it is suggested, should not be an unwieldy tome of rules and procedures but,

> rather, it should be a flexible, responsive framework for collaborative activity and a powerful tool for the management of change. Such a document can only be arrived at by collaboration and dialogue within the school community. (DES 1999b: 16)

So far so good, in the sense that SDP is clearly seen as an internal school process, which although a legal requirement does not demand particular goals, targets or outcomes and recognises that schools 'know their own strengths and the aspects of school life which require further development' (DES, 1999b: 13).

However, at the same time as SPD, the DES introduced the WSE pilot project and proposed like SDP to extend it to all schools eventually. Despite the conciliatory language of consultative evaluation referred to previously, evaluation by any reasonable definition suggests some form of measurement against objectives, aims, goals and targets and a concern with quality assurance and organisational and individual performance. It is clear immediately that there is a possibility for tensions between these two processes. Therefore an important question arises as to whether the relationship between collaborative planning in schools and evaluation designed to provide some degree of fuller accountability can be as uncomplicated and unproblematic as the DES suggest.

Whole-School Evaluation Irish Style

The potentially difficult relationship between planning and evaluation has been the subject of some comment in other countries. Hopkins and Lagerweij (1996: 83) summarise the emerging concept of school development planning and its relationship to evaluation as follows:

> It (planning) provides a generic and paradigmatic process, combining as it does select-ed curriculum change with modifications to the school's management arrangements or organisation. As compared with school review, where evaluation is the initial step in the cycle, development planning emphasises evaluation occurring, often in differ-ent forms, throughout the process.

As these approaches to change management have become more dominant, certain tensions have emerged. For example, there are contradictory pressures for centralised government control over policy and curricula on the one hand and decentralised responsibility for implementation, resource management and evaluation at local level on the other. According to Hopkins *et. al.* (1994: 68),

> the key challenge, as a recent OECD report makes clear, is to find a balance between the increasing demands for centrally determined policy initiatives and quality control and the encouragement of locally developed school improvement efforts.

However, the rhetoric-reality gap between policy and practice is particu-larly hard to break down in relation to school planning when accompanied by evaluation. Teachers in Ireland, particularly second level teachers, have little or no experience of being evaluated or inspected. In fact, since the teacher unions effectively prohibited members from teaching in front of an inspector, most second level teachers proceeded through their careers without ever hav-ing experienced an externally controlled evaluation of their teaching. Moreover teachers continue to be suspicious of imposed or 'contrived' collegiality, partic-ularly when accompanied by targets, performance criteria and appraisal systems. For example, research by Sugrue (1997), which sought the opinions of prima-ry school principals and teachers on inspection and planning, found that most perceived it as a process over which teachers have little control, despite the rhetoric of collaboration. In this climate of suspicion the WSE project was designed with enormous care and the language used was intended to allay any suspicions that judgements were to be made or the work of individual teach-ers criticised.

WSE was developed by the DES as 'a developmental model to serve the Trinitarian purposes of school improvement, school development and school effectiveness' (DES, 1999a: 17). The model stressed that schools were at various stages on a continuum of effectiveness and that schools are 'more' or 'less' effective on the continuum, as opposed to being 'effective' or 'ineffective' in absolute terms. Considerable attention was given to developing an acceptable cultural and contextual language in which the model and its outcomes would be couched. Original documentation referred to the model as a 'whole school inspection (WSI)' using 'performance indicators (PIs)' with a specific focus on evaluating 'the quality of teaching and learning'. Subsequent wide-ranging consultation with the various 'education partners' (e.g. teacher unions, school governing body authorities and national parents' associations) yielded 'valuable insights' which contributed to 'useful amendments' to the original model. As implemented, WSI became known as whole-school evaluation (WSE), using evaluation criteria (as opposed to performance indicators) to evaluate aspects of school life, including the quality of learning and teaching (as opposed to teaching and learning) (DES 1999a: 17–18).

The WSE Pilot project reported on three features of life in the 35 schools:

- The quality of school planning
- The quality of learning and teaching
- The quality of school management.

At post-primary level, the pilot project examined the quality of learning and teaching in a selected number of subjects in each school while at primary level all teachers in the school were evaluated. The final phase of the planning work involved an exhaustive series of meetings between the 'education partners', beginning with a consultative conference attended by delegates from 19 organisations representing teachers, parents, management and trustees and the DES. Subsequent to the conference, which agreed in principle that a professional evaluation of schools was necessary (O'Dalaigh, 2000), long and tedious negotiations took place over the detail of implementation, and particularly the language of the evaluation criteria.

Eventually the general framework agreed stressed that the emphasis of the evaluation would be on the work of the school as a whole and that individual teachers would not be identified in the WSE reports. It was agreed that the data obtained during the WSE project (or elsewhere) would not be used to compare schools locally or nationally or to construct league tables of schools. As indicated above, great care was taken to develop non-threatening language in the design of the criteria to be used in evaluating each of the areas chosen. Finally it was agreed that the process would take into account the unique contextual factors of each school, specifically those factors relating to the socio-economic background of pupils, range of pupil ability and level of resources.

However, importantly, despite these concessions, WSE did maintain many of the key elements of the original proposal and resisted attempts to make the process one of entirely internal self-review or self-evaluation. The original concept had been that the evaluation process would be an external validation of internal evaluation and was likened to holding up a mirror to the life of a school (O'Dalaigh, 2000). It was envisaged that this would involve external evaluation conducted by the inspectorate. Surprisingly this version of WSE was largely agreed, as was, to the amazement of many observers, the proposal that the visiting inspectors could observe post primary teachers teaching and examine their students on their work. In the context of the Irish post-primary sector this represented a very major development (McNamara and O'Hara, 2001).

The bulk of the evaluation work took place in nineteen ninety nine and the process used was as follows (DES, 2000a):

1. An initial meeting took place between the school principal and the relevant inspector. A second meeting was held with all staff members, followed by meetings with the teachers in the areas of the curriculum to be evaluated. A separate meeting was held with representatives of the board of management.

2. Following these meetings the WSE team of inspectors visited the school. The evaluation first focused on planning and management and these areas were discussed with relevant personnel and related documentation (such as the School Plan) was examined. Classroom visits by inspectors dealing with a particular subject area focused on evaluating the quality of learning and teaching in the context of the relevant curriculum. The inspectors observed the nature of teacher-pupil interactions and engaged with the class in a variety of ways, such as asking questions, giving a short written assignment, listening to oral reports of work completed or reviewing a sample of copybooks. When the inspector visit was completed, oral feedback and advice were given privately to each teacher concerned.

3. Shortly after the evaluation visits had been completed, post-evaluation meetings were arranged between the designated reporting inspector and

the principal, the whole school staff and the staff members directly involved in the evaluation. The work of the school was discussed and the findings of the evaluation outlined. Strengths and areas for further development were also discussed. In most schools, a separate meeting was also held with representatives of the board of management at which findings of the evaluation were outlined.

4. Finally a whole-school evaluation report was given to each school. The reports completed by the inspectors discussed the operation of management and planning and the learning and teaching that was seen to take place. They focused on the work of the whole school and not on the work of individuals. There was particular emphasis on affirming positive elements of the school's work and suggesting lines for further curricular, managerial and organisational development. Since all aspects of the reports had been discussed previously at the post-evaluation meeting, the reports themselves were intended to act as a summary of findings of the evaluation in the school and as a basis for further in-school development planning.

Evaluating WSE

Information on how the WSE pilot project developed in practice was obtained from a series of questionnaires sent to all participating schools (principals and teachers) and to inspectors who conducted the evaluation in those schools. In addition, approximately one-third of the schools involved were chosen at random for a follow-up contact, during which principals were asked about their views on the process and its outcomes in their school.

In general the data indicate that WSE as a process in its own right and in tandem with SDP was seen in a largely positive light by principals, teachers and inspectors (although significantly more so by principals than by teachers). Negative outcomes and possible seeds for future problems were also identified, but first the positive findings will be mentioned.

The evaluation report (DES, 1999a: 47) on the WSE pilot project concludes that WSE is a 'viable and effective approach to evaluating the functioning of schools' and was perceived positively by the schools and other parties involved. Unquestionably, the 'consultative evolutionary development of the model' paid valuable dividends (McNamara and O'Hara, 2001:104). A partnership approach, transparent and negotiable, was adopted by the DES at the very outset of the project. More importantly, consultation and discussion with the stakeholders (schools, managerial/governing authorities, religious denominational and other interest groups, parents and teacher unions) was maintained throughout the various stages of the process (and indeed since the end of the pilot project).

The data also suggest that the WSE project succeeded to a considerable extent in generating a whole-school/wider community culture of quality assurance, shared by the key stakeholders (McNamara and O'Hara, 2001). This took much time, resources and an enormous investment of human commitment and goodwill. The buoyant economic climate has enabled a more substantial capital flow into education. In this context, the WSE pilot project was timely. Resources, both human and financial, necessary for its implementation and subsequent development, were not spared. This understandably served to bolster goodwill among members of the inspectorate, teacher unions and teachers but also raised major questions as to whether such an intensive and time-consuming initiative could in reality be spread across the entire school system.

Another positive outcome was the sense in which an interlinked process of planning and evaluation gained a foothold in the education system. It would seem that a more strategic, enlightened eye (Eisner, 1999) view of external school evaluation was potentially now in place in Ireland and that in tandem schools might at last be supported and scaffolded following inspection in order to ensure improvement and development (Sugrue, 1997). School inspection was now clearly linked to capacity-building, enabling schools to identify their own needs, draft their own development/action plan, target their resources, and ultimately build a positive, reflective and collaborative culture of school self-review and consensus. The building of high consensus (Rosenholtz, 1989) schools in which there is an educative climate and agreement on institutional goals and strategies to realise these goals is the core to school improvement and development and SDP/WSE appeared to provide a mechanism to enable progress in this direction. Taken together these positive outcomes represent a considerable success. However, less encouraging outcomes can also be identified.

On the negative side it can be argued (as in a very critical *Irish Times* piece by columnist Fintan O'Toole) that the WSE project by the very nature of its collaborative and non-threatening posture lacked much credibility as an evaluation (as the term is widely understood). As such, O'Toole (2000) suggested, it did little service to any of the stakeholders and indicated a closed and defensive mentality among teachers. There is no doubt that, in making the process acceptable to teachers, the concerns of other stakeholders were downplayed. For example, the concentration on whole school rather than individual teacher performance placed question marks over the future direction and credibility of WSE as did the very limited role given to pupils and parents.

As a result it emerged quite starkly that one of the greatest challenges facing the adoption of WSE as a national model was the manner in which the evaluation criteria employed might be used in schools as a self-evaluation tool, tailored to meet the individual school's needs while at the same time meeting external expectations concerning accountability.

In addition, the absence of evaluation criteria for each specific curricular subject in the original WSE model needed to be addressed, if change was to be effective at classroom level. An increasing body of evidence (Scheerens and Bosker, 1997; Taylor Fitz-Gibbon, 1996) suggests that differential effectiveness exists in schools and that significant variance among pupils' achievements can be attributed more to differences at classroom rather than whole-school level. Furthermore there is a body of evidence from the school effectiveness research which suggests that students' performance may be high in one subject and low in another (Smyth, 1999). How might a model such as WSE, dedicated to improving learning processes and outcomes at school level, accommodate the inherent challenge posed by such research? With its overriding emphasis on overall school performance, could WSE develop strategies to deal with ineffective subject departments and ineffective classroom teaching, particularly at second level?

A further issue arising from the WSE pilot project (which also relates to teacher sensitivities) concerned the commitment to the promotion of a democratic, inclusive approach to evaluation at school level. The views of pupils, as key stakeholders in the teaching-learning process, were not sought during the pilot project. A token gesture of involvement was offered to the parent body (parent representatives on the school's governing body met with the inspectors) during the pilot project. What is worth fighting for in quality assurance? In a democratic, socially inclusive society as Ireland would purport to be, a widely held view is that schools must be enabled to speak for themselves (MacBeath: 1996, 1999). Accordingly, negotiating an appropriate role for the various stakeholders in WSE emerged as a thorny issue in the side of policy-makers, bearing in mind the volatile teacher union context. At the conclusion of the WSE project it appeared certain, however, that national parent organisations, who have gained increased power in recent years, would demand that parents must play a more proactive role in educational evaluation particularly WSE. Equally, it seemed likely that increasing consciousness of their potential role would encourage students to seek a much greater voice in issues concerning their own education.

Another issue which emerged was unhappiness with the allegedly softly softly approach taken. This is very clear from the research with principals and inspectors. Many principals pointedly noted that the WSE framework as tested in the pilot allowed for a detailed evaluation of school management, planning, etc., but not for the evaluation of individual teachers. For this reason it was felt that the process was 'largely an evaluation of management' and that most critically, even where teacher weaknesses were identified, the existing situation where it is possible to do next to nothing about them remained unchallenged. In the words of one principal speaking for many, 'WSE can make recommendations but in itself won't cure weaknesses in any school' (DES 1999a:27).

Similar frustrations were echoed by many of the inspectors involved. Several remarked that, due to lack of regular testing in both primary and post primary education in Ireland, the 'hard data' on which to base 'real' judgements are not available–'access is required to better organised in-school data on pupil performance' and the WSE process 'should involve the collection of hard data' (DES 1999a:20). It became clear that key data which schools in theory possess such as drop-out rates, levels of absenteeism and so on were not available in a usable, accessible format. Likewise individual teachers or subject departments had little in the way of collected or collated information on pupil results, aptitudes or attitudes. In short no process that could remotely be regarded as systematic evidence-based self-evaluation was occurring in schools. Since self-evaluation and the presentation of evidence to support judgements was in theory a foundation stone of WSE this outcome represented a major problem with the proposed system. The lack of usable data whether provided by the schools and teachers or by some other mechanism emerged clearly as a key weakness of WSE which would have to be addressed before the process was mainstreamed.

Lastly 'political sensitivities' to be respected in writing the final reports also irritated the inspectors and involved them in a workload which would be 'untenable if the project was mainstreamed' and resulted in reports which, in the caustic works of one inspector, 'invariably tended towards superficiality' (DES 1999a: 21).

Despite these reservations it must be noted that the data indicate a largely positive response to WSE from both principals and inspectors. Moreover it also emerged that the care taken to allay fears paid dividends in that teachers ranked the improvement of the quality of their relationship with the inspectorate as the most positive outcome of the project. This is in stark contrast to the hostility to inspection that has characterised previous debate around the issue of evaluation.

Principals and inspectors were particularly positive about the relationship between SDP and WSE, suggesting in the words of one principal that both procedures combined 'served as a focal point through which we re-structured all our professional efforts in the school' (DES 1999a: 6). Moreover all categories of respondents tended to see SDP as a natural corollary of WSE in the sense of providing a vehicle through which change and improvement could be implemented when the 'snapshot' of WSE was completed.

A final positive and indeed remarkable outcome was that teachers agreed to be evaluated at all and moreover were then positive (if not as positive as other respondents) in their evaluations of the process. Here again there appears to be a clear link between SDP and WSE in the sense that the data suggest that the experience of the former made teachers rather more confident and less defensive about the latter (McNamara and O'Hara, 2001).

After WSE—The Way Forward

Despite the reservations noted, the first efforts at both SDP and WSE must be regarded as a success, even if a somewhat surprising and unexpected success. The DES (2000b: 3) itself saw the WSE process being mainstreamed with the following improvements:

> Feedback from participating stakeholders highlighted a number of lacunae in the pilot project model and illuminated a more inclusive, contextually sensitive model. Building on this feedback, the proposed WSE model for mainstreaming shortly will incorporate an evaluation of additional areas of school life, i.e. curriculum provision, school ethos and support for students. Upholding the principle of transparency, evaluation criteria will be available to schools and all interested parties. School context variables which impact on learning will be taken into account during WSE e.g. pupil background factors, pupil ability levels and existing resources. Reporting on evaluation in schools will be based on fair, reliable evidence as opposed to impressionistic reportage. The primary focus of WSE will be on the functioning of the school as a whole. In accordance with national legislation the comparative performance of schools in the form of league tables will not be compiled.

The DES (2000b: 3) defined the future relationship between WSE and SDP as a 'twin track developmental approach which will be central to educational policy'. Alongside the conduct of external review by the inspectorate, schools it was envisaged would be increasingly encouraged to use the evaluation criteria as a tool for school self-evaluation. School improvement and quality assurance policy in Ireland was henceforth to be founded on a 'twin-track' approach with school self-evaluation running parallel to whole-school evaluation conducted by the inspectorate. This represented a degree of clarity about future directions which was certainly a new departure.

In addition, the DES suggested that WSE would provide a 'stream of high quality data' for making policy decisions, and offer a 'feedback loop at system level on the overall quality of school provision in the country' (1999b: 12). These data would enable 'like to be compared with like allowing valid, full and reliable judgements in relation to quality assurance'.

At its completion in nineteen ninety nine the WSE project had achieved a significant breakthrough. It had tested a functioning system of school and teacher evaluation which had by and large been positively received in the pilot schools and had aroused no serious opposition among the key stakeholders. On the other hand, fundamental problems with the proposed system had also emerged. Chief among these were a lack of data and evidence on which to base judgements and a very limited role for key stakeholders, particularly parents and pupils. However, these shortcomings were acknowledged in the WSE final project evaluation report and it was therefore reasonable to expect that they would be addressed in the context of the wider expansion of WSE to all schools. In the next chapter, we will examine the model of school evaluation that finally emerged following the pilot. We will do so with a view not only to examining the impact of the WSE experimental model on the final framework but also to see in particular how the critical issues raised by stakeholders were addressed by the DES.

LOOKING AT OUR SCHOOLS

An Emerging Evaluation Framework

Introduction

In common with most European countries, Ireland has been attempting for some years to develop a system of school evaluation which balances external monitoring and inspection with internal autonomy and accountability (CERI, 1995; Nevo, 2002). The first iteration of this process was described in chapter four. It was a pilot project in thirty five schools entitled Whole-School Evaluation (WSE) which was undertaken in the late nineteen nineties and completed in nineteen ninety nine (DES, 1999a; McNamara, O'Hara and Ní Aingléis, 2002). However, a series of rancorous industrial disputes rendered impossible any further mention of evaluation and inspection until two thousand and three. In that year, a new framework for school evaluation building upon WSE entitled *Looking at Our School* (*LAOS*), was published by the Department of Education and Science. The first evaluations of schools under this framework took place in two thousand and four. The framework documents, which set out the new national process of school and teacher evaluation, are analysed in this chapter. The implementation of the new evaluation scheme will be considered in the next chapter.

This chapter analyses the context of the evaluation framework which emerged into a difficult educational environment. Key interests, particularly teachers, are strongly resistant to what they perceive to be reductionist managerialist interference in their professional autonomy. Additionally, the current economic success of the country has been based on cooperation and negotiation between the social partners, a model which is perceived to preclude invasive inspection or appraisal of professionals in their workplace, and requires all change to proceed only after the achievement of consensus. However, other stakeholders, the EU, OECD, and, nearer home, parents, business interests and elements in the media, are increasingly vocal in demanding that hard data about the performance of teachers and schools be made available in a transparent fashion. Likewise it is perceived that maintaining international competitiveness and attracting overseas investment requires evidence that the schools are as effective or more so than in competing countries (Sugrue, 2004). Moreover, it is clear that in one form or another, and whether for bureaucratic and managerialist reasons, or to enhance autonomy and decentralisation, most EU countries are seeking to implement a school evaluation system (Haug and Schwandt, 2003; Nevo, 2002; Scheerens *et. al.*, 1999; Schollaert, 2000). Into this fraught scenario, a model of school evaluation (*LAOS*), based on the pilot project described in the last chapter, was introduced reluctantly and with great caution by the DES.

This chapter begins with a brief overview of the educational policy context designed to make clear the sensitivities around introducing new approaches to evaluation. It continues with an analysis of the *LAOS* documentation which identifies the key elements of the framework and analyses some of its strengths and weaknesses. This analysis is conducted with particular regard to the extent to which the problems identified in the evaluation of the WSE pilot project are addressed in *LAOS*.

Policy Context

In May 2003, the DES in Ireland published twin documents entitled *Looking At Our School, an aid to self evaluation in primary schools* and *Looking At Our School, an aid to self evaluation in post primary schools* (DES, 2003 a & b) (these documents, although designed for different levels of the education system, are so similar in content that they can be treated as one in this chapter and are referred to hereafter as *LAOS* and referenced as DES, 2003). The publications contain a very detailed framework for the inspection and evaluation of schools and teachers, including one hundred and forty three 'themes for self-evaluation' which schools and teachers are invited to consider in preparation for an external evaluation by the inspectorate. The *LAOS* framework is built upon the outcomes of the WSE pilot project which, as was discussed in the previous chapter, had concluded some three years earlier (DES, 1999a). WSE represented a first experiment, a toe in the water of school evaluation, in a system in which evaluation, inspection and appraisal are regarded as deeply controversial, especially by the powerful teacher unions.

The WSE project is described in chapter four, but in short it was designed with an emphasis on cooperation and partnership rather than monitoring and accountability. As we have seen, this softly, softly approach was probably necessary in the context of a system in which the experience of external inspection had been very limited in the previous three decades. In the case of post primary schools, inspection had been virtually non-existent; while in primary schools, though inspection was more widespread, it was conducted in a very benign, irregular and idiosyncratic manner (Sanders and Greaney, 1986; Sugrue, 1999). This tradition of inspection, such as it was, left a legacy whereby most principals and teachers either had no experience at all of evaluation or perceived it to be something external, done to them, rather than something which is part of their professional responsibility. Moreover this lack of experience of inspection and evaluation had been compounded by other factors tending to increase unease and resistance. These included the substantial power exercised by teacher unions, negative reports of school evaluation in other systems, particularly Ofsted in England, and the partnership framework through which public sector change must be negotiated and paid for (Boyle, 1993; Cullingford, 1999; Earley, 1998; Norton Grubb, 1999; Ofsted 1998; Stoll and Fink, 1996).

Despite a commitment at the end of the pilot project to mainstream WSE, no further mention of inspection or evaluation took place until late two thousand and two. During this time, a rancorous and lengthy series of industrial disputes was perceived to have soured the climate in schools, particularly post primary schools. Such was the depth of animosity engendered by these disputes that it was widely felt that whole-school evaluation, or indeed any form of school evaluation or inspection, was a dead letter. Thus, an announcement rather out of the blue in late two thousand and two by the then Minister for Education and Science, to the effect that work on school evaluation was proceeding, and that he expected to see it operational in all schools in the near future, caused considerable surprise. Nonetheless the *LAOS* framework was published in two thousand and three (DES, 2003) and the first round of school evaluations began in late two thousand and four.

Looking at Our Schools (LAOS)

In the *LAOS* documents an elaborate system of evaluation themes is outlined as the basis on which school management and staff can make 'professional judgements regarding the operation of the school' (DES 2003: ix). The evaluation themes in *LAOS* are structured into 'areas' which are in turn made up of a number of 'aspects' each of which have a series of 'components' which in their turn have a series of 'themes for self-evaluation' attached to them (DES 2003 : x). It may be noteworthy that these terms, area, aspect and component, replace terms such as 'evaluation criteria' used in the WSE project - an indication perhaps of the immense sensitivity to anything smacking of evaluation in any form in the Irish education system. There are five 'areas' in total:

- Quality of learning and teaching in subjects
- Quality of support for students
- Quality of school management
- Quality of school planning
- Quality of curriculum provision.

Each area has a number of aspects attached, each of which in turn has a number of components, for example:

Area: Quality of learning and teaching in subjects

Aspects: Planning and Preparation, Teaching and Learning and Assessment and Achievement

Components (of, for example, Planning and Preparation): Planning of Work and Planning of Resources.

Each of the 'components' has in turn attached to it a set of 'themes for self-evaluation' which the document suggests 'can be used by the school as a guide in judging or measuring its own performance'. For example the 'themes for self-evaluation' for the component 'planning of work' are as follows:

Component: Planning of Work

Themes for self-evaluation:

1. Long term planning for the teaching of the subject and its consistency with the school plan.

2. The extent to which planning documents describe the work to be completed within the subject.
3. The degree to which planning is in line with syllabus requirements and guidelines.
4. The degree to which planning provides for differential approaches to curriculum coverage in accordance with the spectrum of student ability, needs and interests.
5. The extent to which provision for corrective action for learning problems or difficulties is an integral part of the planning of work in the subject.
6. Evidence of cross-curriculum planning and integration.
7. The provision for monitoring, review and evaluation of the planning of work in the subject.

The methodology suggested for using these themes 'while engaging in a self-evaluation exercise' is described as follows:

> A school may decide to focus on an area, an aspect or a component. The school will gather information in relation to the theme or themes under evaluation. Having engaged in a process of collecting and analysing this information and evidence, the school will be in a position to make a statement or statements indicating its own performance in the relevant component, aspect or area (DES, 2003: x).

The type of statement regarding each area, aspect or component evaluated which schools are invited to make is described as 'a continuum consisting of a number of reference points representing stages of development in the improvement process'.

This continuum is to be represented for each item by describing the situation discovered by the self-evaluation as one of the following:

- Significant strengths (uniformly strong)
- Strengths outweigh weaknesses (more strengths than weaknesses)
- Weaknesses outweigh strengths (more weaknesses than strengths)
- Significant major weaknesses (uniformly weak).

This four level scale it is suggested will identify strengths but also the areas in which improvement is necessary.

In essence, four of the five 'areas' above are, as it were, concerned with whole-school evaluation, while the fifth, 'quality of learning and teaching in subjects' represents the structure under which individual teachers and subject departments are to self-evaluate and be inspected. The process of inspection of teachers and subjects as outlined in *LAOS* was further developed in a subsequent publication, *A Guide to Subject Inspection at Second Level* (DES, 2004) , supplemented by a series of leaflets on each individual subject area which are gradually appearing. However, as we shall see in chapter seven, lack of clarity regarding expectations of teachers and subject departments, and the process of providing feedback to them on their performance as perceived by the inspectors, represents a significant weakness in the system.

LAOS: A Documentary Analysis

At first glance the two *LAOS* documents maintain that rather uneasy co-existence of external evaluation by the Inspectorate and internal school self-evaluation which characterised the original WSE pilot project. For example in the joint foreword to the two documents, the Chief Inspector sets out the relationship as perceived by the DES between school development planning, school self-evaluation and external inspection (DES, 2003: v):

> The School Development Planning Initiative provides support to schools in the process of internal review and in formulating their school plans. This set of themes for self-evaluation has been prepared by the Inspectorate to further assist school communities in fulfilling their quality assurance obligations. It will also provide a clear framework within which external evaluation of schools and centres of education by the Inspectorate will be carried out.

However as the two documents progress it is noticeable how the emphasis on internal self-evaluation looms increasingly larger and the role of the Inspectorate and external evaluation diminishes. In fact the documents only refer on one further occasion to external inspection (DES, 2003 : viii):

> Ireland is adopting a model of quality assurance that emphasises school development planning through internal school-review and self-evaluation, with the support of external evaluation carried out by the Inspectorate.

In contrast the emphasis on school development planning through internal school review and self-evaluation grows stronger throughout the documents - for example:

The centrality of the school's role with regard to evaluation and development is clear.

Schools themselves have the key role in the task of identifying existing good practice as well as areas for further development.

This document presents a set of themes through which a school may undertake a review and self-evaluation of its own performance.

These evaluation themes will be continually updated so as to be of assistance and relevance to schools in their review and self-evaluation activities as part of the school development and school improvement process. (DES, 2003 : iii-x)

Analysing these documents, it seems reasonable to argue that the evolution of school evaluation in Ireland from WSE to *LAOS* features a degree of movement along the evaluation spectrum described in chapter three above. The direction of this movement is clearly away from external monitoring and towards internal review and self-evaluation. *LAOS* produces a template for schools undertaking self-evaluation and the role of external inspection in this process is significantly downplayed. The model which emerges is remarkably similar to the idea of MacBeath that the role of external evaluation and inspection is merely to ensure that internal systems of evaluation and self review are implemented effectively, 'a model in which external evaluation focuses primarily on the school's own approach to self-evaluation' (MacBeath, 1999: 152).

Insofar as evidence exists, it can be argued that the emerging approach is close to that favoured by Irish school principals. Five Irish second level schools took part in a European Union Pilot Project entitled Evaluating Quality in School Education at Second Level (1998–2000) (DES, 2000a). This project ran contemporaneously with the official Department of Education and Science pilot project, Whole-School Evaluation. The European project was very influenced by the work of John MacBeath and Michael Schratz and was strongly committed to internal self-evaluation (European Commission, 1997; MacBeath *et. al.*, 1999). The WSE project, while extremely cautious and non-confrontational, was nonetheless concerned to a greater extent with outside involvement, specifically the evaluation role of the Inspectorate. Two schools took part in both projects and in subsequent interviews with the present authors the principals of both were significantly more supportive of the EU project than of WSE.

In both cases the principals expressed the view that any form of external evaluation was by its nature superficial, a snapshot, underestimated the achievements of schools other than academic success and tended to raise deep concerns among teachers. In contrast, self-evaluation with no external mandate or monitoring (as in the form of the EU project) was perceived as a major success. One principal stated that 'unlike evaluation by outside individuals, including Department of Education Inspectors, teachers were comfortable with the format and used it constructively'. The other principal expressed a very similar view, 'teachers are prepared to be self-critical and to ask themselves questions they might resent from others'. In general therefore in the climate prevailing in Ireland it may well be that the strong emphasis on self-evaluation in the emerging policy is perhaps the only realistic and achievable approach.

In most other aspects *LAOS* follows the pattern of the WSE pilot. This may be understandable since WSE was, to an extent, perceived to have been a success primarily because it raised no outright opposition from powerful vested interests. However as we have seen, major weaknesses in the WSE pilot were pinpointed in the final evaluation report of that project (DES,1999a). Very significantly, *LAOS* does not refer to any of these issues. As a result a comparison of *LAOS* to the evaluation report of WSE shows continuity in the aspects that were successful but also no discernible attempt to address the significant reservations raised in the WSE evaluation.

In analysing *LAOS*, we will begin with the ways it builds on the successes of WSE. In many ways the evaluation of WSE was, as we have seen, very positive. The project was endorsed by principals, teachers and inspectors and there was a general perception that the process was workable for the future. Inspectors reported a high level of co-operation from the schools involved, principals saw WSE 'making a significant contribution to the planning processes in their schools' and teachers while significantly less enthusiastic than the other respondents found the process 'supportive and affirming'. Moreover potentially difficult developments such as inspector observation of post-primary teachers teaching and subsequent interaction with the pupils were successfully implemented. Final reports were well received with principals by and large of the view that they were 'a fair and objective picture of their school's key strengths and the aspects of its work requiring further development'. Finally each category of respondent felt that WSE had increased the feeling of 'ownership by the staff of the school of its provision and of responsibility for improving on that provision' (DES, 1999a: 25–30). In the light of these positives, the evaluation philosophy and framework outlined in *LAOS* is very much a continuation of that tested in the WSE pilot project.

Despite the positive evaluation findings outlined above serious flaws were also identified. The inspectors involved pointed out that the quality of data available in schools was very poor and that for 'political' reasons the reports they had ended up writing had been very general, 'tending towards superficiality'. Many principals involved felt that the emphasis on 'whole-school' meant 'that it was the management that was evaluated and that while the process might uncover certain issues and problems it did nothing to help schools deal with those problems'. It was also felt that the framework developed was too extensive and detailed to be easily used by schools, the workload imposed on schools and particularly on the inspectors was unrealistic and unsustainable and that key stakeholders particularly students and parents had largely been excluded. Finally the status and ownership of the inspectors' reports was unclear - it was left entirely to the schools to decide whether or not to make them available to parents and the public at large (DES, 1999a:25-30). An analysis of the *LAOS* documents, it is argued, indicates very little attempt to remedy these deficiencies. The following sections illustrate this point.

What Data?

We have already quoted extensively from the *LAOS* framework documents describing how the process of self-evaluation is to work. Schools will 'engage in a process of collecting and analysing information' and on this evidence' 'statements' will be made (DES, 2003: x). This sounds impressive until one realises firstly that these bland assertions ignore the fact that very little data is available about any facet of the operation of schools in Ireland, and secondly, no attempt is made to suggest who should 'collect and analyse' this information or how they should go about it.

This criticism of the original WSE project was flagged clearly in the evaluation report of that project (DES, 1999a). Inspectors involved noted the lack of 'hard data' on which to base reasonable judgements, 'schools need to present us with evidence oral and written in respect of their operations' and again 'access is needed to better organised in-school data on pupil performance' (DES, 1999a : 28). The final section of this report suggested that these points had been taken seriously by the Department. Under the heading 'moving forward ' we read about the need for better quantitative information:

> both individual schools and the inspectors carrying out whole-school evaluation
> would derive considerable benefit from having access to a range of quantitative infor-

mation, including statistical and other information, on patterns of early school leav-
ing and pupil participation and on the catchment area from which the school draws
its pupils. Information of this kind would greatly enrich the WSE process for the school
and should form part of the preparation for the future whole school evaluation. (DES,
1999a : 47–48)

This section goes on to promise that WSE when fully implemented would
yield 'a stream of high quality data which will allow valid, full and reflective
judgements in relation to quality assurance'.

Interestingly, in the strict context of self-evaluation and for internal use
only, the gathering of potentially contentious data proved acceptable in the EU
project, Evaluating Quality in School Education at Second Level, mentioned
previously (DES, 2000 a). One of the self-evaluation instruments developed
by schools in the project included a teacher self-evaluation toolbox including
self-administered questionnaires. In this the teacher graded as satisfactory or
unsatisfactory his or her performance in areas such as 'lesson preparation,
delivery, class control and responding to pupil difficulties' on a purely self-
evaluation basis. This and similar approaches were widely and it seems bene-
ficially used in the work of the project.

Nonetheless despite the clear recommendations in the WSE project and
again in the EU quality project, and despite what seems to be a clear commitment in the final sections of the WSE evaluation report, the LAOS documents
are notable for the lack of any suggestions as to how schools should collect the
data on which the effectiveness and credibility of the whole system must rest.
Why is this? It certainly cannot be that the DES is ignorant of the fact that the
education system as a whole, and individual schools in particular, produce
extraordinarily little data. This is acknowledged in the quotation from the WSE
project report given above in which the necessity for such data is emphasised.

Equally it cannot be that the 'areas', 'aspects' and 'components' in the new
evaluation documents do not require significant data to enable sensible judgements to be made in relation to them. For example, component four, 'overall
student achievement in subject', in aspect C 'assessment and achievement' has
the following 'themes for self-evaluation':

Component: Overall student achievement in subject
Themes for Self-Evaluation:

1. The extent to which students' results in regular assessments and/or
    examinations in the subject reflect levels of achievement commensu-

rate with ability and general expectation
2. The extent to which student achievement in the subject is regularly evaluated in comparison with national norms. (DES, 2003: 28)

Clearly any kind of sensible and useful judgements in these areas require data that in the present system simply do not exist. There are no data regarding the 'ability and general expectations of pupils', still less any 'national norms' of achievement with which comparisons can be made. In the latter case it might be argued that results of state examinations provide 'national norms'. However, a comparison with these results is useless to individual schools since it provides no evidence of the particular performance of a school in 'adding value' to pupil achievement. This is because there is no baseline data and the intake of schools differs enormously. This point is made by Smyth (1999: 208):

> A particular school's average performance in "raw" data terms tells us little about the difference the school actually makes to its pupils. An above average ranking in these terms may merely reflect a selective pupil intake. In contrast another school may have lower exam results but its pupils may have made considerable academic progress relative to their initial ability levels.

Research instruments and tools which would allow schools to gather and analyse the required data exist. Smyth, mentioned above, used a variety of instruments to gather data for her influential work *Do schools differ?* and the EU project, Evaluating Quality in School Education at Second Level, already referred to, also developed a series of research instruments which schools could use in the process of self-evaluation. However none of this work is referred to in the bland statements in *LAOS* nor is it suggested how 'gathering and analysing information' across the very wide range of aspects, areas and components is to be done in practice.

Several alternative strategies, still centred on school self-evaluation but yet enabling schools to generate the data necessary to make such evaluations more than merely impressionistic and unreliable guesswork, certainly exist. For example Smyth (1999: 226) concludes that 'schools could monitor their own attendance and dropout rates etc' but 'information collected at the school level is likely to be of limited utility without comparable information on the National context . . . providing value added analysis to schools would be worthwhile'. Such an approach would require information on pupil ability at the point of entry and additional information (through surveys for example) on pupil background. This information could be used by the school itself in set-

ting targets for improvement and in monitoring the introduction of new programmes or teaching methods.

Clearly without something along the lines suggested by Smyth there is no
way in which schools can hope to obtain any significant data on current performance and therefore ways of improving. Equally nothing short of this can
really be considered to be evaluation by any reasonable definition of the term.
Evaluation whether external or internal, mandated or self-driven requires at a
minimum the collection and analysis of a variety of types of data on which firm
conclusions can be based. There is no danger in this for schools and teachers,
so long as the data is confidential to the schools, not permitted to be used for
advertising and is concerned with school and teacher self-improvement and
professional development.

Several schemes for school self-evaluation using teams of trained teachers
to develop research instruments and collect and analyse data are reported in the
literature (Nevo, 1999; Scheerens *et. al.* 1999; Simons, 2002). A somewhat different approach involving self-evaluation but with external collection and
analysis of data is administered by the CEM centre at the University of Durham
and attracts large numbers of schools in the UK on a volunteer basis (Tymms
and Coe, 2003). Similar initiatives are underway in New Zealand, Australia,
Hong Kong and Estonia. In Estonia, it is the national Ministry of Education
itself rather than a private agency which gathers data and feeds it to schools in
a usable format for self-evaluation (Anton, 2005). In describing this system,
Anton (a senior official of the Estonian education ministry) acknowledges a
point that is often avoided, namely that in-depth external evaluation across an
entire education system is logistically and in terms of resources likely to be
impractical. Therefore, self-evaluation, but based on quality data, is the only
realistic answer: 'in Estonia our strong emphasis on school self-evaluation as the
way to improve is also in part to reduce expensive external evaluation'. These
varying approaches to supporting self-evaluation through systematic research
are considered in greater detail in part three of this study.

For the moment, it is worth noting two key concepts which appear particularly appropriate to the Irish context that underpin the work of these initiatives. The first of these is the concept of 'distributed research' meaning that the
recipients of the feedback, namely schools and teachers, are themselves active
partners in the process, analysing and interpreting the data, rather than simply passive participants (Tymms and Coe, 2003: 639). Related to the concept
of distributed research is the very important distinction made by Tymms (1999:
85) between 'professional monitoring systems' in which the data are used by the

workers themselves and 'official accountability systems' in which the data are used to hold those workers to account. Tymms stresses the role of the former in helping to find and solve problems in a climate free from fear.

Whether such a system might or might not prove ideal for the Irish context is as yet uncertain, although part three of this study describes the early stages of an initiative designed to enable self-evaluation in Irish schools. One thing that is certain however is that individual teachers, principals and schools cannot be expected to collect and analyse the data necessary to implement the evaluation system currently being suggested without a structured and well supported approach to self-evaluation being designed and implemented.

Whose Report and Who Is To Act on the Findings?

A second set of issues raised in the WSE evaluation but not tackled in *LAOS* concerns the ownership and use of the final inspection reports and the responsibility for improving shortcomings identified. In the case of the latter point principals involved in the WSE pilot were sceptical that change would follow the identification of problems. The following was a representative response, 'WSE can make recommendations but in itself won't cure weaknesses in any school' (DES, 1999a: 27). This issue is not referred to in *LAOS* but in a revealing response to a question at a conference of principals in early two thousand and six the Chief Inspector made it clear that as schools were self governing and self-evaluating institutions it was a matter for themselves to address weaknesses identified during inspections. It was forcibly pointed out to the Chief Inspector that schools have little or no control over resourcing or over teacher tenure (subsequent to appointment) or conditions. It was clear that principals were less than satisfied with this position.

A related issue of vital importance to the accountability role of the new evaluation system is access to the final report. As indicated previously, some of the inspectors involved in the WSE project felt that due to the sensitivities involved the school reports tended to be rather bland. The DES position was that these reports were owned by the schools and it was left to them to decide whether to make them public or not. Once again, in *LAOS*, no reference is made to this issue. However, the DES refused requests from the media for access to the first school evaluation reports carried out under the *LAOS* framework on the grounds that it was prohibited from publishing such reports by the section of the 1998 Education Act which prohibits providing information which could be used to compile league tables of schools. This decision was over-turned by the Information Commissioner but was subsequently appealed by the principal of a primary school with the support of the primary teachers' union. A recent Supreme Court judgement (Sheedy v the Information Commissioner, 2005) upheld the school's position and it then appeared to be entirely a mat-ter for school management to decide whether to release none, some or all of the inspection report. However, the Minister for Education and Science caused some surprise by announcing in late 2005 that, despite this judgement, she pro-posed to place completed evaluation reports on the DES website. Regardless of some union opposition she proceeded to do so, and since April 2006 whole school evaluation reports are available on the DES website. This develop-ment took place during the period of the research in schools reported on in the next chapter, and the evaluation reports, together with the early impact of their publication, are considered then.

Complexity and Resources

The WSE evaluation (DES, 1999a: 28) suggested that the evaluation framework piloted by that project was perhaps overly extensive and very wasteful of resources, particularly school and inspector time. However, as previously men-tioned the *LAOS* framework was considerably more extensive than WSE, with some one hundred and forty three themes for self-evaluation. Although it is pro-posed to employ a considerable number of new inspectors to speed up the process, and this has begun to happen, it would seem that the complexity of the system as it stands will limit evaluations to once every five years at best, and probably to longer intervals. This is perhaps another reason why the emphasis on self-evaluation in schools is stronger in *LAOS* than it was in WSE. Significantly, two later documents issued in 2006, *A Guide to Whole School Evaluation in Post Primary Schools* (DES, 2006 a) and *A Guide to Whole School Evaluation in Primary Schools* (DES, 2006 b) attempt to substantially streamline and clarify the inspection process. The long lists of 'themes for self-evaluation' of the *LAOS* documents are subsumed into a short paragraph under each of the five 'areas'. In addition, the evidence which schools were supposed to provide under *LAOS* to support their self-evaluative judgements becomes simply a required list of school plans, policies and other similar documents. The over-all effect appears to be a recognition that the original *LAOS* framework was over elaborate and more importantly that schools don't have and can't generate 'hard data' on their own performance. These new documents were issued during the school research phase of this work and their impact on the actual practice of school evaluation is considered in the next chapter.

Parents and Pupils

A final issue raised in the WSE project evaluation (DES, 1999a: 48) but not confronted in *LAOS* is the appropriate role of parents and pupils in the process. During the WSE pilot the inspectors did meet with parents (usually the parent representatives on the Board of Management) and with pupils (either from the school council or where none existed chosen by the principal). This approach is endorsed in *LAOS* which makes no concessions to suggestions in the WSE evaluation that the views of parents and pupils should be ascertained in a formal and representative way through the use of questionnaires and interviews.

Conclusion

This chapter contains a documentary analysis of the new system of school and teacher evaluation recently introduced in Ireland. The new system was constructed after an extensive pilot project which in turn was influenced by emerging evaluation policies and practices in the EU and in several European countries. The approach to school evaluation taken was also heavily influenced by the work of leading theorists in the field such as John MacBeath and by contextual issues within Ireland such as the negotiated partnership agreements on which economic and social policies rest and the continued strength of the teacher unions.

In consequence the emerging evaluation system is characterised by an emphasis on co-operation and collaboration, and on school and teacher self-evaluation with light touch supportive external monitoring by the Inspectorate. Professional and organisational development is prioritised ahead of accountability and naming and shaming of teachers or schools and comparisons and league tables are strictly forbidden. In summary it is argued that this approach to evaluation is largely in line with international trends as outlined in chapter three and places Ireland more or less at the position on the school evaluation spectrum towards which we suggest most systems are gradually converging.

However due to over-riding concerns with negotiation and the avoidance of conflict it is also suggested that the model adopted displays serious weaknesses. In particular there is a strong reluctance to engage in the serious data collection and analysis necessary to underpin an improvement strategy. There is also a marked reluctance to develop a serious role for parents and pupils or to use the evaluation reporting system to tackle serious problems or reduce the culture of secrecy endemic in Irish education. However this is how it seems from an analysis of the documentation—we now need to examine whether the new evaluation system as implemented in the schools displays these characteristics in practice.

The above analysis of both the strengths and weaknesses of the new school evaluation system as it is outlined in the documentation was used to generate an interview schedule for research with a number of school leaders and teachers whose institutions were among the first to be evaluated under the *LAOS* framework. It is to this research that we now turn our attention.

· 6 ·

LOOKING AT OUR SCHOOLS

Stakeholders Respond

Whole School Evaluation: Processes and Procedures

The key framework document for whole school evaluation in Ireland, *Looking at Our Schools* (DES, 2003), provided, as we have seen in the previous chapter, an extensive set of themes for self-evaluation, divided into five categories: management, planning, curriculum provision, teaching and learning, and student support. This framework, while designed to 'facilitate self-evaluation as a central component of the continuous planning process' was also to be utilised 'by the inspectorate in conducting whole school evaluations and as a basis for other external evaluation of the work of schools' (DES, 2003:ii).

As indicated in the previous chapter, it was always unlikely that such a detailed framework could in fact be closely followed for either of the above purposes and in fact a series of more manageable documents designed to clarify and streamline the process of whole school evaluation have been produced by the DES in the meantime. These begin with *The Professional Code of Practice on Evaluation and Reporting for the Inspectorate* (DES, 2003 c), *Procedures for Review of Inspections on Schools and Teachers under Section 13 (9) of the Education Act 1998* (DES, 2003 c) and *Publication of School Inspection Reports, Guidelines* (DES, 2006 c).

The most significant of this series of documents however are *A Guide to Whole School Evaluation in Post-Primary Schools* (DES, 2006 a) and *A Guide to Whole School Evaluation in Primary Schools* (DES, 2006 b). As with the original *LAOS* documents, these two publications are so similar that they can be considered as a single entity and they will be referred to hereafter as *Guide* and referenced as (DES, 2006). The *Guide*, although referring to *LAOS* as the key framework document, actually represents a considerable change of focus and policy. It appears to have been produced to meet criticisms that the inspection process, as outlined in *LAOS*, was overly complex and did not make clear enough what was expected of schools and teachers. In consequence, in the *Guide*, the list of themes for self-evaluation under each of the five category areas is reduced to a very general paragraph on each, and there is no longer any mention of the school making judgements on its own performance in each area on a four point rating scale as suggested in *LAOS*.

These changes would appear from our research in schools simply to reflect the reality of the inspection process as it is being implemented. Even before the *Guide* was published in two thousand and six, inspectors were not requiring schools to respond under all the themes laid down in *LAOS*, nor indeed did we come across a single instance where the rating scale is even mentioned. The *Guide* clarifies (2006: 5) the WSE procedures and processes in considerable detail (an omission from *LAOS*) and also, very significantly, spells out the policy documents and other information which schools (but not teachers) are required to present before and during WSE. This consists of a list of plans and policies which schools are obliged anyway to have prepared under various legislation. It also, very significantly, includes a new document, 'WSE: School Information Form' which seeks basic information on pupil numbers, staffing etc and short, self-evaluatory comments under headings such as 'progress so far and future priorities for school development planning', and 'the supports provided for the inclusion of students from minority and disadvantaged groups'.

Although not specifically asking for evidence to support any claims or statements made, the *Guide* 'WSE: School Information Form' is in other respects not dissimilar to the 'Self Evaluation Form' used by Ofsted in England and may therefore represent a small beginning towards a more evidence-based approach to evaluation.

This notion is reinforced by the inclusion in the *Guide* of the information that the inspection team will seek examination results for the school for the past four years from the State Examinations Commission, and that these may be discussed with school management and staff, although 'not presented in the WSE report' (DES, 2006: 25). Despite these developments, however, our research indicates that as yet there is very little indication that the inspection process is obliging schools to adopt more systematic forms of self evaluation or evidence-based practice.

The *Guide* does not set out to clarify what is expected from individual teachers, both in terms of preparation in advance and during inspection. This is left to a series of guides to inspection in each subject area which are gradually being prepared and published by the DES. However, our research indicates that teachers, as opposed to subject departments where things are a little clearer, still perceive a very considerable lack of clarity regarding what is expected of them and the problems in this regard are among the chief issues with WSE discussed later in this chapter.

The *Guide* was issued in early two thousand and six in the middle of a series of school visits being undertaken by the authors. It quickly became apparent that schools recognised and welcomed the simplification and clarification of the structures and processes of WSE and that the *Guide*, rather than the *LAOS* documents, has effectively become the source used by schools to prepare for inspection. Before examining the research case studies in the schools, we will briefly consider the research methodology employed.

Research Methodology

As indicated earlier *LAOS* has only begun to be implemented in schools relatively recently. There are more than three thousand primary schools and over seven hundred post primary schools in Ireland, but only a small minority had undergone a full evaluation at the time of this research.

In designing this study, the authors decided to focus primarily on what appeared to them to be the key emerging issue, namely the extent to which schools and teachers are producing or indeed are capable of producing systematic research data to underpin self-evaluation or external evaluation judgements. This, after all, is the rationale on which the evaluation scheme is supposedly based. This does not mean that other issues were not considered in the research but only that priority was given to the research capacity available in schools since this, or the lack of it, is central to the credibility of school and teacher self evaluation.

The research reported in this chapter, therefore, emphasises the extent to which the new evaluation system is both requiring and supporting schools and teachers in developing systematic self-evaluation research methodologies. It is for this reason that the school case studies reported here confine themselves to teachers and school leaders (principals and deputy principals) and did not include other key stakeholders such as parents, pupils, members of boards of management or indeed the inspectorate or general public.

The chief methodology used in this phase of the research was semi-structured interviews. Based on the analysis of the *LAOS* framework documents reported in chapter five, two interview schedules were developed. These were piloted with the principal and a teacher in each of two schools; one primary and one post primary. The interview schedules were revised slightly in light of the pilot, and were then used in case studies of some twenty four schools, twelve primary and twelve post primary. The schools were situated in the greater Dublin area and throughout the rest of Leinster and were chosen from among those which had already had undergone a full whole school evaluation. The sample was not stratified since there was no indication that size, location, gender or other variables would influence the response to whole-school evaluation. However the pilot did indicate that schools classed as disadvantaged might have a different perspective on WSE and five such schools were included in the case studies.

The interviews were semi-structured in the sense that the same question schedule was followed in each case but supplementary questions were asked as and when interesting responses could be further explored. In the twenty four schools studied a total of twenty eight school leaders were interviewed since in some cases although either was sufficient for the research both principal and deputy principal volunteered to take part. It had been hoped to interview at least one recently inspected teacher in each school but in six schools this was not possible for various reasons. In all twenty interviews with teachers were conducted drawn from eighteen schools, two schools each providing two interviews and the reminder one each.

The interviews were conducted in the schools except for four interviews with principals held in the University and three teacher interviews conducted by phone. The question list was sent to all respondents in advance and all interviews were recorded. The interviews ranged in duration from fifteen to ninety minutes with the average interview lasting thirty five minutes. All interviews were transcribed and analysed using the NVIVO data analysis package.

Two other significant sources were also used in this phase of the research. The first is the final evaluation reports of the schools case studied. The second is a piece of research conducted by MORI Ireland for the DES on schools' responses to whole-school evaluation (DES, 2005). This work, hereafter referred to as 'Customer Survey', involved a questionnaire sent to some one hundred and fifty schools which had undergone WSE.

Whole-School Evaluation: Research Findings

The findings which emerged from this research are explored below in the following sections:

- ◻ Whole School Evaluation: Processes and Procedures.
- ◻ Whole School Evaluation: Positive Responses.
  1. Happy 'Customers'.
  2. Comprehensive.
  3. Collegiality.
  4. Impact on Improvement.
  5. 'Worth Doing'.
- ◻ Whole School Evaluation: Negative Responses.
  1. 'Evidence-Free Evaluation'.
  2. Feedback to Schools and Teachers.
  3. Evaluation Reports, 'From Effusive to Merely Positive'.
  4. The Role of Stakeholders.

Whole School Evaluation: Processes and Procedures

Schools report that the Guide (DES, 2006) sets out very clearly the processes and procedures of WSE from 'notification of inspection' through to 'publication of the report and school response'. The process as outlined is divided into three distinct phases, pre-evaluation, in-school evaluation and post-evaluation. In each phase the steps involved are clearly described and this research confirms the findings of the DES Customer Survey (2005) with regard to the positive view of these procedures taken by schools. For example, more than 83% of those polled in Customer Survey (2005:14) agreed or strongly agreed that 'appropriate notice was given of the general inspection visit and all the meetings were agreed in advance'. A small number of the interviews did throw up criticisms of aspects of the procedures, for example, a short lead-in time, compelling schools (usually the principal) to 'burn the midnight oil' getting 'the mountain of documents' required into readiness. A more common criticism referred to sometimes prolonged periods between the in-school phase and the final report. Comments here included 'the enthusiasm which had built up was allowed to dissipate', or more prosaically, 'people had long forgotten the whole thing'. In general, however, it appears that the administrative and procedural elements of WSE are widely regarded as satisfactory.

Whole School Evaluation: Positive Responses

1. Happy 'Customers'

It will be remembered that the analysis of *LAOS* documents outlined in the previous chapter suggested that the process in action might display both positive and negative aspects. On the positive side it was suggested that the framework, developed as it was through long and detailed negotiations with the stakeholders and stressing the centrality of school improvement through self-evaluation, would be received positively by schools and teachers. The research evidence bears out this expectation.

All the respondents indicated in one way or another that despite considerable fear and trepidation in advance (schools researched received on average about three weeks notice of the inspection) the schools found the process to be 'positive, affirming and renewing'. The professional, collegial and non-threatening approach of the inspectors was stressed time and time again. The initial phase of the inspection involves preparatory meetings between the inspection team and school management. The next phase involves the team of inspectors (in most cases three or four but in one large post primary school five) conducting the evaluation (over a three or four day period). The inspection itself breaks down into two almost separate processes: whole-school and department/subject inspection. The latter consists of meetings with subject teachers, examination of plans and schemes of work, classroom observation, and looking at pupil work. In the case of the primary schools all or most teachers received classroom visits from inspectors while in the post primary schools two, three (or in one case four) subjects were evaluated.

With regard to whole school evaluation, the process is primarily one of meetings with the board of management, senior management, middle management, all staff and particular groups of teachers such as special needs, guidance and so on and meetings with pupil and parent representatives. These meetings

are described as largely being about the school producing and explaining policy documents which it is required to have in relation to such areas as planning,
admissions, guidance, discipline, bullying and so forth. The final phase of the
process involves discussion between the leading inspector and the principal
about the content of the final report, a draft of which is given to the school for
comment before issue of the final version. Almost without exception the
respondents indicated that the inspection teams managed this potentially
fraught process in such a way that the schools, while relieved to have it over,
regarded it as a positive and worthwhile experience. This interpretation is
confirmed by the *Customer Survey* (2005: 12), which reports overwhelmingly
positive responses from both teachers and principals to statements about WSE
such as 'inspectors adopted a professional approach in their interactions with
me' and 'inspectors were courteous and respectful of my professionalism'.
Overall, all the evidence suggests that the schools evaluated to date can be
regarded as happy customers.

2. Comprehensive

The majority of schools also felt that the framework, by covering such a wide
set of 'themes for self-evaluation' was able to obtain a comprehensive picture
of all the schools' activities and not just academic outcomes. One principal stated that 'the framework is very broad, reflecting the wide role of schools and this
is as it should be as schooling is about more than skills' was a typical comment.
This point was particularly stressed by respondents from the schools designated disadvantaged who felt very strongly that the 'affirmation of good practice'
provided by the inspectors was of 'extraordinary importance to teachers in disadvantaged schools who rarely feel valued or supported'. These schools stated
that the final reports did manage to capture, 'the context and the problems in
which these schools and teachers work'. This finding is again confirmed by the
Customer Survey (2005: 14) which reports that close to ninety per cent of
teachers supported or strongly supported the view that 'inspectors took account
of school/class context factors during the evaluation process'. Likewise it was
felt by many respondents that as the framework was so extensive it could be used
as a 'scaffolding' for improvement strategies. One principal suggested that
WSE creates 'a template under so many headings of where we are trying to go'
and is 'an excellent start, heading in the right direction'. However, the very
extensive nature of the evaluation framework also drew criticism which will be
reported later in the chapter.

3. Collegiality

Respondents also repeatedly stated that the WSE process brought staff togeth-er to prepare and gave them a new sense of focus and collegiality. Comments here included 'a lot of staff learned what others are actually doing', 'the big advantage is it gets teachers to cooperate' and 'the focus of the entire school was on getting ready, it really brought us together'. In each of the post prima-ry schools only perhaps three or four specific subject areas were included. Principals remarked on how the rest of the staff rallied around to help the 'unfortunate ones'. Interestingly one principal claimed that so 'positive' and 'affirming' and 'helpful' were the subject inspections that by the end of the process those who had 'escaped' were sorry not to be included! Similarly with the 'whole-school' aspects of the evaluation respondents were grateful and indeed a little surprised that more junior staff gave a great deal of help in preparing the 'mountain of paperwork' required. Several respondents suggest-ed that by far the greatest benefit for the school of *LAOS* was the way in which it tended to get the staff working together, although there were sugges-tions that for various reasons this might be a short term gain, 'but in the long term it is unrealistic because there is so little time available'.

4. Impact on Improvement

Although, as we shall see, both teachers and school leaders tended to be scep-tical about the longer term impact of WSE, nonetheless many instances of pos-itive change, at least in the short term, resulting from the process were mentioned. Particularly interesting is the perception of many respondents that these improvements were connected to an 'agenda', being 'pushed' by the inspectors, to which schools and teachers felt constrained to respond. For example, planning at subject department level was high on this alleged agen-da and thus, one school reported, 'we now have a lot of subject meetings, common exam papers and sharing of resources', and another stated that 'sub-ject teachers are now meeting more regularly and we are now big on collabo-rative work in subjects'. One principal summarised it as 'it certainly helps you to get the teachers to plan—some have not really thought about what they do for twenty or twenty five years'.

More use of ICT was also seen as being high on the inspectorial wish list and the purchase and use of laptops and data projectors seems to have moved up the agenda of many schools as a result. Predictably, perhaps, this also brought criticism of the fact that limited resources, both in terms of the timetabling of meetings and the purchase of ICT equipment, were conveniently ignored in the inspection reports.

Somewhat more controversially, many schools felt that the inspectors' agenda was opposed to banding and streaming and in favour of mixed ability teaching, and that WSE was being used to push this policy. Comments here included, 'they were against our banding system and we now have a task group looking at it' and, again, 'they were very concerned about ethos, how the kids are treated and pro mixed ability teaching, we may have to change but it will be a big culture shock for staff and parents'. Another principal remarked that, like the inspectors, she was against the streaming system in her school but would not have raised it but for WSE, 'the report gives you the authority to do things'.

Other examples of the alleged agenda being pursued by the inspectorate which came up regularly were concern about adequate provision in the related areas of pastoral care, guidance, and social, personal and health education. Schools were questioned closely on these areas, and a number were warned to increase timetable provision which was judged to be below required levels in these areas.

Although in general this DES agenda of improvement being driven through WSE was reasonably well received, nonetheless pursuing these issues through the WSE process may in time prove increasingly controversial. Several of them, streaming for example, relate to key issues of ethos which schools regard as primarily internal and there were several examples in the research data of resentment at what were perceived as bullying, hectoring tactics by the DES.

5. 'Worth Doing'

To sum up on the positive side, the consensus was that the *LAOS* framework as implemented by the inspectors, was 'worth doing', had 'affirmed teachers and schools', dispelled fear of evaluation and convinced school staffs that 'this is the way to do it'. At times, endorsement was rather lukewarm, 'every so often it is good to have a spring clean' (teacher) and 'no harm to get policies up to date' (principal), but on the whole more fulsome compliments were common, such as 'made us totally think through all our priorities'. This had been achieved, it was by and large agreed, by taking a softly, softly approach and by downplaying inspection and up-playing school self-evaluation. Predictably therefore perhaps, given the care and caution of its construction and execution, *LAOS*, in the opening iteration, has been positively received, regarded (to an extent, as we shall see) as worthwhile and become, at least so far, an accepted addition to school life. The latter alone is a considerable achievement in an educational community deeply suspicious of evaluation, inspection and appraisal.

Whole-School Evaluation–Negative Responses

1. 'Evidence-free Evaluation'

A particularly interesting outcome of this research was the extent to which the respondents alluded to *LAOS* as a once-off event to be prepared for and gotten over. It became very clear that the central idea of the *LAOS* framework, namely that self-evaluation would be an ongoing process between inspections, had failed to take hold. Questions about plans to continue the process of self-evaluation after *LAOS* were met with puzzlement. Further probing elicited the clear perception that insofar as it had been considered at all it was assumed that the school development planning process (SDP), which is also a statutory requirement of schools, would be the vehicle for ongoing development/improvement work (DES, 1999b). The clear implication here is that significant reconsideration may have to be given to the relationship between SDP, ongoing self-evaluation and evaluation by the Inspectorate. It may well be that these frameworks are far too extensive (the SDP framework is as complex as *LAOS*) and similar to exist side by side (O'Dalaigh, 2000; Simons, 2002). Moreover the two frameworks show the same strengths and weaknesses in that both contain comprehensive definitions of the areas to be planned or evaluated but little in the way of criteria against which to make judgments or research methodology to gather evidence. Based on this small sample, a strong case for the rationalisation and integration of these two processes appears to exist, although rationalisation in itself is unlikely to encourage evidence-based practice.

Like the response to the questions concerning ongoing self-evaluation, those asked about data collected and evidence generated in preparation for *LAOS* largely evoked puzzlement. It became clear that although 'endless meetings' were held and a 'mountain of paperwork' was prepared for both subject and whole-school evaluation, this consisted almost entirely of bringing together and updating existing planning and policy documents–class plans, homework policy, school plan, discipline code, admittance procedures and so on. The only exception to this was some additional material in the form of class tests in some subjects and pupil copybooks. The concept that the success or failure of, for example, the discipline code might be evaluated through some process of data collection and analysis was completely alien. Further probing in this area resulted in some interesting new thinking. One principal remarked 'I suppose when you think about it, it is not evaluation really, it is just impressionistic'. Another stated: 'we do have lots of data—absence and late lists and so on—but it is never analysed and used—it would be a big job'. In the same vein another principal remarked that 'schools have evidence yes, but it is not joined-up evidence' and went on, 'I suppose what this really is, is evidence-free evaluation'. A theme that emerged in these responses was that such data might well be useful and desirable but schools were not equipped, nor staff trained to do it. 'Is the balance correct? The *LAOS* framework is good but we need training to make it work' and, again, 'we are not good at knowing how we are doing, we concentrate on inputs'.

A minority view, very negative about any idea that evaluation needed to be based on more systematic research, was also evident—'in teaching much of what we do is not measurable, giving pupils a sense of belief, hope, helping emotional needs, social work, and we should not try to measure it'. On the other hand, there were examples of schools which were engaging in more systematic forms of self-evaluation and evidence collection. These respondents were very critical of the WSE process and the inspection teams, alleging that, not only were schools not encouraged to rigorously self-evaluate, but where they had done so, no interest was shown in the evidence produced. One principal remarked that 'they (the inspectors) were afraid to make use of it, they only judged the structures, no evaluation of implementation or outcomes'. In another school the principal said that the literacy scheme for less able pupils was not achieving its targets but, 'we got a glowing report because we have a team and regular meetings, but we have huge problems—they did not want to know.' Another principal remarked: 'how well are you evaluating yourself, they say, but they do not want to see any evidence, all they want to see is the processes we have in place for homework or discipline or whatever—nothing re outputs'.

Several teachers expressed a similar viewpoint, saying that no internalisation or adoption of the process was taking place among school staffs, and this was at least partly because there was so little inspectorial interest in evidence or self-evaluation data. Comments here included, 'no interest in the teacher-researcher idea' and 'they never ask for evidence if they wanted to they could say "what is your evidence for doing it that way", but they never do'.

There is evidence from another source which supports the notion that a lack of school-based research is a major issue at the heart of school planning and evaluation. The DES recently published *An Evaluation of Planning in Thirty Primary Schools* (DES, 2006 d) and noted that only twenty percent of schools could be considered 'good' in the area of using evidence to track improved school attainment. The few schools that showed good practice in this area are described in the following terms:

> A comprehensive policy on assessment, measuring attainment systematically, devising formats for plotting progress and monitoring improvements in attendance . . . evidence of change of pupils' behaviour and improved attendance. (DES, 2006 d: 73)

What is interesting here is two-fold. Firstly, our research shows that, where the schools and teachers studied had gathered evidence, little interest was shown by the inspectors, and moreover schools and teachers are not aware that such evidence gathering is required, expected or even welcomed. At the same time, it seems clear from the above quote that the DES wishes schools to gather systematic data and evidence but yet has done absolutely nothing to support, encourage or train schools and teachers to respond. Somehow, the twenty percent of good practice mentioned above has emerged as it were of its own accord, but our research implies that this is a rare phenomenon. It seems clear, therefore, that the empowerment of schools and teachers to self-evaluate will have to come from sources other than the DES, and the research reported in part three of this study is one effort to begin that process.

2. Feedback

The second major negative finding in this research can be summarised as poor feedback, and was a common theme in the interviews with both principals, deputy principals and teachers.

Principals tended to have two major criticisms concerning feedback, one being the general and/or impractical nature of advice given and the second more strident, the lack of any mechanism or indeed responsibility being provided by the DES to follow up problems identified during WSE.

In the case of the former, there was considerable annoyance along the following lines: 'they put in recommendations when they know there are no resources to do the things suggested' or, again, 'they said a bigger library and more IT, but we have no money, so it's all just forgotten about now'. Other suggestions made in inspection reports were regarded with open cynicism, particularly relating to posts of responsibility, a subject which came up regularly. The following was a typical comment 'they feel they have to say that but they know reorganising posts of responsibility is a very touchy IR issue which is not really on'. Equally, with regard to another regular recommendation, more subject team meetings, many school leaders made clear the difficulties involved. The following was a common response, 'they know I cannot timetable meetings as most teachers are on full hours, so it's just goodwill, and that will not last'.

Ironically, in light of the above, even greater annoyance was caused by things not said in the final reports. By far the most common complaint from school leaders in the course of these interviews refers to 'the elephant in the room', dealing with poor teaching and underperforming teachers. This topic, alleged many principals, is 'avoided like the plague' since 'despite WSE, there is still no mechanism to deal with a weak teacher'. One principal remarked, 'if this system is about accountability at all, it is about management accountability, certainly not teacher accountability'.

This attitude among principals in fact seems at odds with evidence mentioned in previous chapters, that Irish school leaders favour internal evaluation over external inspection. What may be happening here, though, is that, given that such a resource intensive system of evaluation has been put in place, principals feel that it should, in order to justify itself, be able to deliver tangible results on key issues such as increased resource allocation and tackling poor teaching. With regard to feedback, a somewhat similar view can be traced in the interviews with teachers.

In interviews with teachers a high level of dissatisfaction with the level and quality of the feedback received after inspection was uncovered. It must be acknowledged that this finding is at odds with the *Customer Survey* (2005:15), which found that approximately seventy seven percent of teachers agreed or strongly agreed with the statement 'inspectors provided opportunities for me to discuss their observations and listen to my viewpoint' (it may be significant that over twenty one percent disagreed or strongly disagreed with this statement, by far the highest negative response in the *Customer Survey*). At all events, in the interviews, teachers reported feeling 'demeaned', 'upset' and 'amazed' at the haphazard nature of the subject inspections and feedback. Among the comments made were the following:

'Very badly informed in advance'
'No clear indication what they wanted to see'
'Advice very general, of no real use'
'Nothing given in writing'

'Wrote all the time in my class on green and red sheets–I suppose green good and red
bad, but did not show them to me or refer to them afterwards'
'Ten minutes in the corridor after the class, very unprofessional'.

A regret expressed regularly by teachers was that no reference was made by
inspectors to good practice or ideas from elsewhere, 'no real advice on methods and no sense of telling you that there is good practice elsewhere and bringing it to you'. Another teacher remarked, ' not worth it–nothing new, exciting
or challenging'. Overall, the sense that comes across from teacher interviews
on this area is that, while the process is very stressful, 'no other profession would
put up with it', it might still be regarded as 'worth it' if the quality of feedback
were higher. In summary, the findings in relation to teacher feedback in WSE
are as follows:

◻   A need for more time for class teachers to have discussions with
     inspectors.
◻   A need for more specific recommendations, whether criticisms were
     offered or not.

A final point relating to feedback made by both principals and teachers was
that what they perceived to be the determination of the inspectors to stick to
a 'very rigid', 'very inflexible' approach to their work inhibited any spontane-
ity which might have helped to improve the quality of advice and support.

'Would not deviate from the structure laid down for them'
'Would not go into other areas'
'Had to do everything in a certain order at a certain time, in order, they said, to be the
same everywhere–why, when no comparisons are made?'

3. Evaluation Reports: 'From Effusive to Merely Positive'

Another recurring theme in the interviews conducted is the nature of the
reports produced by the team of inspectors after the external phase of the
evaluation and the subsequent follow up of issues and problems identified. A
document outlining the reporting process, *Publication of School Inspection
Reports, Guidelines*, was published in two thousand and six (DES, 2006 c).
Under these *Guidelines*, a draft version of the final evaluation report is sent to
the schools for comment before it is finally issued. School leaders found this re-
assuring and amongst the schools researched there was a unanimous view that
the draft report (positive in each case) was a fair reflection of the evaluation

and indeed of the work of the school. (This is not, however, always the case in that is it understood that a number of schools evaluated to date have used the mechanism of appeal to the Chief Inspector against the report, which is part of the process.)

On the other hand, among those interviewed for this research there was a clear sense of doubt and scepticism that the evaluation report would ever be critical regardless of the reality of the situation, 'we do not have a concept of positive criticism here and it is just as well the report is very softly, softly'. Or again, 'there is no sign that we will get any help (from the DES) to deal with under performing teachers so it is just as well that these reports don't go down that route'. This last point, the question of pursuing issues raised by *LAOS*, is, as has already been indicated, another theme that continually recurs. Among comments here were the following: 'if problems are identified schools will be left to their own devices', or, again, 'no one believes the DES will intervene and of course schools can't solve all problems themselves in-house, that is a fiction'.

As previously explained, the question of the right of access to the inspection reports was before the Courts when this research commenced. Most of the early respondents felt that the decision on what groups should have access to the reports should be left to each individual school although all but one claimed that they would favour full publication of the report on their own school when it arrived. Although the Courts found in favour of schools themselves deciding on the question of publication, the Minister for Education and Science decided that all evaluation reports should be published on the DES website, and this has been the case since April, two thousand and six (DES, 2006) .

As part of this research, an analysis of the reports pertaining to the schools studied was undertaken. It is hard to disagree with one principal who remarked that the reports seem to range 'from effusive to merely positive', or even perhaps with the response in the national newspapers, well represented by the heading and sub heading in the *Evening Herald* (22 June, 2006: 1), 'Whitewash–Sea Views, Praise for Science Classes, But Where Are the Hard Facts, Minister?' More nuanced was the *Irish Times* (23 June, 2006: 8) which headed its piece, 'Minister denies reports are bland' and carried a column by Ombudsman Emily O'Reilly which, under the heading, 'A first small step in the right direction', speaks of 'beginning to peel back the curtain of secrecy in education'.

These negative views of the utility of final evaluation reports were widely echoed in the research interviews:

'Nothing dynamic to enthuse and challenge'
'Written in a way that the ordinary person would not and could not read'
'Recommendations very superficial'
'Pretty predictable stuff-all very general, superficial, following a formula'.

However some perceptive critics suggested that on closer scrutiny there might be more to the reports than meets the eye:

'Very little criticism–but you have to learn how to read them'
'Very bland but because of that any specifics are noticeable'

This notion of 'learning to read' the reports or 'reading between the lines' became clear to the authors as more reports were analysed. Bit by bit in a sea of supportive affirmation nuggets of critical advice emerged in a small number of the reports studied. For example in one school a particular subject department was told that 'some students get good feedback and correction'. In another school the level of absenteeism was commented on unfavourably while other schools and departments were gently chided on a lack of planning, limited use of varied methodologies, lack of student work displayed on the walls and so on.

Overall it seems fair to say that despite the publication of the inspection reports, those, particularly in the media, demanding accountability, clear definitive judgements and the outing of weak teachers are doomed to disappointment. However, this, as has essentially been argued throughout this study, is likely to be a good thing rather than the reverse. These rather gentle, rambling reports may not set the pulses racing, but they may form the basis for some improvements and reforms and, more importantly, are unlikely in their present form to damage school and teacher morale. Nonetheless, given the resources committed to WSE, it may well be that better school based research, improved feedback and more substantive reports could all contribute to getting substantially more developmental gain out of the system without damaging its essentially unthreatening character.

4. The Role of Stakeholders and the Question of Resources

Finally it is worth referring briefly to a number of other issues which arose in the course of this research. Firstly, it was suggested in the analysis of the *LAOS* framework that the vast number of 'aspects', 'components' and 'themes' was unrealistic and that no school or inspection team could deal with them all. In fact this seems to have been recognised in practice and the schools researched report that the inspection team tackled the various areas 'generally' and made no attempt to 'checklist' or 'tick off' each theme for self-evaluation. As has previously been noted, this de facto situation was recognised by the DES when it issued the greatly simplified *Guide* (DES, 2006). This outcome seems to have satisfied the schools but in effect it renders the apparent comprehensiveness and exactitude of the *LAOS* framework fairly meaningless and surely supports the argument that a much reduced and more focused framework would be more conducive to a meaningful evaluation.

The second area defined as one of potential difficulty, but which only emerges fleetingly in this research, is the role of parents and students in the evaluation process. The final report of the WSE pilot project (DES, 1999a) suggested that more account would have to be taken of the rights of key stakeholders such as parents and pupils to an input into school evaluation. However, there was no reference to these stakeholders in the *LAOS* documents, in fact if anything the emphasis was greater than ever on management and staff. However, none of the interviewees in the present research reported any issues raised by parents or students and neither the parent or student representative bodies nationally have made any critical statements in relation to *LAOS*. In the interviews conducted for this work it was reported that the evaluating inspectors did 'speak to parents' (usually the representatives on the Board of Management) and 'students on an ad hoc basis'. No question of any structured research to ascertain the views of the broad body of parents or students appears to have arisen.

A third issue, that of resources, particularly time implications for schools, did arise but not as strongly as might have been expected. What emerged here and has been noted earlier, was the tendency to see WSE as a once-off chore, to be prepared for and gotten through. Both principals and teachers spoke of many meetings and long nights updating documents, plans and policies. One principal described this period as 'us against them, working together to defeat the invader'. However, when asked in general terms if WSE was worth the expenditure of effort and resources, responses ranged from 'definitely' to 'I suppose so', or 'just about', with the majority in the middle somewhere. Perhaps tellingly, however, when the question was more specific, such as, 'would you spend the resources going into WSE on it or on, for example, more money for special needs or ICT, none of the respondents opted for WSE.

Conclusion

As we have seen, the *LAOS* framework for school evaluation and self-evaluation was developed, in theory at least, with the insights generated by the original WSE pilot at the forefront of everyone's mind. Despite, or perhaps because of this, the *LAOS* document is very long and detailed containing five areas of evaluation, sub-divided into one hundred and forty three themes for self-evaluation. As has been discussed, the emphasis in the framework is very much on self-evaluation. Schools are required in theory to gather evidence and then to make judgments about their own performance on a four part rating scale in respect of each theme for self-evaluation. This process of self-evaluation is then to inform the work of a visiting team of inspectors which would carry out a whole-school evaluation at unspecified intervals, probably not more than once every five years.

Chapter five set out to analyse the *LAOS* framework in the context of the outcomes of the WSE pilot project which proceeded it. The authors suggested that *LAOS* places greater emphasis on school self-evaluation than did WSE and significantly down plays external inspectorial evaluation. It is also suggested that the language of *LAOS*, for example replacing the 'evaluation criteria' of WSE with 'themes for self-evaluation' further demonstrates that the acceptability of the process to schools and teachers is the central concern of the DES.

For similar reasons the authors also suggests that weaknesses identified in the WSE report are not tackled to any degree in *LAOS*. Key among these issues are: the un-realistic extent of the framework itself (subsequently simplified by the publication of the *Guide* in two thousand and six); the lack of required data collection and evidence generation to support schools' statements about their strengths and weaknesses; lack of quality and depth in feedback both to schools and to individual teachers, and related concerns about the insubstantial nature of the final reports; lack of clarity about responsibility for following up issues identified; and, finally, the role of the key stakeholders particularly parents and students in the process. In order to examine the implementation of the new evaluation framework in practice, case study interviews with school leaders and teachers were conducted in twenty-four schools.

The outcome of this research indicates a mixed response to the WSE system. The experience of the schools is described as extremely positive, affirming and supportive. Senior staff report that the process provided a focus for schools as they prepared for it and had benefits in terms of increased cohesion and collegiality. The work of the inspection teams is invariably described as professional and supportive and the final reports were well received (to an extent) and perceived as fair and somewhat helpful. No negative feeling (rather than pre-evaluation nerves) or reservations is reported.

As against these positives several negatives also emerge. It is clear that the wide-ranging nature of the framework means that a great deal is not specifically considered during the evaluation. It is also evident that the concept of ongoing self-evaluation has not taken hold in schools and that there is a great deal of overlap between the *LAOS* framework and that of school development planning. An integration and rationalisation of these two policies will need to be considered urgently. It also emerges that there is no concept in schools of collecting and analysing data to build evidence on which to base evaluation judgments. Most of what counted as evidence in the schools visited consisted of professional judgments by staff and inspectors largely using existing paperwork such as school policies and plans. This is not to say that such judgments do not count as valuable evidence, only that they are but one of many possible sources of evidence (McNamara and O'Hara, 2004; Thomas and Pring, 2004). The lack of any guidelines in *LAOS* as to criteria or research methods that might inform judgments has led to what amounts to data free evaluation in practice. Moreover it is clear that without such guidelines and the provision of training and research support for schools, the situation is not likely to change.

A second key problem identified in the research was the quality and usefulness of the advice and feedback given by the inspectors during and after WSE. By and large, both principals and teachers felt that the feedback was either somewhat cynical (suggesting things that could not be done, whether for resource or 'political' reasons, or bland and superficial). In particular, teachers appeared hungry for good advice and ideas. This, as Winch (2001) points out, is a key marker of a good inspection/evaluation system—the extent to which developmental, professional gains outweigh the negatives inherent in all such systems, including teacher stress and damage to autonomy and morale. High quality feedback is the key to this and the current research indicates major shortcomings in this area.

In the case of both these negative outcomes, low levels of school and teacher internal research and self-evaluation, and poor feedback, it seems to us that significant improvements could be made to WSE without impairing its widespread acceptance. In fact, it seems clear to us from this research that greater clarity and support in both these areas would be welcomed by schools and teachers. Moreover, since as this chapter demonstrates vividly, many principals and teachers are sceptical, or at least not fully convinced of the benefits of WSE, overcoming these feelings is crucial to the future of the process. As Leithwood *et. al.* (2004: 4) put it,

> the chance of any reform improving student learning is remote unless . . . schoolteachers agree with its purpose and appreciate what is required to make it work. Local leaders must, for example, be able to help their colleagues understand how the externally initiated reform might be integrated into local improvement efforts, provide the necessary support for those whose practices must change, and must win the cooperation and support of parents and others in the local community.

Other negatives also emerge from this research, but are perhaps not as problematic as the above, in that they could, arguably, be tackled in the context of increasing the self-evaluation capacity of schools, including generating more and better evidence from a wide variety of sources. For example, the very limited role for parents and students contained in the *LAOS* framework has not as yet resulted in much negative comment and a greater role for key stakeholders would surely emerge in the context of more systematic school self-evaluation. Equally, among the schools researched there is deep scepticism regarding the extent of any remedial action being taken by the DES in cases where the evaluation indicates problems, and final evaluation reports are regarded as positive but superficial. Again, however, it could hardly be otherwise when there is so little research data available in schools on which to base more in-depth reporting and recommend credible remedial interventions.

This research indicates that *LAOS* is very much a process still developing and evolving. It is clear that the first priority of the DES is to establish it as an accepted part of the system by proceeding with extreme caution and stressing the co-operation, partnership and self-evaluation aspects. Whether, as time goes by, the rigour and quality of the research underpinning the process can be raised to a level where the judgments made are regarded as robust enough to support follow-up remediation remains to be seen. What does seem beyond doubt is that schools, to paraphrase John MacBeath, are not in a position to speak for themselves in that there is little evidence of any self-evaluation capacity in the system. Unless the situation can be improved, it is hard to see how WSE can deliver on its very considerable potential as a tool to enhance school and teacher development. There is consequently a significant danger that external forces may use this lack of internal capacity to impose narrow and reductionist forms of evaluation and appraisal on schools and teachers. It seems, therefore, a priority to work towards the development of teachers and schools with the self-evaluative mindset and the skills necessary to undertake internal evaluation. Part three of this work will concern itself with developing an approach to this difficult task.

· PART 3 ·

DEVELOPING THE
SELF-EVALUATING TEACHER

Introduction

In the opening two parts of this work, an overview of the international and domestic origins and current operation of the Irish school evaluation system was presented. Perhaps unsurprisingly, given the extensive consultation that took place prior to its introduction, many of the themes and trends that emerge in the international research on the area of school and teacher evaluation have been replicated within the Irish system. One of the most interesting of these themes is the ongoing debate as to whether it is possible for an externally mandated, accountability focused and inspectorate led system of school evaluation to successfully engage with and indeed nurture a culture of internally driven, improvement focused and teacher led self-evaluation. It has been suggested in this work that, internationally, reconciling these imperatives has become a goal of most school evaluation systems, with what degree of success it is perhaps too early to say. In the Irish context what has become clear is that, in theory at least, this is also the goal that the DES is seeking to achieve.

However what our research in schools demonstrates is that, as yet, the concept of the school and teacher as self-evaluating agents has failed to take hold. This cannot be regarded as surprising since other than rhetoric and exhortation little or no support or guidance has been given to empower such a development. Therefore given that the entire WSE process is effectively built on this foundation it seems timely to engage with the concept of the self-evaluating teacher and school.

In this part of the study an account will be given of how an education department in an Irish university designed and tested a programme that would prepare a diverse group of teachers at various stages of their professional careers to embrace the theory and practice of self-evaluation. It was hoped that this would prepare them to subsequently engage with the emerging system of evaluation in Irish schools. Because, at a rhetorical level at least, the Irish approach to school evaluation seeks to build on evaluation work supposedly already being undertaken by school communities the programme developed had to prepare teachers to actively undertake this work. This meant not only providing them with the essential research skills to engage in a self-evaluation process but also putting in place the structural support necessary to allow them continue this engagement over an extended period of time. This was particularly important for the teachers taking part in this study for, unlike many of the groups mentioned in the international literature, these teachers do not come from one or even a related cluster of school communities (Neil *et. al.*, 2001; Simons, 2002). Therefore rather than having the school group as the locus of the self-evaluation training process in this study the individual teacher working with a broader community of likeminded professionals becomes the centre of the training.

A further complicating factor was the reality that the system of evaluation being proposed for Ireland was only being rolled out piecemeal at the time that this research was being conducted. This meant that while there was some clarity at a documentary level as to what was expected from teachers engaging with the system, little information was available as to the practical requirements imposed on teachers and schools undergoing inspection. For this reason it was decided to design the training programme in an iterative fashion, experimenting with different elements over a three year cycle with a view to producing a final programme that was culturally and systemically relevant.

This part begins with chapter seven, an analysis of how the focus of school and teacher evaluation systems has shifted in recent years and explores in some detail how other education systems have supported the development of self-evaluation skills at a range of levels. It continues in chapter eight with a description of how the insights generated by this analysis of the international literature were used to design the programme of training under discussion. An outline of the different stages of the programme developed is then provided with a discussion as to the reasons for the inclusion of different aspects. Chapter nine goes on to provide a detailed analysis of the data generated in the course of the implementation and evaluation of the training programme, paying particular attention to its success as a method for helping professional educators to develop self-evaluation skills.

· 7 ·

SUPPORTING SCHOOL AND TEACHER SELF-EVALUATION

The European Experience

Quite an amount of time has been spent in this study charting the journey of the concept of the self-evaluating teacher from the periphery of systems of educational evaluation to their centre. This chapter continues this analysis and takes it one stage further, examining not only the increasing acceptance of self-evaluation at an official level but also exploring what this means in practice in a range of educational settings.

The chapter begins with an analysis of the reasons behind the increased acceptance of the notion of self-evaluation, concentrating on a series of robust models generated in the late nineteen nineties by a number of European researchers. It goes on to explore the practical implications of this acceptance at both a general European level and also at a local systems level in a number of EU countries. Considerable attention is paid to the way in which individual education systems have sought to support the development of a culture of self-evaluation and in particular a detailed analysis of the recent English experience is provided. The chapter concludes with an examination of a trans-European evaluation training project which, somewhat unusually, focused on the development of a network of committed individuals as the chosen method for ensuring the spread of self-evaluation skills in a range of educational settings. This project significantly influenced the research work in Ireland reported in chapters eight and nine.

The Triumph of the Self-Evaluation?

In a recent work on school evaluation, Professor John MacBeath states that, 'self-evaluation is now seen as a matter of priority in most economically advanced countries of the world' (2003:2). Given MacBeath's championing of the concept of self-evaluation over a number of decades, it might be possible to dismiss this statement as the analysis of a partisan voice in an increasingly passionate debate. However MacBeath's statement has been echoed by a range of commentators from all sides of the school evaluation debate. At a European level, the *Recommendation of the European Parliament and Council on European Cooperation in Quality Evaluation in School Education* (2001) clearly argues that improvements in European school evaluation provision are dependent on the enhancement of schools' abilities to evaluate themselves. Specifically the *Recommendation* calls on Member States of the EU to 'encourage school self-evaluation as a method of creating learning and improving schools' (2001). This analysis is echoed in the recent highly influential OECD report on the future of the teaching profession, *Teachers Matter* (2005). This report sees the development of self-evaluation skills within the education system as being a critical component of the drive to improve educational provision in OECD member states.

Perhaps most surprisingly of all, the system of school evaluation most often associated with externally imposed, low trust accountability, the Office for Standards in Education (Ofsted) in England has recently decided to make school self-evaluation a central plank of its approach to monitoring educational quality. So radical has the change been, that in a recent article MacBeath speaks of, 'the new relationship in England' (between schools and the State) (2006:5). Official documents now state that 'self evaluation evidence (is) at the heart of inspection' (Milliband, 2004 cited in Swaffield and MacBeath, 2005:6). The newly produced Self-Evaluation Form is to be considered 'the most crucial piece of evidence available to the inspection team' (Ofsted, 2004: 24). Indeed the British government minister with responsibility for the area at that time, David Milliband, publicly celebrated the emergence of a new 'simplified school improvement focus, where every school uses robust self-evaluation to drive improvement' (Milliband 2004:3). Official Ofsted documents now state that:

> Intelligent accountability should be founded on the school's own views of how well it is serving its pupils and its priorities for improvement. This is what is meant by school self-evaluation. (Ofsted, 2004: 7)

To get a sense of the radical shift in emphasis these statements represent one need only refer back to public statements by the former Chief Inspector of English schools who attacked a number of teacher unions for 'promoting something as subversive as self-evaluation' (McAvoy, 2004: 19).

So, are we now entering into the era of self-evaluation where divisive, intrusive and ultimately destructive forms of externally imposed accountability are a thing of the past? Perhaps, but it is by no means as clear cut as that. While the rhetoric of school evaluation now officially celebrates the role of self-evaluation this is nearly always presented within a context where an external, inspectorate- led accountability structure is still in place. This can perhaps be best seen by continuing the quotations provided above. After celebrating the triumph of self-evaluation in economically advanced countries MacBeath goes on to say that, 'in most of these countries there is a concern to align it more closely with external inspection' (MacBeath 2003: 2). The European parliament goes on to argue in *Recommendation 1e* that Member States must 'clarify the purpose and the conditions for school self-evaluation, and to ensure that the approach to self-evaluation is consistent with other forms of regulation' (European Parliament, 2001: *Recommendation 1e*). Finally, Miliband having celebrated the centrality of self-evaluation argues that it should be seen as being part of 'an accountability framework, which puts a premium on ensuring effective and ongoing self-evaluation in every school combined with more focused external inspection' (Miliband, 2004:11).

It is arguable that what we have seen emerge in recent years, as exemplified by the above quotations, is a re-framing of the debate surrounding the relationship between internal modes of school improvement and external forms of accountability. There is, to quote Nevo (1995), a growing realisation that the relationship between school communities and inspectorates should be based on 'dialogue' rather than conflict. Of course the concept of dialogue is a little nebulous in itself. Questions as to who participates in the dialogue, their relationship, the format that the dialogue is to take and the hoped for results are often posed (Nevo, 1995, 2002, 2006). Notwithstanding these caveats, the move towards acknowledging the centrality of self-evaluation is an important one and it has led to a number of attempts to develop a comprehensive framework of school evaluation that includes all elements of the emerging dialogue in a structure that demonstrates their relationship. Perhaps the most detailed of these frameworks is the one developed by MacBeath in collaboration with Schratz and others over the past decade (1999, 2000, 2003) and it is to this that we will now turn.

Allowing Schools to Speak

Initially produced as part of the 'Schools Must Speak for Themselves' and 'Evaluating Quality in School Education' research projects, MacBeath and colleagues designed a model which sought to provide a multi- dimensional view of school development and evaluation.

The framework developed was entitled 'The Cube Model of Evaluation' (MacBeath *et. al.*, 2000: 93). A simpler version of the model, drawing from the work of MacBeath, Schratz and Austrian colleagues, was previously published in 1999 (see Figure 7.1) (MacBeath *et. al.*, 1999).

The less complex model suggests that there are three dimensions involved in school evaluation, the top down/ bottom up, the external/ internal and the support/ pressure. The explanations of these dimensions are fairly self-evident. The internal/ external dimension 'represents a continuum from self-evaluation to evaluation from an outside source' (1999: 2). The pressure/ support dimension relates to individuals' or schools' perception of the amount of assistance or coercion they experience in the course of the evaluation. The top down/ bottom up axis,

> represents how a system sees and implements change. At one extreme it is delivered from above, by dictat, by legislation, by national structures. Alternatively it can come entirely from below, from class teachers, from pupils and parents, building on day-to-day school and classroom practice. (MacBeath *et. al.*, 1999: 2-3)

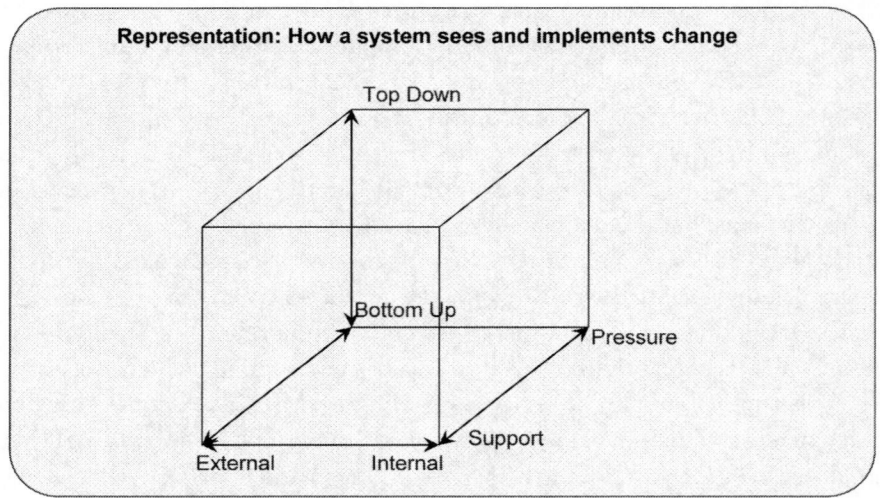

FIGURE 7.1: THE INITIAL CUBE MODEL OF EVALUATION (MACBEATH *ET. AL.*, 1999: 3)

The model was updated in the year two thousand with the addition of ref-erences to internal and external evaluation, self-evaluation and development and accountability (see Figure 7.2).

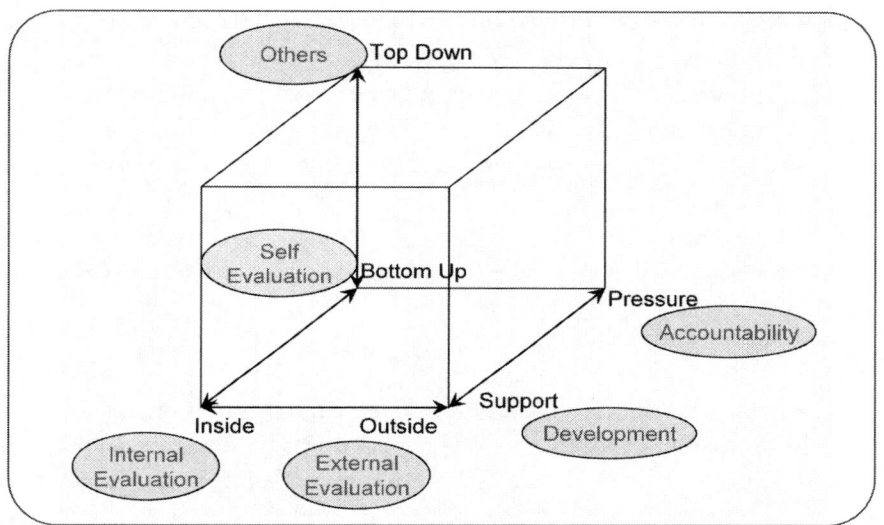

FIGURE 7.2: THE UPDATED CUBE MODEL OF EVALUATION (2000:93)

In essence what the revised model argues is that within the three dimen-sions outlined there is a 'particular point that defines the nature and describes the process of evaluation' (MacBeath *et. al.*, 2000: 93). Naturally identifying this point is a difficult process, as each of the 'corners' of the cube model iden-tified seek to exert influence and pull the focus of the evaluation in their par-ticular direction.

However what is of equal importance in this model is the emphasis on the dynamic relationship between all of the elements included. Altering one ele-ment of the model will have an impact on all other elements and will change the location of that 'particular point' mentioned above.

This conceptualisation of the interconnectedness of a number of elements in school evaluation systems is an interesting one and MacBeath *et. al.*, seek to tease it out. They argue that if we accept this way of looking at evaluation then we must be willing to acknowledge that 'top-down approaches need bot-tom up responses. External expectations have to meet internal needs, and pressure will not work without the push of some internal direction or vision'

(2000:93).

Thus a system of evaluation that seeks to emphasise the importance of self-evaluation will have to consider, amongst other things, how:

▢ The internal priorities of the school community engaging in an evaluative process can be matched with the external requirements of a publicly accountable inspectorate system?

▢ A culture of school improvement which seeks to emphasise reflection, development and trust can interact with a system of school accountability which seeks to prioritise measurement, standards and at times sanction?

▢ The need for an objective 'snapshot' of the quality of work being undertaken by a school can be met by the data produced by the school community itself?

These and similar questions have been posed with increasing frequency at a number of different levels within European education systems in recent years. While the focus of many of the answers has been at a systemic level, for example the re-structuring of the Ofsted system in England and the development of the *Looking at Our Schools* (*LAOS*) system in Ireland, other interventions have sought to tease out the implications of the questions at a schools level. The schools- based research reported in the previous part of this work seems to support the absolute necessity of focusing on school and teacher self-evaluation if systemic reforms are to have any chance of succeeding in practice. It is to this group of interventions that we will now turn. In particular we will examine a range of initiatives that have tried to enhance the ability of individual teachers and school communities to engage in the oft cited 'dialogue' that is considered to be at the heart of successful self-evaluation on a more or less equal footing with other key stakeholders (Nevo, 2002).

Experiments in Supporting the Self-Evaluating Teacher: The Broader European Experience

The year 2004 saw the publication of perhaps the most comprehensive comparative study of evaluation systems within the European Union (EU). Entitled *Evaluation of Schools providing Compulsory Education in Europe* and published by Eurydice under the auspices of the Directorate-General for Education and

Culture, the report sought to provide a comprehensive analysis of the multi-faceted 'approaches to the evaluation of schools providing compulsory educa-tion' within the EU (2004:9). In the context of this study, one of the most interesting sections of the report is that dealing with so-called 'supporting measures' (2004:122) provided for internal evaluators of schools. The follow-ing table, taken from the report, provides some indication of the allegedly com-prehensive nature of the supporting measures available at the time (see Table 7.1). Given the growth in interest in self-evaluation methodologies outlined earlier in this chapter, one might assume that the range of supports now avail-able to the self-evaluating school within the European Union might have been significantly enhanced in the interim. In reality however our work not only in Ireland but further afield suggests that much of this reported support for self-evaluation is overstated to put it mildly. While, as we have seen, rhetori-cal support for self-evaluation has grown rapidly, practical support remains limited. The value of the table is less as an indication of what is in fact hap-pening and more as a summary of the type of things that would need to hap-pen to underpin the widespread implementation of systematic self-evaluation.

A cursory glance at the table below indicates that while very few EU countries have all of the supports offered nearly all claim to have some support for self-evaluation built into their systems of evaluation. In terms of populari-ty, the provision of training and resource persons are the most popular inter-ventions across the countries surveyed closely followed by the production of evaluation frameworks and indicators. In commenting on this hierarchy in pop-ularity of support measures the reports' writers suggest that, 'support through training personnel . . . reflects a long-term investment' (2004:126). This is an interesting insight as it suggests that the creation of genuinely self-evaluating schools is not something that can be done overnight. Rather, it implies a requirement to concentrate on enhancing the skills of the school communities seeking to engage in evaluation over an extended period of time. This process, the report suggests, will require governments, education departments and other support agencies to offer 'human, financial (and) material resources' (Eurydice, 2004:126) if it is to succeed.

While the table on the next page may be rather exaggerated, nonetheless a good deal of interesting work on the process of encouraging self-evaluation has been undertaken and some of this is considered in the next section.

	Be fr/de	Be	DK	DE	EL	ES	FR	IE	IT	NL	AT	PT	FI	SE	UK	UK SC	IS	LI	NO	BG	CZ	EE	CY	LV	LT	HU	MT	PL	RO	SI	SK
A	x	x		x	x	x					x		x		x	x	x		x							x	x	x	x	x	x
B		x			x	x	x		x	x	x	x	x								x										
C		x	x			x	x	x	x				x	x	x	x	x	x	x				x							x	
D			x		x								x	x	x	x			x					x			x				
E		x								x			x		x	x									x			x			
F		x				x				x			x	x	x	x			x									x			
G						x				x			x	x	x				x				x								
H		x		x	x					x			x	x									x						x		x
I											x	x	x	x					x						x						
J		x		x											x																
K		x				x		x					x	x																	

TABLE 7.1: SUPPORTING MEASURES AVAILABLE TO INTERNAL EVALUATION OF SCHOOLS, COMPULSORY EDUCATION 2001–2002

A= Training
B= Evaluation Framework and Models
C= Resource Person
D= Indicators on the education system (including results)
E= Research and other publications on evaluation
F= Guidelines and Manuals
G= Website
H= Criteria, indicators and procedures used in external evaluation
I= Exchange of Experience / sharing good practice
J = EFQM Good practice model
K = Financial support (Eurydice, 2004: 124)

Supporting the Self-Evaluating Teacher: Models of Best Practice

Recent years have seen a range of resources produced at local, national and transnational levels aimed at supporting schools and individual teachers who wish to engage in a process of self-evaluation. At the risk of over simplification, it is possible to categorise the support mechanisms under three broad headings:

1. Supports designed to facilitate the local collection of data to enable schools and teachers to meet the requirements of state mandated self-evaluation systems.
2. Supports designed to engage teachers with the theory and practice of school self-evaluation with a view to their developing their own contextually sensitive models of evaluation without reference to external requirements.
3. Supports designed and implemented by some outside agency to collect and analyse data independently and feed it back to schools to underpin internal evaluation.

We will examine some recent initiatives under these broad headings.

Supports Designed to Facilitate the Local Collection of Data for Centrally Mandated Self-Evaluation Systems

As we have already seen in the earlier part of this chapter, one of the more interesting recent developments in school evaluation has been the extent to which the English system which had largely concentrated on emphasising the centrality of 'objective' external evaluation has now begun to recognise the necessity of internal or self-evaluation in any comprehensive system for measuring quality in schools. However some authors, most notably MacBeath (2003, 2005) Simons (2002) and Scheerens (2002) would question whether centrally mandated self-evaluation should ever properly be identified with the developmental, improvement focused nature of genuine self-evaluation. Yet in England at a rhetorical level at least there is a strong commitment to,

> introducing a new inspection system which puts more onus on a school to demonstrate that it can diagnose where its strengths and weaknesses are and do something about improving and developing them. (Ofsted, 2005: 1)

At the centre of this change in focus is the promotion of the use of the Self-Evaluation Form (SEF). Its champions in Ofsted claim that using the SEF can enable inspectors to, focus inspections on your evaluation of your strengths and weaknesses which helps to make inspection sharper and more helpful while still providing evaluations against a national framework. At the same time, we can lighten the burden of inspection on you. (Ofsted, 2005:1)

Ofsted encourages schools to use the SEF 'to develop their own process of self-evaluation and to fit the completion of the SEF into their core systems as best suits them' (Ofsted, 2004:7). This is an interesting approach to mandated self-evaluation. The central authority does not provide a prescribed methodology for producing data on which judgments will be made but it does insist that all data produced must fit into a template designed externally to the schools. In addition, Ofsted is clear about the elements that make up an effective self-evaluation. According to its publications, there are six acid tests of effective self-evaluation:

- It asks the most important questions about pupils' learning, achievements and development.
- It uses a range of telling evidence to answer these questions.
- It benchmarks the school's and pupils' performance against the best comparable schools.
- It involves staff, pupils, parents and governors at all level.
- It is integral to the school's central systems for assessing and developing pupils and for managing and developing staff.
- It leads to action. (Ofsted, 2004: 7)

What this means in practice is that the SEF asks schools:

- To evaluate their progress against an inspection schedule.
- To set out the main evidence on which this evaluation is based.
- To identify strengths and weaknesses.
- To explain the action the school is taking to remedy the weaknesses and develop the strengths. (Ofsted, 2005: 1)

The SEF requires contextual information on the school, covers all relevant aspects of the school's work and evaluates compliance with statutory requirements. It is envisaged that the SEF be filled out prior to the school inspection and be used as a basis for that inspection although it is not compulsory for schools to use it. This latter point is emphasised throughout but yet there is considerable pressure put on schools to view this as a critically important document:

The SEF is intended to record the outcomes of your self-evaluation. As such, it should be an accurate diagnostic document with all conclusions fully supported by the evidence. It should indicate key strengths and weaknesses, and what needs to be tackled to effect improvement. Inspectors will make considerable use of the SEF when discussing their arrangements for inspection. The impact of your self-evaluation in helping to bring about improvement will be a major factor in their judgments about the effectiveness of your leadership and management and your capacity to improve in the future. (Ofsted, 2006: 3)

The form is thirty seven pages long and is divided into three sections:

◻   Part A dealing with self-evaluation.
◻   Part B dealing with factual information about the school.
◻   Part C dealing with information about compliance with statutory requirements.

It provides a set of indicators which seek to assess the quality of the school under a range of headings (see Table 7.2).

The Whole School
Teaching and Learning
Pupil Guidance and support
Leadership and management
Pupil Achievement
Curriculum
The school in the community

TABLE 7.2: SEF HEADINGS

Staff are expected to rate the school on a four point scale:

◻   Inadequate.
◻   Satisfactory.

◻   Good.
◻   Outstanding.

One of the innovative aspects of the SEF is the facility provided by Ofsted that allows schools to enter the material online and provides a range of reporting and editing functions that should, in theory at least, enable the school awaiting inspection to tailor their data to the requirements of the visiting team.

There is deep disagreement as to whether this is actually a form to encourage self-evaluation or whether it is simply a summary of existing data (MacBeath, 2003). Also, because of the central importance of the SEF to the overall judgement made about individual schools there are serious doubts as to whether schools will actually include all relevant information as is recommended in improvement focused self-evaluation (Hofman, Dukstra and Hofman, 2005) or whether positive information will be cherry picked and included in an attempt to present the school in the best possible light. To a number of writers, MacBeath being the most vocal, this type of evaluation is more accurately described as 'self-inspection' rather than proper self-evaluation as it can be argued that it is 'simply doing the inspectors job for them'. This interpretation is further strengthened by the inspectorate's maintenance of their position as the ultimate arbiters of quality in the school. While they might 'take into account' the schools own analysis of its work, the final decision still rests with them. As MacBeath points out, 'there is no pretence that this is an equal partnership' (2006: 7).

Whatever about its status as a instigator of valid self-evaluation, the complexity of the SEF has resulted in the development of a series of support materials, both on paper and online, to enhance the usage made by schools of the document. These support materials can be divided into two main types, those which try to explain the SEF and assist in its completion and those which seek to complement the SEF and offer 'complementary processes which schools can use on an ongoing basis rather than simply for review' (MacBeath, 2005:2).

Explaining the Self-Evaluation Form

When faced with the requirement to complete a thirty seven page long, complex and vitally important document that could have a profound influence on the future of their school, many school leaders asked for help. Indeed Ofsted explicitly acknowledges the need for help when engaging in this type of high stakes reporting by encouraging a number of external stakeholders 'to develop a range of tools, aids and training in self-evaluation which schools can pick and choose from' (Ofsted 2004: 7).

Among the most common types of help offered is that provided by Bristol Children and Young People's Services. This type of support consists of an explanatory document that provides advice and suggestions for the completion of each part of the SEF. The document emphasises that these suggestions 'are not part of the SEF and have been drawn together as an aid' (Bristol Children and Young People's Services, 2005). What is interesting about this is not only the fact that a local authority feels the need to provide such a guide but also that quite subtly it is used to influence the manner in which the SEF is completed. The provision of 'suggestions that are not part of the SEF' while not binding, is naturally going to influence what is included in the final report. Many other Local Education Authorities in England (see for example Hertfordshire and Sheffield) have developed similar tools and models to act as evidence gathering templates for schools.

The Bristol guide offers a twenty nine page commentary on the completion of a thirty seven page form. As can be seen from the examples below (Figures 7.3 and 7.4) the commentary provided is very detailed, providing a wide range of sources and ideas but also what amounts to a set of directions for completing the SEF.

PART A: SELF-EVALUATION

1. CHARACTERISTICS OF YOUR SCHOOL
What are the main characteristics of your school?

Drawing on Section B and C of this form and other relevant data, write a brief description of its features.

(Please note that this is an opportunity for a brief summary of the main characteristics of the school and it is not necessary to repeat tables of data.)
1a Please outline the main characteristics of the learners, including:
  - their attainment on entry and how you know this;
  - their social and economic backgrounds, indicating the level of prosperity or deprivation.

FIGURE 7.3: QUESTION 1 PART A SEF FOR SECONDARY SCHOOLS

The guidance document from Bristol tries to provide the necessary information on how to successfully answer the above. One question results in ten prompts for possible answers (Figure 7.4). Serious questions must be raised about whether this is actually an example of self-evaluation. It is arguable that it is more akin to what Davies and Rudd term 'a limited preliminary inspection process' (2000:5) which prepares schools to face the more daunting external examination. We do not really see a 'bottom-up' approach in which the school seeks to tell its own story using its own words and highlighting its own concerns.

PART A: SELF-EVALUATION

1. CHARACTERISTICS OF YOUR SCHOOL
What are the main characteristics of your school?

Drawing on Section B and C of this form and other relevant data, write a brief description of its features.

(Please note that this is an opportunity for a brief summary of the main characteristics of the school and it is not necessary to repeat tables of data.)

1a Please outline the main characteristics of the learners, including:
◻   their attainment on entry and how you know this;
◻   their social and economic backgrounds, indicating the level of prosperity or deprivation.

Advice and Prompts
◻   Refer to KS2 attainment evidence against national attainment at KS2 - state which areas are lower/higher - what does this say about the strengths and weaknesses of your pupils and indicate any significant trends?
◻   Refer to any analysis of the Level of Social Deprivation, based on the Ward Level indices of Deprivation 2000, Sure Start local programmes data and January PLASC Postcode Data and PANDA information and comment on
    ◻   A breakdown of the wards where pupils live
    ◻   Educational background of parents
    ◻   Employment domain
◻   Comment on parental aspirations.
◻   Comment on number of free school meals, falling or rising.
◻   Comment on numbers on SEN register, falling or rising, numbers of statements
◻   Comment on ethnicity of pupils (see PLASC, include Traveller information here)/EAL information/information on any Asylum Seeking families.
◻   Comment on Looked After Children/children at risk if appropriate.
◻   Comment on pupil mobility and patterns.
◻   Comment on significant changes affecting the school or its locality e.g. establishment of temporary housing and accommodation in local area, changes in Council Housing patterns.
◻   Comment on progression post 16 and post 18 where appropriate

You need to convey clearly the impact of the above on your school, the provision you make and pupil outcomes. This is also an opportunity to talk about the indicators positively, expressing high expectations as well as those indicators which the school has to address in order to achieve high standards.

FIGURE 7.4: EXPLAINING THE SELF-EVALUATION FORM

Moving Beyond the SEF—
Self-Evaluation, Planning and Improvement

Other self-evaluation support systems take a rather different approach to the Bristol one. Among the most interesting of these is the 'Matrix' jointly designed by the National College for School Leadership (NCSL) in the UK and the British Educational Communications and Technology Agency (BECTA).Designed to support self-evaluation and action planning as well as offering access to online resources, this web based tool allows schools to assess their current position in a range of areas by asking them to review their practice against a set of level statements. Schools are subsequently provided with an action plan which draws from their own analysis of their current practice.

To begin the process, the user–either an individual teacher, group of teachers or management group - chooses to enter any one of thirteen individual areas (see Figure 7.5). Each of these areas contains a number of individual matrices. Users are asked to choose a matrix and to begin the process of assessing the quality of their school's work in the particular area under discussion.

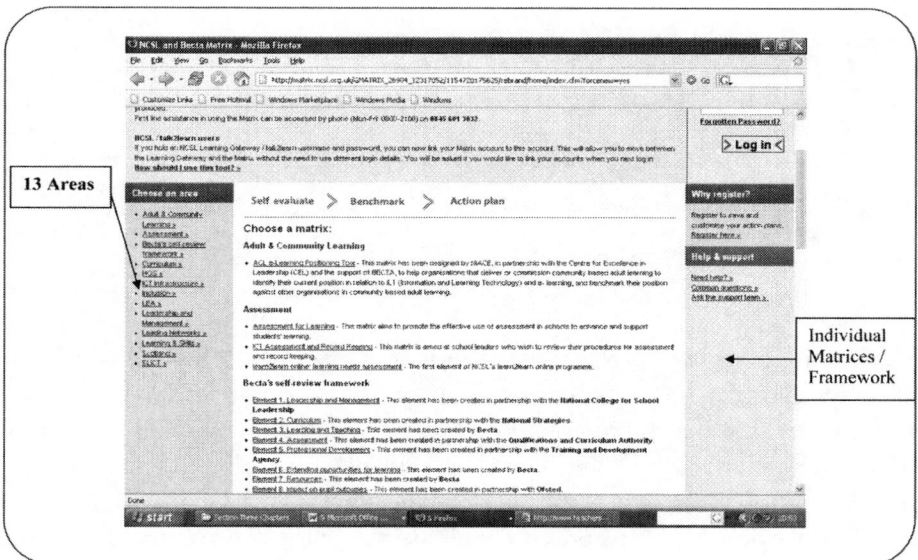

FIGURE 7.5: NCSL/ BECTA MATRIX AREAS

Having entered into an individual matrix users are asked to make a judgment relating to the quality of their school's work in this particular area against a series of five level statements. The levels are labelled not applicable, preemergent, emergent, established and advanced. Users are asked to choose the one that most accurately describes the current reality of their school in this area. An opportunity is also given for the user to enter independent comments and perhaps most importantly statements of evidence (see figure 7.6).

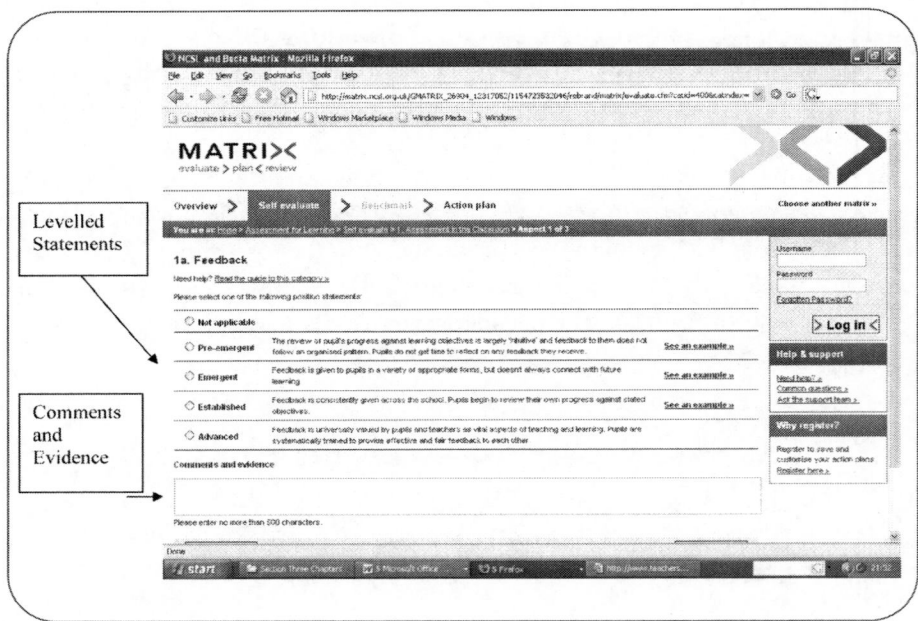

FIGURE 7.6: NCSL MATRIX STATEMENTS AND EVIDENCE

Having completed a rough average of about twelve of these sections the matrix is considered complete. The next stage is the automatic generation of an action plan using the responses provided. This is accompanied by a series of recommendations and advice as to how the plan might best be implemented. One of the key aspects of the action plan is that it can be edited and therefore can take account of the priorities and insights of the team or individual (see figure 7.7). Finally schools are led to specific online resources that might assist them in following through on the action plan decided.

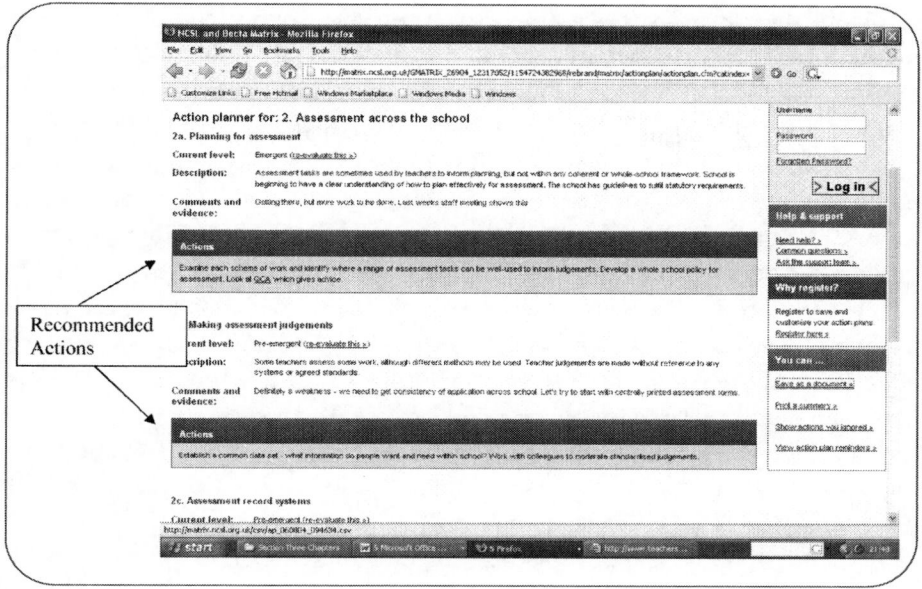

FIGURE 7.7: NCSL MATRIX RECOMMEND ACTIONS

What is particularly interesting about this methodology for supporting the self-evaluation process is that it clearly links the concept of self-evaluation with that of action planning and improvement. This latter point is critical in an organisation's understanding of the purpose of self-evaluation. Nevo (2002) and Scheerens (2002) emphasise the need to clearly identify the concept of self-evaluation in schools with that of ongoing improvement rather than seeing its sole purpose as being linked to an external accountability framework. In practice this is what seems to happen. Data provided on the BECTA site indicates that sixty seven percent of respondents believed that use of the Matrix would help them quite significantly to deliver continuous improvement in their schools (BECTA, 2006). Other research reports discussing practical implementation case studies of the matrix describe its use as a focus for internal dialogue between different groupings within schools. One such report, produced by the University of Southampton, suggests that a scenario be established which would encourage,

staff and senior management to work through some of the matrices separately. Then they could compare their assessments with the other group and discuss the suggested action plans together. (Halnan *et. al.*, 2006:4)

Here then is a good example of the use of a support mechanism as a methodology for both encouraging internal dialogue and providing the necessary data on which to base any improvement strategies. The school is to a large extent responsible for the generation of the data as well as for the future steps taken as a result of this process. The fact that much of this data could also be useful when trying to complete the SEF is an incidental but welcome side effect.

Other somewhat similar initiatives include the Transforming Learning programme developed by the Hay Group (2006) which allows key stakeholders in schools to evaluate important aspects of the school and classroom environment. Based on research conducted by the Hay McBear group into teacher effectiveness, the online facility provides, amongst other things, 'anonymous aggregate data on classroom climate, indicating trends across the school' (Hay Group, 2006). The data is sourced from all levels of the school organisation, including pupils, and is used to provide tailored advice and action plans for individual teachers, subject departments and schools as a whole.

A similar, though more Ofsted focused support system is provided by Cambridge Education (School Centre.net: 2006). In essence this is a compilation mechanism where schools are given an opportunity to produce a self-evaluation plan drawn from an evidence base that can be attached to the final document. Staff are encouraged to interact with the material being gathered with a view to developing 'organic plans' that evolve over time. Again these plans can be focused at a range of levels from that of the individual teacher through to the school as a whole. One of the key selling points of this system is the fact that it includes the SEF form and submits it automatically to Ofsted for the school!

The examples provided above indicate that there has been growth in the provision of support mechanisms for schools in the English system who are seeking to move to a more self-evaluation focused approach to school accountability. What is interesting in the context of the debate about the nature of school evaluation discussed earlier in this chapter is the type of support available. For the most part schools and teachers are being offered methodologies for recording their own data and given arenas for presenting their own evidence. However they are also being asked to use frameworks, formulae, matrices and forms designed by some other group, normally external consultants, to gather and present that data. For this reason, it is possible to argue that this is a form of school evaluation that is being guided from outside rather than growing organically from within. In the next section we will look at systems that have emerged from the bottom up to facilitate schools telling their own story, using their own resources and developing their own mechanisms for drawing together and validating data.

Supports Designed to Engage Teachers with the Theory and Practice of School Self-Evaluation with a View to Their Developing Their Own Contextually Sensitive Models of Evaluation

As we have seen in earlier sections of this work, the concept of self-evaluation is one that has been discussed in educational literature for a number of decades. The work of Elliot (1995) is a good example of an earlier attempt to examine the implications of transferring responsibility for the public presentation of a narrative regarding the quality of educational provision from a centralised bureaucracy to individual school units. While Elliot would argue that this effort to create a schools focused, self-evaluation culture was ultimately unsuccessful, his location of this emerging strand of evaluation within the practitioner research movement is an interesting one. The primacy of the needs and insights of the local over and above the demands and impositions of the national is a constant theme throughout much practitioner research. This form of research, far from disappearing in the late nineteen seventies as its self-evaluation component seemed to, has emerged as one of the strongest streams within educational discourse in the latter years of the twentieth and first years of the twenty first centuries (Schon 1983; Silverman 2004, 2005; Gorard with Taylor, 2004). Given its increasing popularity and emerging strength it is perhaps inevitable that practitioner led research into the potential role to be played by self-evaluation in the future of school evaluation systems would re-emerge.

In this section, we will examine two projects which were designed with a view to producing a local model for evaluating what happens in schools in a sensitive and realistic way. The first of the projects, entitled Schools Must Speak for Themselves, occurred in the UK in the late nineteen nineties. It sought, in the words of one of its sponsoring organisations, to provide a 'bottom-up model for teachers and other school communities to gain information and a picture of their own schools which they could act on' (McAvoy, 2004: 19).

The second project was called School Self-Evaluation- Towards a European Dimension and was funded by the EU under the Comenius programme. This was very much a micro project which sought to examine different methodologies for training individuals to take part in self-evaluation in schools. To some extent these projects represent the two ends of the scale of 'bottom up' research in the area of self-evaluation and for this reason it is valuable to examine them both in some detail. In the next section we consider the work of MacBeath and colleagues and in the subsequent section the Comenius project is analysed.

Schools Must Speak for Themselves: Giving a Voice to the School Community

The research that was eventually to lead to the publication of the highly influential *Schools Must Speak for Themselves* in 1999 (MacBeath) began life in the mid nineteen nineties. In nineteen ninety four, the National Union of Teachers (NUT) in Britain commissioned a study from Strathclyde University into self-evaluation in primary and secondary schools. This study resulted in an initial report entitled, *Schools Speak for Themselves* (MacBeath *et. al.*, 1996) which was published in January nineteen ninety six and distributed to every primary and secondary school in England and Wales. A follow up study conducted by the same researchers on the impact of the initial report on school evaluation practices resulted in the now celebrated nineteen ninety nine publication.

Although beginning life as a UK project, this work has been highly influential not least in its contribution to a subsequent Evaluating Quality in School Education EU project which involved one hundred and one schools in eighteen countries (MacBeath *et. al.*, 2000). In addition, the methodology proposed by the project has been adapted and adopted by several European countries including Greece which launched its own version of it in two thousand and one. In what follows, the two UK Schools Must Speak projects and the subsequent EU wide project are considered together.

These projects provide an interesting counterpoint to the type of top down, imposed system of school evaluation that was being implemented in England and Wales during the period in which the research was taking place. From the outset MacBeath was clear about the reasons why he argues that schools must have a voice in the self-evaluation debate. He opens the book by stating that:

> Schools speak for themselves. They sometimes do so unconsciously, conveying implicit messages about their priorities and values. Some schools are able to speak for themselves with a higher degree of self-awareness and self-assurance. They know their strengths and are secure enough to acknowledge their weaknesses. (MacBeath, 1999:1)

Thus in MacBeath's understanding of evaluation, all schools have a right to a voice in the debate on to quality, accountability, judgment and value in education. It is just that some are more able or more aware of how to use that voice. A critical element of the research underpinning his work is the idea that schools must be facilitated to find a way of presenting their views on all of the key questions relating to school evaluation to a wider public. MacBeath sees this as being a critical aspect of any workable system of school evaluation. He argues that:

> There is an emerging consensus and body of wisdom about what a healthy system of school evaluation looks like. Its primary goal is to help schools to maintain and improve through critical self-reflection. It is concerned to equip teachers with the know-how to evaluate the quality of learning in their classrooms so that they do not have to rely on an external view, yet welcome such a perspective because it can enhance and strengthen good practice. (MacBeath, 1999:1)

Here then is a blueprint for what evaluation should entail. It should:

☐   Facilitate improvement through critical self-reflection.
☐   Equip teachers to make judgments about quality and remove the need for reliance on an external view.
☐   Develop a confidence in teachers to engage with and see the value in an external perspective on their work.

While not revolutionary, these ideas flew in the face of an educational establishment that, at that time at least, celebrated the primacy of the external view of the inspectorate over the internal opinion of teachers and anecdotally at least perceived a system that sought to prioritise the views of teachers as being in some way seditious (McAvoy, 2004:19).

It is important to emphasise that what was produced both from the initial *Schools Speak for Themselves* report and the subsequent research that went into *Schools Must Speak for Themselves* was not a dry analysis of the potential of self-evaluation in schools. While there was undoubtedly a deal of advocacy for the principle of self-evaluation, there was also a commitment to providing practical advice for schools and teachers seeking to engage in self-evaluation. Thus the initial research resulted in the production of a 'framework for self-evaluation' which could be used by schools for quality assurance and school improvement This framework MacBeath describes as 'guiding principles' rather than 'neat and tidy set(s) of prescriptive steps'. He is clear about the necessity of seeing the proposed framework as flexible and adaptable (MacBeath, 1999: 104).

> It would not make sense for every school to invent its own framework from scratch, neither would it be realistic to expect a single, national framework to be equally applicable to all schools across the country and across sectors. Research has consistently shown that 'ownership' of the criteria and of the process is crucial if lasting and sustainable improvement is to occur as a result of such self-evaluation. (MacBeath *et. al.*, 1996: 72)

The framework developed consists of four key elements:

- An overarching philosophy.
- Procedural guidelines.
- A set of criteria or indicators.
- A tool kit.

Many of these elements are common to other approaches to self-evaluation (Eurydice, 2004). However what is interesting about this approach to developing capacity in teachers and schools is the order in which they are presented.

By choosing to begin with what is essentially an explanation of the principles underpinning the framework, *Schools Must Speak for Themselves* (MacBeath, 1999) clearly seeks to engage teachers from the outset. This is in keeping with a view of teachers and other stakeholders as active determinants of the success or otherwise of any model of school evaluation. Teachers must believe that their opinions are valued, that the methodology for making decisions about what happens in their school is relevant and that any framework for valuing the quality of their work is fair. If this does not happen, the critical sense of ownership mentioned in so much of the literature on self-evaluation is virtually impossible to achieve.

It is only when there is a level of conceptual commitment to the idea of self-evaluation that it is possible to establish procedures and practical steps that will allow the vision implicit in the approach to evaluation be realised. The initial framework suggests five key steps at this stage. They are:

1. Start with the end in mind—be aware of where the evaluation will lead and what it will achieve for all of the key stakeholders.
2. Create the climate- self-evaluation needs a climate of trust, collegiality and openness to succeed. The creation of climate, while potentially time consuming, is critical to the implementation of the framework.

3. Promise confidentiality–because of the perceived career challenging element to any form of evaluation, it is critically important that participants feel free to be open when engaging with the framework. One way of doing this is to promise confidentiality and non-disclosure of identifying details when presenting data about the school.

4. Take a risk- engaging in self-evaluation can be risky and this must be acknowledged. Stakeholders should be encouraged to assess these risks and to ensure that they fully understand that not all they discover in the course of the evaluation process may be to their liking, The critical factor of course is to convince them that the end product will make the initial challenges and difficulties worthwhile.

5. Engage a critical friend- because of the potentially threatening reality underpinning the honest analysis of an organisation, it is advisable in the view of MacBeath, to appoint an external person who can act as a sounding board, facilitator and supporter. Given the title of 'critical friend' this individual is potentially central to the success or otherwise of the self-evaluation endeavour in any particular school.

The next stage of the self-evaluation process suggested by this project is the establishment of criteria, 'the yardsticks for what self-evaluation measures' (MacBeath, 2003:5). There are two possible ways of generating criteria:

1. Adapt the extensive range of options available for the particular context faced by the school.

2. Through a process of dialogue and reflection within the organisation, develop a set of criteria that accurately reflect the interests, abilities and concerns of all stakeholders involved.

While the former might be viewed as a quicker and less resource intensive process, the latter is seen as guaranteeing a far greater sense of ownership of the final product. This in turn, it is suggested, will ultimately lead to a greater cohesion and commitment within the organisation. The original *Schools Speak for Themselves* research gives an example of the type of criteria that might be developed by a school in the course of a reflective dialogue in preparation for self-evaluation. These criteria, developed in the course of the research, provide an indication of what is to be measured, the type of evidence that might be amassed, and the methods for uncovering this evidence. The structure is simple, practical and accessible (see Figure 7.8).

The final stage of the model of self-evaluation proposed by MacBeath and colleagues involves the design of suitable tools for gathering useful and relevant data. A range of practical and realistic advice is offered, particularly when attempting to deal with what should be measured. The suggestion that it is 'important not to be tempted into measuring only what is easily measurable' is added to a warning that schools should 'not yield to the temptation of using the tools most immediately to hand'. Indeed schools are warned that, 'the things that are most important to you are likely to be the hardest to measure' (MacBeath, 1999:112).

Indicator: There is a shared sense of teamwork among all staff

Quantitative evidence: Opportunities for joint staff working within the timetable. Participation in school committees and working parties. Incidence of shared planning/teaching.

Qualitative evidence: Staff feel that their views are valued. Staff seek out colleagues for support. Staff feel ownership of policies. Staff value use of INSET. Staff offer constructive criticism or advice.

Methods/Instruments: Survey of uses of staff time. Review of school documentation. Staff feedback forms e.g. evaluation forms after INSET. Peer observation/feedback.

(MacBeath *et. al.*, 1996: 98)

FIGURE 7.8: SAMPLE SCHOOLS SPEAK FOR THEMSELVES CRITERIA

There is a strong recommendation to be circumspect when choosing what to measure. Rather than attempting to measure everything schools are encouraged to concentrate on what is important to them at a particular time and measure that well.

Here then is both a philosophy and methodology of self-evaluation. Instead of a quick fix which may provide banks of easily digestible data of questionable value, there is a commitment to developing a system of evaluation that will become part of the school's daily life. This approach to evaluation hopes to convince of its value before even contemplating asking questions about what is to be examined.

MacBeath is not afraid to explore the broader policy implications of this philosophy of evaluation. He is fully prepared to acknowledge the challenge they pose not only to modes of evaluation current in many EU and OECD countries but also to the very question of how we value and judge education. In the final section of the nineteen ninety nine publication he argues that the public debate on education must, as a result of this study, ask the following questions:

◻   What are schools for and who are they for?
◻   What counts as important and what makes for improvement?
◻   How should success and improvement be measured? (MacBeath, 1999: 150)

He suggests at the end of the book that there are four key priorities that flow from this four-year study. They are:

◻   Self-evaluation should be central in any national approach to school improvement.
◻   Accountability and self-improvement should be seen as two strands of a single interrelated strategy.
◻   Provision of time and resources has to feature as a key issue in school improvement.
◻   School inspection should continue to be a feature of the drive towards school-improvement, but as part of a collaborative strategy with schools and local authorities.   (MacBeath, 1999: 150)

What is interesting about the above list of priorities is how subsequently they have moved into the mainstream of most official and academic discourse about school evaluation. Even the most cursory review of the material presented in the earlier parts of this work will give a sense of the extent to which much of what MacBeath proposed has become accepted wisdom in many European education systems.

School Self Evaluation—Towards a European Dimension; Training Individuals to Self-Evaluate

The School Self Evaluation—Towards a European Dimension project was an EU Comenius Programme intervention. The project set out to design and implement a training programme for school leaders who had an interest in or experience of self-evaluation. As such the project is of particular interest to those who are seeking to prepare networks of school leaders and teachers to begin the process of evaluating their own work.

One of the key initiatives of the 'Towards a European Dimension' project was the creation of a transnational network of practitioners willing to share experiences relating to self-evaluation. The mechanism for achieving this was the design and delivery of an intensive twelve unit training programme on the principles and practical application of self-evaluation in a school setting. From the outset of the project, there was a clear focus on combining the practical with the theoretical with a view to producing something usable for school leaders from a range of educational settings. Thus the initial proposal set itself the task of creating a course that would:

a)   Provide an overview of evaluation systems of schools.
b)   Encourage an exchange of experiences.
c)   Increase awareness of self-evaluation techniques.
d)   Train participants in the use of self-evaluation instruments.
e)   Design training materials and tools useful for future activities through open and distance learning (ODL) (ISOC, 2006)

The co-coordinators summarised the course inputs as follows:

◻   Context and principles influencing external evaluation and self-evaluation programmes in the European educational context.
◻   Origins of school self evaluation, definitions, approaches, methods and implementation issues.
◻   The instruments used to gather information on school self-evaluation.
◻   The use of the information gathered. (Barzano, 2002: 84)

The course was designed over a two-year period and was eventually presented to twenty-one head teachers from twelve different European countries. It was subdivided into twelve workshop units which were presented over the course of a week. (see table 7.3)

Unit 1: Introduction to course	Unit 2: Self Evaluation and External Evaluation: an international perspective
Unit 3: School self-evaluation: origins, definitions, approaches, methods and implementation issues	Unit 4: Presentation of a range of instruments
Unit 5: Data analysis and introduction to group work	Unit 6: Use of information gathered
Unit 7: Presentation of key elements of Italian education system	Unit 8: Fieldwork in school visits
Unit 9: Preparation for final 'consortium'	Unit 10: Course evaluation
Unit 11: Final Consortium	Unit 12: Poster session

TABLE 7.3: TRAINING PROGRAMME DESIGNED BY THE SCHOOL SELF EVALUATION
TOWARDS A EUROPEAN DIMENSION PROJECT

As is the norm with Comenius projects, there was an extensive evaluation of the course which was used to assess the participants' opinions. In general there was a welcome for the course with particular attention being paid to:

◻ The quality of the organisation.
◻ The usefulness of the experience–particularly the mixture of theory and practice.
◻ The opportunities to share experiences with practitioners from other educational contexts (Barzano, 2002: 94–95).

In particular participants highlighted a number of important aspects which allowed them to develop a genuinely interactive network. They included:

- ◻ The development of a common language when dealing with self-evaluation, which allowed them to transcend the terminological difficulties which almost inevitably emerge whenever individuals working in different educational settings begin to communicate.
- ◻ The intercultural aspect of the interactions. Individuals were introduced to the realities of other approaches to self-evaluation which were influenced by specific national and regional contexts.
- ◻ The creation of personal relationships and the development of plans for future collaboration.
- ◻ The enormous benefit to be derived from belonging to a dynamic, engaged and international group of professionals with similar interests. (Barzano 2002: 94–95)

There were of course some suggestions for improvement, which while being important for the particular group, tended to deal for the most part with organisational issues. However some of the more widely focused suggestions included:

- ◻ Greater terminological clarity when discussing evaluation in an international context.
- ◻ The need for a comprehensive framework when discussing self-evaluation in a transnational setting.

Perhaps the greatest testament to the success of this project as an instigator of international partnerships was the decision of a number of key partners to continue their research relationship in a subsequent Comenius 3 project. Entitled, 'Developing European Schools into Learning Organisations (DESLO)', this project sought to incorporate the insights generated during the 'Towards a European Dimension' study into a project with an organisation development focus. Specifically it sought 'to develop and/or highlight within schools key approaches which contribute to the setting up of a learning organisation such as self-evaluation'. (DESLO, 2006)

The 'Towards a European Dimension' study is important for two reasons. Firstly it successfully developed a way of enhancing the self-evaluation skills of key individuals in school communities. Secondly it created a network capable of supporting, challenging, engaging and enabling the individual self-evaluator. In this particular study the network was transnational and involved the development of relationships between educators that took them beyond the confines of their own contexts. It is possible to see how a similar dynamic might be created between individuals working within the same national but different sectoral contexts with much the same results. What is important in the creation of such networks is:

1. The development of a common language for explaining what actually happens in the course of a self-evaluation process.
2. The provision of a safe, encouraging space for the development of network relationships.
3. Clear, focused and useful inputs designed to stimulate discussion and future work.
4. The provision of an opportunity to engage in practical activities related to self-evaluation in real educational settings.

While the creation of the conditions outlined above is challenging it is not impossible and the success of this project influenced the design of the training initiative described in the final chapters of this book.

Supports Delivered by External Agencies Designed to Collect and Analyse Data for Schools to use in Self-Evaluation

In addition to the two major models of self- evaluation support discussed already a third almost hybrid system has been pioneered by the Curriculum, Evaluation and Management Centre (CEM) at the University of Durham. In practice what the CEM centre offers is a methodology whereby data is collected from schools by an external body, analysed and fed back to the school. What makes the model interesting is that at all times the data remains the property of the education community from which it is drawn and they alone can decide what to do with it. At no stage does CEM offer the data to any external body and even goes so far as to forbid participating schools from using its information for comparative publicity purposes. In an attempt to summarise what CEM seeks to achieve, Coe and Tymms state:

> The CEM Centre's work seeks to improve the educational system within which it finds itself, rather than simply to research them from the outside . . . The CEM Centre has always sought to value evidence rather than authority, solve problems rather than

blame, to generate high quality data and to promote randomized controlled trials and efficiency. (2003:639)

The essential philosophy of this type of support system is summed up by the paragraph above. It is:

- ◻ Located within the community.
- ◻ Data led.
- ◻ Organisationally empowering.
- ◻ Solution not blame focused.

As mentioned previously, CEM chose to use the term 'distributed research' (Fitz-Gibbon, 1996) to encapsulate this philosophy. Coe and Tymms suggest that at the core of this concept is the,

idea that the recipients of the feedback (i.e. teachers in schools and colleges) are themselves active researchers in the process, analysing and interpreting the data, rather than simply passive recipients. The research is seen as a collaborative process. (2003:641)

The central argument is that CEM and the schools form a partnership to produce and analyse data which can be used to investigate key aspects of the schools performance. While it is a partnership, it is one with clearly defined roles. CEM collects and analyses the data while the school interprets and uses it in any way that it sees fit. This is a very particular type of collaboration but one that CEM rightly points out provides a strong 'evidence base' from which to make decisions.

The process of generating the evidence that is at the heart of the CEM approach relies almost exclusively on the application of a series of 'information systems' (CEM:2006). Each of these systems covers a set period of schooling of between one and four years in length. The process begins with the collection of a baseline assessment and finishes with the recording of an outcome measurement. (Table 7.4) The next stage involves:

Residual gains (being) calculated between the two, allowing students' achievements on the outcome measure to be compared with the achievements of a national sample of students who started from the same point. (Coe and Tymms, 2003: 643)

CEM Information Systems		
System	Age Range	Description
ALIS—A Level Information System	16–19	Measures value added at A-level using GCSE as baseline. Also gathers attitudinal data on teaching
YELLIS—Year 11 Information System	14–16	Baseline fro GCSE grades examining maths, vocabulary and perceptual reasoning
MidYIS—Middle Years Information System	11–16	Curriculum free assessment to generate baseline for value added measures
PIPS—Performance indicators in primary schools	5–12, Infant and Junior	Baseline data generated at all stages of primary school. Also looks at attitudinal and self-esteem data
PIPS—Performance indicators in primary schools	4–5. On-entry baseline and follow up	Assesses baseline entry data for students
ASPECTS—Assessment Profile on entry for Children and toddlers	3–4	Gathers information from home and pre-school to feed into schools and PIPS

TABLE 7.4: CEM MAJOR INFORMATION SYSTEMS

Alongside the statistical data other contextual and attitudinal material is collected which can add to the depth and quality of the overall analysis provided.

What is immediately noticeable about the system is its comprehensive nature. Every stage of a school child's life, at least in the UK setting, is covered by a sophisticated and apparently contextually and chronologically appropriate instrument. This information is tailored in a majority of cases to tie in with the state mandated measurement stages such as Key Stage tests and other national tests including GCSE and A-level (CEM, 2006). In addition, there is a pronounced concentration on the measurement of the individual student performance not only against a national norm but also against their own potential performance as indicated by their baseline scores. This latter measurement, known as the value added dimension, produces some useful and at times challenging data for parents, pupils and teachers (Fitz-Gibbon, 2000).

The CEM instruments can also be used as a methodology for evaluating the quality of data being generated and used by external bodies such as Departments of Education. Here the independent nature of the Centre becomes a vital part in the process. It has both the ability and the standing to allow it to take government data and critique it both methodologically and conceptually. A recent research report commissioned by the English National Association of Head Teachers used the CEM expertise to critique the publication of value added data. As well as providing a comprehensive report, Tymms and Dean were able to make the statement that,

> although value-added information is an essential tool for professionals, the publishing of value-added indicators in their current form is misleading and should be discontinued. (2004: 5)

Here we see an independent evaluation unit using its data generating and analysis reputation to enter into the policy making arena in order to facilitate a genuine dialogue between schools and external stakeholders.

As well as specific examples such as the one above, Tymms and Coe (2003) suggest that the availability of independent data has resulted in significant strides being made by CEM in the area of evaluation research practice in general. Citing three research themes, they argue that CEM reports have provided a valuable national insight into the value of practice and policy in the areas of standards, the long term impact of effective schools and the influence of different homework policies (2003:649). While interesting in themselves, these reports are important in that they demonstrate how the process of generating data can, over a period of time, facilitate the dialogue that in theory at least exists at the heart of any successful evaluation system.

The CEM model is a fascinating one in the context of developments in school evaluation systems and as such it deserves to be included in any analysis of emerging support systems. It is quite different to the Ofsted type of external supports discussed earlier in the chapter and closer to the 'bottom up' approaches championed by MacBeath and Barzano. However there is one major difference from the latter approach and that is that there is no real attempt to develop teachers as knowledge generators. Rather than giving them ownership of the process of data production, CEM seeks to give them ownership of a rich and detailed stream of data. This is a subtle though significant difference. Teachers now have the information on which to base the telling of their story to any external body however they have been provided with this by someone else. The impact of this on their own engagement with the data produced is difficult to assess. A site visit conducted by the authors certainly demonstrated clearly that management in the schools which chose to use any of the CEM instruments tended to be very pleased with the data it gave them. CEM newsletters also seem to suggest that the process provides interesting information for teachers to use in individual classes. However, there is no sense of teachers taking charge of the data and making it their own in the way that many self-evaluation theorists would argue was essential for a genuinely engaged dialogue to take place.

A second issue of debate surrounds the context within which CEM was developed. The UK, and in particular England, has by now a tradition of demanding statistically robust and high quality data from individual schools on a regular basis. For this reason, schools are used to the requirement to keep and communicate vital data. This is not the case in all countries and in particular it is not the situation that exists in Ireland. Indeed it could be argued, and has been in an earlier chapter, that the absence of data and evidence in the Irish system places great obstacles in the way of a supposedly data- led school evaluation system. The CEM approach therefore is an interesting one that may, in time, find its way into an Irish school setting. However the current structure of the Irish system with its ambivalent attitude towards statistical data would seem to suggest that this time could be an extended one.

Conclusion

Self-evaluation is now a mainstream concept and most education systems throughout Europe are to some extent scrambling to find ways of integrating it into the everyday lives of schools. The considerable number of initiatives and interventions being developed by governments and transnational bodies gives an indication of the seriousness with which the development of self-evaluation capacity is being viewed. Virtually all methodologies proposed concentrate on enhancing the school's ability to gather data relevant to its own operation. Some choose to do this by forcefully guiding schools down a particular pathway using detailed frameworks and forms whereas others seek to give schools the opportunities to develop their own frameworks through which to tell their stories. While the school is undoubtedly the locus of investigation when it comes to self-evaluation, there is a recognition of the value of establishing networks of schools and indeed individual professionals who have an interest in augmenting their capacity to evaluate themselves. These networks are important in that they allow different perspectives emerge and challenge preconceived notions that are embedded in all school communities.

At the end of part two of this book it was argued that the lack of a self-evaluation capacity in Irish education represented a major handicap to the implementation of the new system of school evaluation. The above chapter charts both how widely the importance of such a capacity is increasingly valued in other countries and describes a number of approaches to developing and supporting it. In the light of this need, and guided by the experiences of the various projects and initiatives described above, the researchers set out to design, implement and evaluate a pilot programme of education in self-evaluation for teachers, appropriate to the Irish context.

· 8 ·

DEVELOPING THE SELF-EVALUATING TEACHER

A Pilot Project

Introduction

In earlier sections of this work we have examined the emergence of an Irish system of school evaluation and the issues that have arisen as a result of its gradual implementation. In common with many other European education systems, the Irish education community has struggled to balance the at times apparently irreconcilable demands for public accountability and oversight alongside those of professional development and autonomy (McNamara *et. al.*, 2002). It is partly the difficulties inherent in balancing such demands along with more specific industrial relations issues that resulted in the implementation of the Irish system taking almost a decade. Thus while the pilot project for the system was finished by the late nineteen nineties it wasn't until two thousand and four that the first evaluations under the designated *LAOS* framework, took place (McNamara and O'Hara, 2006).

This lengthy lead-in time left course providers in the initial teacher education (ITE) and continuous professional development (CPD) areas with something of a problem. By the beginning of this decade it was obvious from the statements of the Department of Education and Science (DES) that some form of evaluation system was to be introduced (DES, 1999a; DES, 2003a). It was equally obvious that this evaluation system was going to involve an element of self-evaluation (DES, 2003a; Eurydice, 2004). As self-evaluation almost by definition requires teachers to engage in a process of data collection and analysis (Nevo, 1995), this would have implications for the structure and content of both ITE and CPD programmes offered in Ireland. The essence of the problem facing providers in this period was that while it was clear that some training would be needed, there was a lack of clarity in a number of key areas. In particular, there was no real certainty as to the structure that would be put in place, how this would relate to the proposed evaluation framework and how all of this would come together when inspectors actually began visiting schools. What follows is an account of how the School of Education Studies at Dublin City University (DCU), sought to deal with these uncertainties while at the same time developing a self- evaluation training programme for use with a range of teacher education students at various stages of their careers.

This chapter examines the training programme developed, explores its influences and provides an outline of the different development stages engaged in prior to and during its final roll-out in the two thousand and five to two thousand and six academic year.

The Training Programme

The training programme in self-evaluation developed at Dublin City University School of Education Studies was heavily influenced by the work of scholars such as MacBeath, Schratz and Barzano and their projects as described in the previous chapter. The training programme as it finally emerged consisted of a twelve week module offered to science teachers in year three of a four year initial teacher education programme and to serving teachers undertaking a postgraduate programme in education. The two groups were taught separately and hereafter the former is referred to as the Initial Teacher Education (ITE) group and the latter as CPD (Continuous Professional Development). The groups' responses were researched separately but as we shall see there was not a great deal of difference in what emerged from each.

Many of the writers promoting the idea of school self-evaluation emphasise the centrality of the school community to the process of developing capacity in the area. Since the participants in this project were drawn from many schools the researchers were forced to examine ways of creating an environment that contained all the positive characteristics of a school community while acknowledging the lack of a pre-existing structure. This led the researchers to experiment with ICT and in particular with its content delivery and CMC (Computer Mediated Communication) functionalities. The former included an investigation of the potential offered by DV (Digital Video) technology. The latter involved the extensive use of the MOODLE Virtual Learning Environment (VLE) to provide participants with both a forum and methodology to engage in focused reflective dialogue about their understanding of self-evaluation. At a broader level, this use of ICT was located within a programme structure that possessed many of the classic characteristics of a blended mode of programme delivery (Rothery, 2004; Reece and Lockee, 2005; Vaughan and Garrison, 2005). In practice this meant that participants were encouraged to engage with the online communications aspect of the programme to as great a degree as was possible. However there was also an acknowledgement that the face-to-face and more traditionally structured inputs that formed a core part of the teaching on the programme would have an influence on how that online interaction was structured and developed.

A final, though equally important, element influencing the design of the training programme was the broad policy context within which it was developed. The movement by the DES to develop a system of school evaluation took a number of years. As a result of this, the researchers decided to adopt an iterative developmental approach. This used a three year development cycle and allowed the researchers to concentrate on different aspects of the programme at different stages while at the same time giving them the freedom to integrate any new initiatives produced by the Department as and when they arrived.

The following ideas formed the backbone of the training programme:

- A concentration on the area of teaching and learning.
- A focus on the practical experience of the course participants with a view to using this as a basis of knowledge creation.
- The provision of background material on different models of evaluation.
- The use of ICT to enhance the process of community building and reflection.
- The development of models of data collection which could be used across a range of educational settings.

Table 8.1 provides a brief summary of each of the activities undertaken and is followed by a more detailed explanation of each year's tasks.

	Year One		Year Two		Year Three	
	ITE	CPD	ITE	CPD	ITE	CPD
Use of Online Discussion Forum	x	x	x	x	x	x
Provision of Multi-media material to aid reflection	x	x	x	x		
Provision of training input—reflective engagement on current practice	x	x	x	x	x	x
Identification of criteria for structured reflection	x	x	x	x		
Links to academic and other resources	x	x	x	x	x	x
Provision of training input—models of evaluation	x	x	x	x	x	x
Working with information—using data to make judgements	x	x	x	x	x	x
Introduction of LAOS evaluation framework			x	x	x	x
Provision of training input—development of online communities of practice			x	x	x	x
Design of data collection instruments			x	x	x	x
Provision of training input—school evaluation models			x	x	x	x
Production of original DV material to aid reflection					x	
Design of data collection instruments—using T&L section of LAOS framework					x	x
Provision of training input—autonomy, accountability and self-evaluation					x	x

TABLE 8.1: OVERVIEW OF THREE-YEAR TRAINING PROGRAMME

Years One and Two.

The first and second years of the programme were quite similar and included:

- ◘ Use of online fora.
- ◘ Provision of a range of inputs on the themes of online communities and reflection.
- ◘ Provision of a range of stimulus material including multi-media packages.
- ◘ Focus on teaching and learning and use of practical experience as a basis for guided reflection.
- ◘ Learning to work with different types of data.
- ◘ Use of this experience as a basis for defining criteria for reflection.

As well as these similarities there were a number of changes. Perhaps the most significant was the introduction of the *LAOS* framework to both participant groups. The Framework had been published in the course of year two of the programme and was used to provide an additional input to aid the process of criteria selection. The researchers took the opportunity to suggest the use of the Quality in Learning and Teaching and Learning 'area' of the *LAOS* framework as a basis for discussion and reflection (DES, 2003b : 23–28). This section contained three 'aspects'. An aspect is defined as a concept which 'represent(s) the different activities collectively constituting the area of the school's operation that is to be evaluated' (DES, 2003b: ix). Each aspect was further broken down into components (see Table 8.2 below). The participants, interestingly, saw the benefits of linking their self-evaluation experiments to the national framework and it became clear that this provided a degree of relevance and motivation to the work in their eyes which it may have lacked up to that point. From here on the participants decided to develop their research instruments based around the areas and aspects below.

Aspect A: Planning and Preparation	
Component 1: Planning of Work	Component 2: Planning for Resources
Aspect B: Teaching and Learning	
Component 1: Methodology	Component 2: Classroom Management
Component 3: Classroom Atmosphere	Component 4: Learning
Aspect C: Assessment and Achievement	
Component 1: Assessment of modes and outcomes	Component 2: Record Keeping and reporting

TABLE 8.2: BREAKDOWN OF THE *LAOS* FRAMEWORK

In addition, experience from year one of the programme resulted in more specific inputs on:

◻ Developing online communities of practice—it was decided that more discussion needed to take place regarding the process of community formation, the practicalities of online interaction and the use of professional practice as a basis for individual and group reflection / discussion.

- ◻ Models of evaluation–the publication of the *LAOS* framework led to a more focused concentration on school evaluation models as opposed to the general discussion on evaluation conducted in the first year.
- ◻ Experimentation with different models of online facilitation–these ranged from the focused research question to a more 'hands off' approach designed to allow participants to develop their own online discussion leaders and facilitators.

The programme ran for a full semester in its second year and there was far greater spread of activities within that twelve-week period for both cohorts of participants. Again, the programme finished with a comprehensive evaluation which led to a substantial restructuring of the third and final year of the intervention.

Year Three

In year three some further changes were made to the course. While no significant elements were dropped, some were combined with different aspects being highlighted. In addition, the sequence in which different elements of the programme were introduced was altered with a view to emphasising particular areas of the *LAOS* programme.

The revised programme undertaken by both ITE and CPD participants is presented below.

Phase One—Preparing to Self-Evaluate

Autonomy and Accountability in Education:
- ◻ National and transnational influences.

Evaluation in an Irish Context:
- ◻ The *LAOS* system–origins, influences and implementation.

Developing an online learning community:
- ◻ Strategies, goals and exercises.
- ◻ Reflecting in an online setting.

Gathering information in Schools:
- ◻ Models, modes and techniques of data collection and analysis.

Phase Two—Working as an evaluating community

Using the *LAOS* framework to evaluate Teaching and Learning:
- Designing data collection instruments.
- Using the instruments in a professional practice setting.

Phase Three—Reflecting on self-evaluation

- Reflecting on self-evaluation in practice.
- Critiquing the data collection instruments.
- Evaluating self-evaluation.

The final iteration now follows the traditional training model which begins with providing background material, continues with the development of ideas and actions and finishes with the implementation of and reflection on those actions.

In the first phase, the background material section, a clear and focused input was provided not only on evaluation but also on important elements of the programme including online communities and data collection. This took the form of a series of lectures and training workshops where participants were encouraged to engage with both the information being presented, and perhaps more importantly, with each other. In both the CPD and ITE courses participants were broken up into sub-groups and encouraged to work on a series of training exercises in those groups. This process was used as a way of creating vital interpersonal links between individuals that could hopefully be built on later in the programme

The second phase concentrated on applying this background information in a practical context. The major work here was the design and use of data collection instruments. In order to streamline the process of instrument generation, it was decided to use sub-groups created in the earlier part of the programme as the basic units of development. Each of these sub-groups was given the task of generating an instrument which they considered appropriate for the purposes of fulfilling the evaluation requirement set down by one of the *LAOS* Teaching and Learning area components (see Figure 8.1 below).

Considerable thought went into the process used to train individuals and groups to generate their own self-evaluation instruments. The researchers were mindful at all times of Nevo's warning of the need to clearly differentiate between the methodological training necessary for individuals to engage in formal educational research as opposed to that needed by educational professionals seeking to understand their own work in a self-evaluation setting (Nevo, 1995). For this reason, the training was always presented in the overall context of facilitating the process of investigating participants' own teaching.

This element of the training programme was delivered in three discrete though linked stages. The first stage began with an overview of possible self-evaluation methods including documentary analysis, peer evaluation of teaching, surveys of student opinion , interaction analysis and so on. It continued by providing participants with a basic though comprehensive introduction to dif-

---

Teaching and Learning Methods

Themes for Self Evaluation (LAOS)

The appropriateness of teaching strategies and methodologies employed and the account taken of the range of pupil abilities, needs, and interests

The extent to which lessons are structured so that content and pace are appropriate to the class and to the time available

The degree of variation in teaching strategies and methodologies used in the curriculum area

The effectiveness with which teaching strategies and methodologies in the curriculum area are used

The appropriateness of the range of professional and material resources used to support the teaching of the curriculum area

The account taken of best practice in relation to health and safety and environmental requirements in the teaching of the curriculum area

Questions you might ask about the themes above include:

Rank the following methods in order of your preference (Question Type Hierarchical Scale)

Are the methods I use appropriate to my class group? (Open Question)

Which of the following methods do I use when teaching?

Groupwork, Discussion, Role Play, Experiment   (Scale)

FIGURE 8.1: DESIGNING DATA COLLECTION INSTRUMENTS: STAGE TWO

ferent types of question categories used in survey instruments. It had been realised as a result of the evaluation carried out on the second year of the programme that participants needed an easy to follow guide that dealt with the specifics of question design in surveys. This resulted in a short document being produced which was distributed to all students and used as a basis for a workshop on instrument design In this workshop participants were asked to produce a concise three-question survey and to provide a rationale for the inclusion of each type of question.

The second stage of the process was to provide themes from *LAOS* on which the participants could base their self-evaluations and a range of examples of research instruments from other projects.

The third and final stage saw sub-group participants brainstorming around the theme they had chosen and producing a draft of the data collection instrument (see below for an example of one such instrument). This process was facilitated by the researchers and other members of academic staff and participants were assisted with some of the more technical aspects of questionnaire design when this was requested. On completion of this process, each sub-group took on the responsibility of formatting the instrument and distributing electronically to the broader participant group.

Teaching and Learning

Name   **Class**

Date

Q1 Please indicate your level of agreement with the following statements

	Yes	No	NA
Did students seem interested in the topic?			
Did learners learn better through interaction?			
Did learners learn better individually?			
Was the material relevant to the students' learning?			
Were learners motivated to learn by receipt of a reward?			
Do you feel it is necessary to self evaluate one's practice			
Was participant learning inhibited by a disability?			

If participant learning was inhibited by a disability please comment

_____

_____

_____

Q2 In your class, which methodologies did you use?

Demonstration   ☐

Group work   ☐

Lecture   ☐

Discussion   ☐

Practical Exercise   ☐

Other (Please List)

_____

_____

_____

Q3 Did your environment impact on the teaching methods you chose?

Yes   ___   No ___

Please explain

_____

_____

_____

Q4 Please indicate your level of agreement with the following statements

	Strongly agree	Agree	No Opinion	Disagree	Strongly Disagree	NA
My teaching methods were very effective in enabling me meet my objectives						
I had sufficient resources to adequately support my teaching methods						
My teaching methods supported the development of a safe learning environment						
I used a variety of appropriate teaching methods						
I catered for a variety of learning styles						

Q5 Please rate the extent to which students' learning is affected by external influences (1 being little effect, 5 being greatly effected).

1   2   3   4   5

Q6 Please rate the extent to which the teacher's attitude affects the participants learning (1 being little effect, 5 being much effect).

1   2   3   4   5

Q7 Please indicate your level of agreement with the following statements

	Strongly agree	Agree	No opinion	Disagree	Strongly disagree
Peer pressure has an effect of students learning					
Low levels of literacy inhibit participants' learning					
Participant learning is affected by lack of self-esteem					
I found the self-evaluation questionnaire helpful in evaluating learner participation.					

Q8 Which methodology was the most successful in today's session?

Why?

_____

_____

_____

Q9 Which methodology was the least successful in today's session?

Why?

_____

_____

_____

What Was Developed?—Examining the Data Collection Instruments

The design process engaged in required both the CPD and ITE cohorts to produce and distribute four data collection instruments. The areas of professional practice to be evaluated using the questionnaires were:

◻ Planning.
◻ Classroom Management.
◻ Teaching and Learning.
◻ Assessment.

Each of these formed part of the *LAOS* Teaching and Learning area.

The design process took place early in the programme with participants being given the opportunity to review the operation of the data collection instruments both during and after this period. There was a common order of usage adopted by the two programmes with each beginning with the planning instrument and moving onto a new instrument each week (see Table 8.3). As a result of the initial review, the CPD cohort decided that the designated area of classroom management be changed to classroom management and learning atmosphere as they felt this more accurately represented their understanding of the role of that particular theme in their professional lives. At a later stage in the process, the ITE group decided that the design process be revisited and that a different type of daily evaluation instrument be produced and used in place of the assessment instrument. This meant that the process design resulted in the production of three thematically linked and two discrete instruments (Table 8.3).

Data Collection Instruments Designed	
CPD	**ITE**
Planning	Planning
Classroom Management	Classroom Management and Learning Atmosphere
Teaching and Learning	Teaching and Learning
Assessment	Daily Evaluation Sheet

TABLE 8.3: DATA COLLECTION INSTRUMENTS DESIGNED

Categorising the Instruments

To assist the process of evaluating these instruments it is proposed to examine:

1. Their general type as defined by Airasian and Gullickson's 'Categorization of Self-Evaluation Examples' (1997:18).
2. Their structure in terms of numbers and type of questions.

Airasian and Gullickson (1997) designed their 'Categorization of Self-Evaluation Examples' in order to provide education professionals with a series of templates with which to examine their own work. They suggest that any process seeking to improve educational practice needs to base itself on solid information. In their opinion, the only way to get this information is to examine professional practice through multiple lenses and from multiple perspectives. In essence they argue that, even with the current popularity of systems of professional development based on the concept of reflective engagement, before we can meaningfully reflect on practice, before we can chart avenues that need change, before we can make meaningful decisions about practice it is necessary that we have a clear awareness of our teaching practice; our actions, assumptions, beliefs and effects. (1997: 16)

The model suggests therefore that data collection instruments that seek to allow educators examine their professional practice should be grouped under the area practice that they are trying to assess. The four areas identified by Airasian and Gullickson (1997:18) are:

◻   Beliefs–Underpinning values of educator relating to subject / pupils/ profession.
◻   Knowledge–Professional knowledge and expertise.
◻   Practice–What actually happens in a learning situation.
◻   Effects–How this impacts on students / colleagues / learning organisation.

The process of categorising the instruments developed in the course of this project required the researchers to examine each of the questions and assign it to one of the areas of interest. Instruments can cover more than one area.

There are a number of notable issues that emerge from the process of categorising the instruments. The first is the total lack of instruments coded in the category that seeks to examine the 'effects' (1997: 18) of professional practice. This is all the more striking as at least one of the instruments, assessment, is meant to be primarily concerned with the assessment of student learning. Interestingly, one of the programme participant groups raised exactly this issue as a criticism of the instruments designed. They claimed in their final report that they,

found that the questionnaires were focused on me even when they should have been focused on the students! We found this really confusing at times. How can we examine assessment without looking at what students do? Also, why does self-evaluation only seem to value what teachers say about themselves? Do the other people involved in education not have a voice? (Final Report: Group B)

Another somewhat more pithy response to the online forum makes a similar point about one of the CPD instruments:

Again I seem to have a block with regard to this questionnaire as I find it difficult to see how one can self-evaluate a participant's learning. (CPD Online Discussion: Using the Teaching & Learning Instrument)

Categorization of Self-evaluation Instruments					
		Area Assessed			
Course	Instrument	Beliefs	Knowledge	Practice	Effects
CPD	Planning	✓		✓	
	Classroom Management	✓	✓	✓	
	Teaching and Learning	✓	✓	✓	
	Assessment			✓	
ITE	Planning	✓		✓	
	Classroom Management	✓		✓	
	Teaching and Learning	✓	✓	✓	
	Daily	✓	✓	✓	

TABLE 8.4: CATEGORIZATION OF DATA COLLECTION INSTRUMENTS
ADAPTED FROM AIRASIAN AND GULLICKSON, 1997.

A second significant outcome is the discovery that all of the instruments designed have some form of practice focus built in. This is understandable, particularly given that the broader thematic area of Teaching and Learning is concerned with the mechanics of practical engagement in an educational setting. It also confirms something of the general point made in the participants' contribution above. The instruments were designed to focus on what happened in individual learning encounters and for most participants this was co-terminous with their actions as teachers.

A third interesting outcome of the process involves a comparison of the thematically linked instruments designed by the two cohorts. The planning and teaching and learning instruments follow the same categorisation pattern with the former including questions that address areas of beliefs and practice only and the latter dealing with beliefs, practice and knowledge. The instruments diverge at the classroom management / learning atmosphere instrument level with the CPD using this instrument to assess beliefs, practice and knowledge and the ITE participants indicating an interest in only their beliefs and practices.

The Structure of the Instruments Designed

Participants were encouraged to use as broad a range of question types as possible in the final instruments designed. This was done in order to vary the type of data generated but also to give the participants the opportunity of considering alternative ways of examining recurring issues in their professional practice.

A number of respondents commented on precisely this aspect of the design process in their final evaluative reports. One mentioned that,

> we deliberately included questions that provided both quantitative and qualitative data. This provided the writer with a framework by which she could review her practice and helped the reflection process by triggering thoughts, views and opinions that might otherwise not have occurred. (Terminal Evaluation Report)

At the end of the design process, as we have already seen, the two cohorts produced eight discrete data collection instruments. Each of these instruments, even those which were thematically linked, had a different structure and included different question types. A number of general patterns emerge from the table below. It is interesting, for example, to note that the ITE participants were significantly more willing to use open questions. In particular, the daily evaluation questionnaire designed by this group in the latter stages of the programme was made up almost exclusively of open questions. In addition, the average number of questions used was in or around ten other than on the CPD Assessment questionnaire which limited itself to four.

Types of Questions Used in Data Collection Instruments					
Course	**Instrument**	**Open**	**Closed**	**Combined**	**Total**
CPD	Planning	1	6	6	13
	Classroom Management	0	9	1	10
	Teaching and Learning	2	4	3	9
	Assessment	1	2	2	4
ITE	Planning	1	8	2	11
	Classroom Management	1	5	3	9
	Teaching and Learning	5	1	4	10
	Daily	8	1	0	9

TABLE 8.5: TYPES OF QUESTIONS USED IN DATA COLLECTION INSTRUMENTS
(NOTE, QUESTIONNAIRES LISTED IN ORDER OF WHICH THEY WERE USED)

When the instruments were finalised, participants were encouraged to use them for a specified period in their workplace and were required to post their evaluations of the instruments on the MOODLE VLE. While the programme developers tended to take the lead at the beginning of each weekly discussion, there was a gradual effort to give to the course participants the opportunity to take control of the discussion fora where possible. In addition, the programme developers modelled different modes of online facilitation at different stages of the process including that of the critical friend, social facilitator and lurker (Rafaeli et. al., 2004).

It should be noted that there was an additional element of the programme introduced for the ITE students alone. They were supported in the creation of original DV material for use as a stimulus for reflective discussion and self-evaluation. The materials concentrated on the use of specific teaching and learning skills, specifically the microteaching skills (McIntyre, McCleod and Griffiths, 1977; Brophy, 2004) studied by all education students at DCU. Participants were asked to record, edit and place a clip of thirty seconds to one minute online and to invite discussion as to its value as an exemplar of good teaching. It was the self-generated element that was considered most important as participants were being encouraged specifically to use examples of their own practice to assist the development of the knowledge base of the online community of which they were a part. The limitation of this aspect of the programme to the ITE students was a logistical one alone. As full time students they had more free time on campus to make use of the equipment available to record and edit their material. The CPD participants were in a much more time pressured situation and it was not considered practical to require them to produce such material. In subsequent iterations of the programme the greater availability of portable DV technology has led to this element of the programme being extended to all participants.

Conclusion

By the end of the three-year development cycle there was in place a comprehensive and complex training programme designed to facilitate the development of the ability to self-evaluate in two linked groups of educational professionals. By adopting an iterative approach which built towards a final programme structure in its third year, the researchers acquired the freedom to experiment with different ways of approaching a potentially controversial subject area. The iterative cycle also allowed the researchers to take account of the rapidly changing external policy context which had a major influence on the final shape of the programme. What eventually emerged from this process of development was a blended approach to the development of self-evaluating educators which managed to combine the benefits of traditional face to face teaching with the potential of emerging ICT systems to enhance the professional skills of course participants (see Figure 8.2). The model below tries to capture the blended nature of the training approach developed.

Of course, providing a training programme to empower professionals to become self evaluating is only a first step and indeed is of little use unless it influences the ongoing professional development and practice of those undertaking it. The impact, if any, therefore, which this training programme had on the teachers who undertook it, is the key question and an evaluation of the outcomes is the subject of the next chapter.

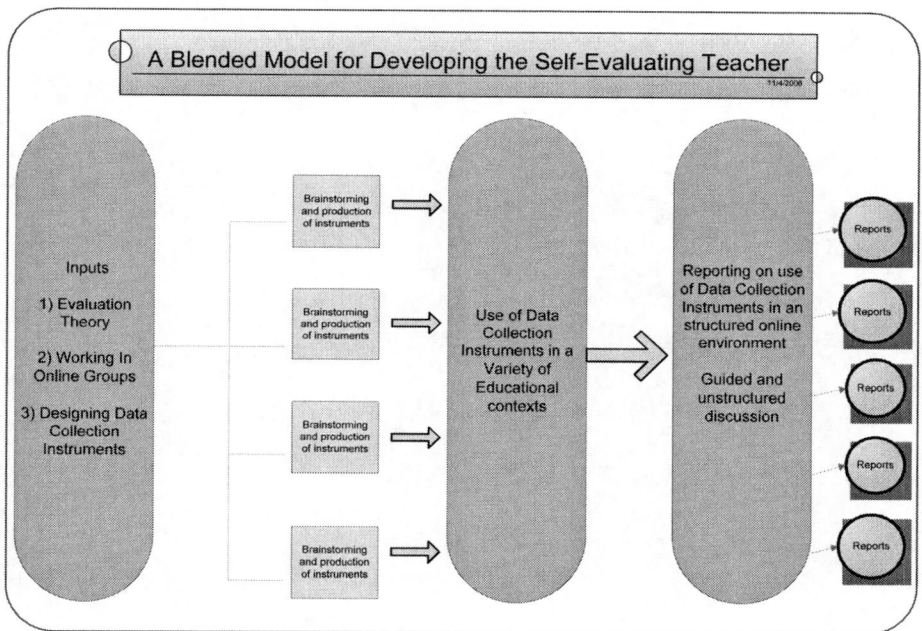

FIGURE 8.2: A BLENDED MODEL FOR DEVELOPING THE SELF-EVALUATING TEACHER

DEVELOPING THE SELF-EVALUATING TEACHER

Exploring the Project Outcomes

Introduction

The course was designed to develop education professionals who were capable of evaluating their own practice in such a way as to give them both the information and the confidence to engage in a process of dialogue with a new, national system of school evaluation. Previous sections of this study have explored in some detail those elements in any system of professional development that are considered essential when attempting to prepare educators to engage in a process that requires them to evaluate their own practice. In summary, what writers such as Nevo (1995, 2002, 2006), MacBeath (1999, 2003, 2004) and Simons (2002, 2004) argue is that any approach to developing self-evaluating professional educators must be:

◻ Community centred.
◻ Practice oriented.
◻ Focused on helping teachers to gather accurate and usable data about their own practice.
◻ Capable of engendering a sense of ownership and commitment on the part of teachers to the concept of self-evaluation.

Given that the programme described here in its final form sought to include each of these elements, it seemed logical that the analytic model designed to examine the data generated should also address these areas (see Figure 9.1 below).

As can be seen from the diagram below, the model designed was a dynamic one that sought to explore not only the discrete elements identified by evaluation theorists but also to capture the complex interconnections that exist between those elements.

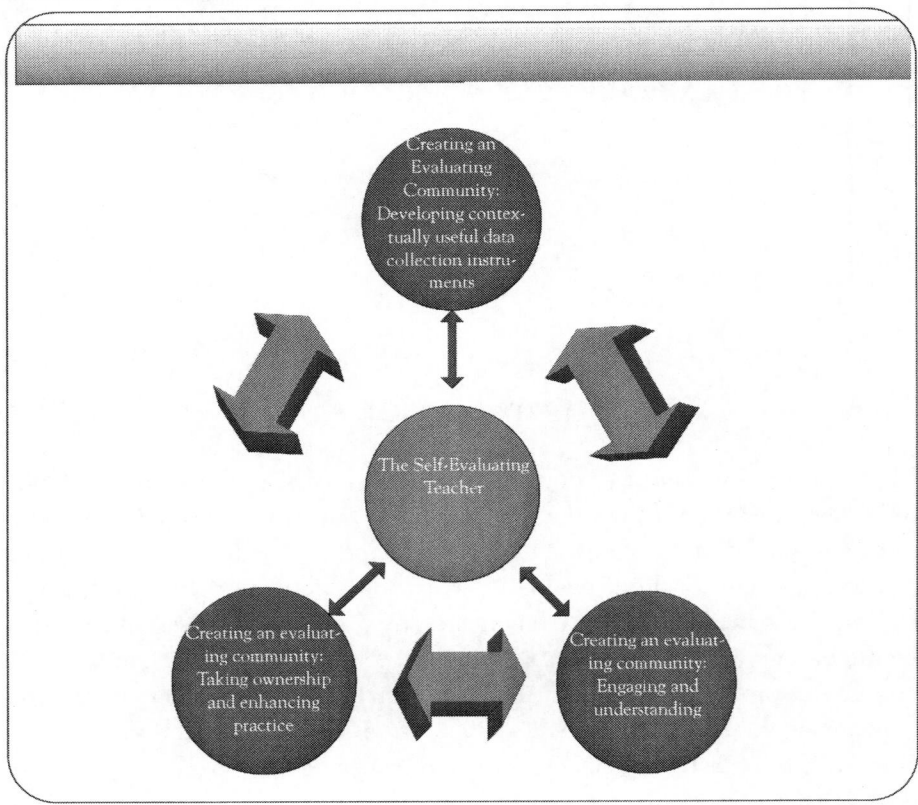

FIGURE 9.1: DEVELOPING THE SELF-EVALUATING TEACHER: AN ANALYTIC MODEL

An essential element of the model is the importance assigned to the concept of community. Building not only on the work of MacBeath but also on that of Hargreaves (2006), Lave and Wenger (1991) and Darling-Hammond (1996) the model examines the role of the professional community in the development of self-evaluation capacity. In this particular case the type of community was not a school community in the traditional sense. Rather it was made up of teachers from different schools and at different stages of their careers seeking to enhance their professional skills.

The analytic model was used therefore to examine relevant data under each of its three dimensions with a view to deciding whether or not the programme designed actually did develop self-evaluating teachers capable of engaging in dialogue with external stakeholders. The rest of this chapter will provide a detailed analysis of the findings generated by the use of this model.

Methods of data collection

The evaluation of the training programme relied heavily on data generated through the use of the MOODLE Virtual Learning Environment which was the ICT platform for the project as well as more traditional formats such as interviews and surveys (see Table 9.1 below).

Data Collection Methods	
ITE	CPD
Questionnaires	Questionnaires
Interviews	Interviews
Online Discussion Postings	Online Discussion Postings
VLE Generated Statistical Data	VLE Generated Statistical Data
Individual Reports	Individual Reports
Group Reports	Group Reports
Group generated digital video material	

TABLE 9.1: A SUMMARY OF DATA COLLECTION METHODS

The rise in popularity of systematic, theory led qualitative research over the past number of decades has resulted in the emergence of a number of support mechanisms for researchers working in the area. Among these has been software to assist the process of qualitative data analysis. More properly known as computer assisted qualitative data analysis software or CAQDAS (Bringer, Halley Johnston and Brackenridge, 2006) its use has become so commonplace that MacMillan and Koenig were able to state that 'the issue is not whether to use CAQDAS but how it should be used' (2004:180).

Seale, when analysing the advantages of CAQDAS, lists the benefits of the software under four broad categories:

a. Speed at handling large volumes of data, freeing the researcher to explore numerous analytic questions.
b. Improvement of rigour, including the production of counts of phenomena and searching for deviant cases.
c. Facilitation of team research, including the development of consistent coding schemes.
d. Helping with **sampling** (emphasis in the original) decisions, be these in the service of representativeness or theory development. (2005:189)

Following an extensive study of the different CAQDAS available a decision was made to use the NVIVO 7 package, one of newest and most powerful of the many tools available. As well as offering all of the functionalities suggested by writers such as Weitzman (2000), it also had a powerful multimedia analysis tool which was to prove particularly useful in this study. In practice, the NVIVO software proved to be, to coin a phrase, fit for purpose. The large quantities of data produced were stored, analysed and repeatedly accessed. Theories were developed, challenged and modified and reports made and argued over.

The second use of data analysis software in this study was a statistical analysis package to manipulate the quantitative data generated (Gorard and Taylor, 2004). The software used in this case was the SPSS package, one of the most widely available of all statistical analysis software. Described by its developers as 'the leader in providing predictive analytics solutions that help educational institutions make better decisions' (SPSS, 2006:2) the software helps researchers to:

◻ Collect, prepare, analyze, and manage research data.
◻ Discover important concepts and relationships in journals, publications, and research databases.
◻ Produce high-quality output for reports and publication (SPSS 2006: 3).

In reality, it was the first of these functionalities, the ability to manipulate research data that was of most use to the authors.

We will now consider the findings of the research using the analytic framework outlined above.

Developing Contextually Useful Data Collection Instruments

Stage One: Developing Contextually Useful Data Collection Instruments

At earlier stages in this study we have examined the importance attached to the process of empowering teachers to generate useful, appropriate and relevant data collection instruments for use in their own professional settings. MacBeath (1999, 2005) argues that the act of generating information about elements of professional practice considered to be of value by the teacher is what differentiates self-evaluation from self-inspection. Nevo (1995, 2002) suggests that the process of training teachers to evaluate their own work using materials generated by the learning community in which they are located is a critical initial step to developing the dialogue that is at the heart of his understanding of the self-evaluation process. Barzano (2002), Simons (2002) and Scheerens (2002) also acknowledge the importance of preparing educational professionals to formally investigate their own practice and argue that it should be at the heart of any professional development process seeking to address the area of school evaluation.

For this reason each iteration of the programme included a section which was devoted to assisting participants to develop their own evaluation instruments. By the third cycle of the programme, this element had developed into the three-stage process outlined in the previous chapter. In summary, the three stages involved were:

1. Development of the data collection instruments–including,
    a. The identification of the particular aspects of *LAOS* Teaching and Learning section to be evaluated by each sub-group
    b .Provision of training on the process of generating data collection questionnaires
    c. Brainstorming around the area
    d. Production of the instrument by the sub-group
    e. Distribution to the broader programme group.

2. Use of the data collection instrument by all programme participants.
3. Evaluation of the instrument both online and in final programme reports.

In this section of the study we will assess the reaction of the course participants to the process described above. It should be noted that the research reported in the remainder of this chapter was conducted exclusively with the participants in the third year of the project, consisting of thirteen trainee teachers and twenty four experienced teachers taking a postgraduate diploma in the two thousand and five to two thousand six academic year.

Evaluating the Process of Instrument Development

When asked their opinion on the usefulness of being facilitated in developing their own self-evaluation instruments, a clear majority of both the CPD and ITE programme participants indicated that they found the process helpful (see Figure 9.2 below).

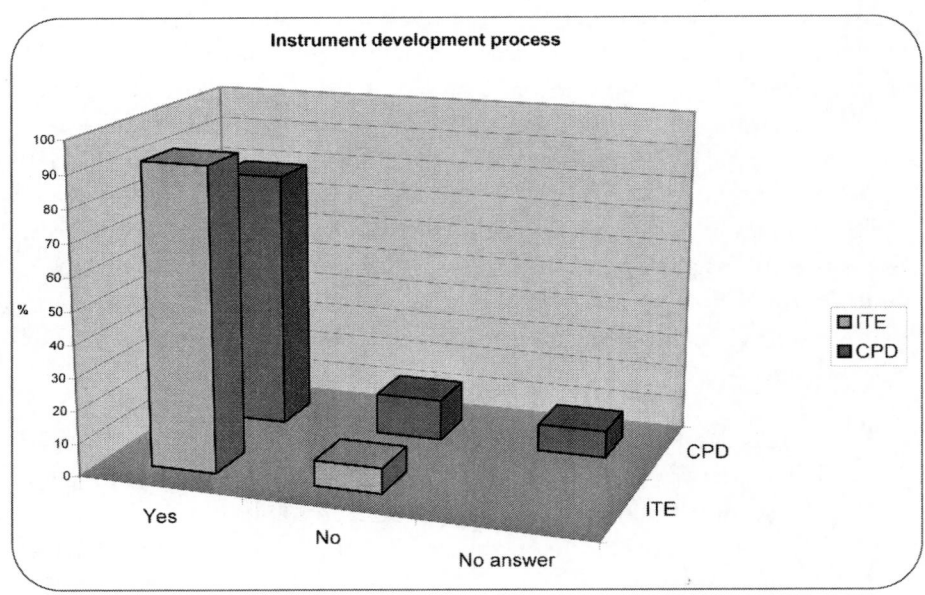

FIGURE 9.2: IN YOUR OPINION WAS THE INSTRUMENT DEVELOPMENT PROCESS USEFUL?

(ITE *N* = 13 ; CPD *N* = 24)

With approximately seventy nine percent of the CPD and over ninety two percent of the ITE participants respectively indicating their overall satisfaction with the process, it would seem, on the surface at least, that the three-stage model developed was considered a success. A close examination of the qualitative data generated in the course of the study indicates a similar pattern. One participant, in response to a question posed in an end of programme evaluative survey, encapsulated this viewpoint when stating that,

> due to the class diversity a great amount of information and experience went into the creation of the questionnaires which were used in the process of self-evaluation. These questionnaires I found invaluable and I doubt if I could have developed such questionnaires on my own. . . . If you have other people on board during the development of the instruments tools, it makes the whole thing more relevant and it stands a better chance of overall success. (Respondent 14: End of Programme Evaluation Survey)

Here the diversity of the group is seen as adding to the usability and durability of the instruments created. In addition, the very process of working in a group is seen as being an essential prerequisite to the process of instrument creation.

Another participant, writing in her final report on the programme, developed this understanding of the importance of group diversity pointing out that,

> the questionnaires used in this self-evaluation process, being developed by so many people with so many diverse backgrounds in the class gave the author a much broader outlook of the areas in which she might improve her teaching practices. (Respondent 12:Terminal Evaluation Report)

The broad range of professional contexts represented in the group encouraged the respondent to ask questions of her practice that she may never have previously considered. This type of response directly addresses one of the potential criticisms of the self-evaluation process, namely its perceived tendency to avoid asking difficult or uncomfortable questions (Davies and Rudd, 2000).

The theme is taken up by a third member of the CPD cohort who links the cycle of instrument development to the cycle of reflection that is at the heart of much of the professional development and self evaluation literature. In outlining the different stages of the development cycle she explained that her,

> group began by brainstorming. We were from very different backgrounds. The process

identified multiple and varied ideas. Over a period of time we reviewed and reflected on the relevant material in the area of evaluation. This was critical to the process. We devised a definitive set of themes and questions based on our reflection. (CPD Online Dialogue: General Evaluation Discussion Forum)

Another response to the final evaluation survey emphasises the impact of the group design process on individual interpersonal skill when it states that,

During the development of self evaluation instruments my communication skills were vastly improved. This occurred as a result of the deep reflection that was required when structuring the questionnaires with other people. I had to be able to make my points about what I thought was important and listen to others who mightn't have agreed. (Respondent 8: Terminal Evaluation Survey)

Another indicated that they,

liked this part of the process a lot. It gave us a chance to use the experiences we were having in schools and to put them into the questionnaires. It was also great to have the groupwork to focus our conversations on topics that were really relevant to us. (CPD Online Dialogue: General Evaluation Discussion Forum)

In both of these responses the group is seen as adding to the process by acting as a sounding board.

Another theme to emerge from this part of the data was the value that participants placed on having a clear structure to follow when designing their questionnaires but also a recognition that it was mostly through trial and error that their research skills improved.

Participants felt that the provision of clear instructions and a designated area of investigation was particularly helpful. A comment from the general evaluation forum sums up this perspective:

The stuff from *LAOS* and Ofsted was really useful when we were designing the questionnaires. It helped us to concentrate on what was important in the area we were asked to look at. This was really important when we were working on areas that we didn't agree on. I think we would be still there arguing now except that we were able to point to your notes and say no that is not what we are being asked to do. (CPD Online Dialogue: General Evaluation Discussion Forum)

Another participant, picking up the theme in their final programme report, suggested that,

I felt a bit confused by the questionnaires early on. I knew that I was meant to be asking questions about my teaching and I knew that I had to agree them with others but I wasn't too sure about what sort of questions to use. The notes were really detailed but it was a bit hit and miss when I went to use them in the class. I think we got better at this and when we decided to change things around at the end I liked that we all sort of agreed about what type of questions were best. (Respondent 17: Terminal Evaluation Survey)

A final comment from another participant had a forward look to it:

I think I will be much better at this thing next time I try it. Going through the process of designing and using the questionnaires once really taught me a lot about how you need to put them together. Looking back on it now, a lot of the questions we put in weren't needed and we left out a lot that we did. It was frustrating but I suppose that is how you learn. (Respondent 2: Terminal Evaluation Survey)

Aside from the welcome commitment to the idea of repeating the process at some future date, the three quotations indicate the vital importance of the process of using the instruments to the participants' overall perceptions of the value of the process of design.

Using the Data Collection Instruments—Cycle of Implementation and Impact

In theory at least, the provision of appropriately designed instruments not only allows practitioners' to judge the quality of their own work, it also provides them with the information and vocabulary with which to engage other key stakeholders in the education process (Nevo, 1995; MacBeath *et. al.*, 2000; Simons, 2002).

The use of the practitioner designed data collection instruments by both cohorts of participants gave the researchers an opportunity to investigate the validity of these claims. In particular, the availability of weekly online postings combined with final evaluative reports and survey material allowed us assess the extent to which the use of the data collection instruments moved from something that was in reality imposed by the dynamics of the programme to something that participants valued and would continue to employ in subsequent years.

In essence the analysis of the various data sources suggested that both cohorts followed a similar implementation cycle when using the data collection instruments (see Figure 9.3).

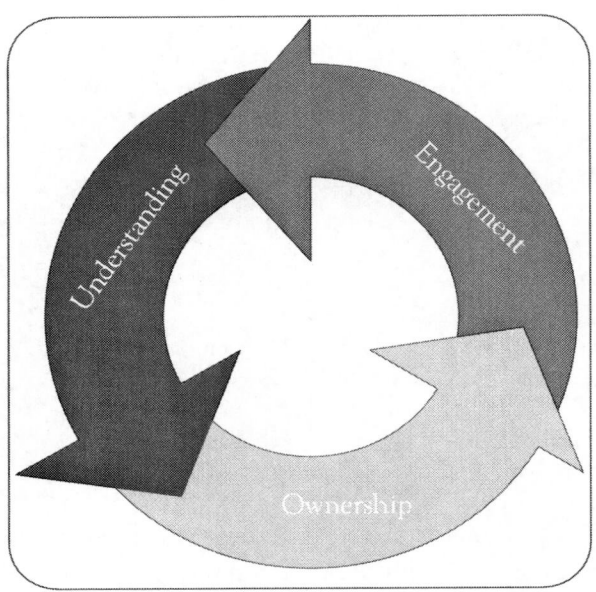

FIGURE 9.3:
DATA COLLECTION INSTRU-
MENT IMPLEMENTATION CYCLE

The cycle begins with an initial engagement with the process of instrument use which, if we are to be honest, is at times an imposed engagement. In most cases however it moves from this to a voluntary engagement which in turn results in the emergence of an understanding of the value of the process. The final stage of the cycle sees participants take ownership of the process of instrument use. This final stage is identifiable as participants begin to alter the research instruments to make them more usable in their own professional context. In this way they move from being products of a group to being the property of the individual. However, because the individual is part of the broader community which produced the initial instrument, they bring their own context-based understanding of how to improve the instruments back to the larger group and, in the process, add to the knowledge base of that professional community.

Initial Engagement

The initial postings relating to the use of the data collection instruments concentrated on how the surveys were designed. Among the most commonly posted comments were those relating to the overall length of the questionnaires and the format of questions posed. A typical posting of this sort was made by a CPD participant who when asked to comment on the use of the planning instrument generated by her group stated that:

> I felt that 13 questions was a lot to answer. If I were to keep up the self evaluating I would be more likely to answer less questions on a regular basis and keep them on file. It seemed a lot for just one area - i.e. planning. There are also the other areas to consider. (CPD Online Dialogue: Using the planning instrument)

Another in the same forum claimed that,

> it showed me that there is room for improvement but also I found it very long and time consuming to fill in. (CPD Online Dialogue: Using the planning instrument)

One of the ITE participants, reacting to his cohort's planning instrument, made much the same point,

> there are just so many questions and a lot of them are asking you for the same stuff in different ways. Also it was really time consuming. I am teaching five classes in a row some days and I just don't see the point in having to fill out a long questionnaire after each one. (ITE Online Dialogue: Planning)

Gradually, however, deeper issues than merely the length of the survey begin to come to the fore. For example the following from a CPD participant demonstrates how individuals start to move from one part of the cycle to another.

> In the initial stages of the process I thought that the questionnaires should be quick and easy to use. As I engaged in self-evaluation further, I began to realise that while it does need to be user friendly, I need to learn from it. It needs to be useful to me as a professional practitioner. I cannot compromise on length to the detriment of the quality of information gained. It is important to use a form that is relevant to my work. However it should be capable of feeding into and useful to any existing evaluations in the organisations or groups I work for. (CPD Online Dialogue: General Evaluation Discussion Forum.)

The phrase, 'I cannot compromise on length to the detriment of the quality of information gained', presents a perfect example of a practitioner coming to terms with the philosophy underpinning self-evaluation.

A similar process is evident in relation to issues of question type and format. Here we see participants begin to realise that closed tick box type questions while quick and easy are in fact are of limited use as an aid to reflection and self-evaluation. For many, completion of questionnaires with a predominance of closed questions involved little more than ticking a box. Contributors to the MOODLE site expressed the frustration induced by this format of question quite eloquently:

> After each lesson or at the end of the day i'd sit down take out a pen and tick the boxes. That was it.

> There were definitely things in the sheet that have the potential to make you think about planning in a different way, the way it was set out though, tick this box tick that box, it was just too easy, you could do it without thinking at all.

> I didn't find it particularly helpful at the time nor do I think I will find completed ones helpful in the future. There was no room for explaination (sic) or expansion.'The methodologies I planned to use were effective'- box ticked, big deal, what were they? (ITE Online Dialogue: Planning)

Another respondent to the same forum echoed the criticism when she said:

> I just filled it in after every class. it made me think about how i planned my class and it helped me to appreciate the fact that not all plans go according to plan. it wasn't that helpful because when filling it out it was just mostly ticking yes and no and there wasn't enough questions to make you think how you could really change the lesson and to improve it. (ITE Online Dialogue: Planning)

What is interesting about this response is the reason given for the dissatisfaction with the question format. The respondent suggested that 'there wasn't enough questions to make you think'. This point was taken up by another respondent who went on to explain her dissatisfaction with the closed question in terms of the limitations placed on the user by the format:

> The questions posed were really good and could certainly help you to improve your planning, but the required response was inadequate. I'm not suggesting that we should write an answer to each question individually, but more use them as a set of guidelines for writing relevant information for ourselves, so that we can make it useful. It's not the did it work or did it not that really matters, it's the what was it and why. (ITE Online Dialogue: Planning)

What comments such as the last one cited above indicates is that through use of the instruments and engagement with the ideas presented during online dialogues, participants begin to come to an understanding of the underpinning principles which guide both the development and use of the different evaluation methodologies disseminated.

Developing an Understanding

The examples cited above clearly demonstrate the process whereby the use of the evaluation instruments causes participants to move from a stage of initial engagement to one where they are beginning to develop an understanding of both process and issues. In the following posting we can see more clear evidence of a participant moving beyond the surface issue of question type to the real issue - the type of evidence required for effective self evaluation to take place:

> The fact that it's quick and simple to do makes it inticing (sic) and one might think that because of this it might encourage people to self evaluate. But it is this very fact that means you don't really have to think about it. So are you evaluating at all? Self evaluation to me is a means of trying to improve your skills as a teacher and I think a big part of that is being able to look back and see where you have failed or succeeded in the past. And what in particular aided that outcome. This evaluation sheet doesn't allow that. You might be encouraged to fill out the sheet but to do some constructive self evaluation? (CPD Online Dialogue: Assessment questionnaire)

A second critical part of the understanding phase involves the user developing an appreciation of the potential of the information produced by the data collection instruments to change their future practice. At times this involves little more than a statement of some vague future intent. However more often than not this is accompanied by a rationale for potential future uses. For example, one of the ITE participants indicated her willingness to use the classroom management questionnaire at a future date stating that,

> I would, but not as an everyday self evaluation questionnaire. I would use for classes which I am having classroom management and discipline problems. It is limited to classroom management so I would only use it on a particular troublesome class. So if I feel I need to evaluate a particular class which im having trouble in terms of discipline I will start to use this questionnaire for a few days and sort out my problems. (ITE Online Dialogue: Classroom management)

There are clear signs here of an understanding of the need to be sure of the reasons underpinning the use of a particular data collection instrument. In this situation future use is dependent on perceived need.

In other situations, future use is predicated on an understanding that teachers might not be fully aware of what is actually happening in every learning situation they engage in. There is an explicit statement in this next posting of the need to engage in future episodes of data collection in order to understand what is happening in the average classroom. Asked if he would use the classroom management instrument again, the ITE participant said:

> Absolutely, there is no way I can know where I will be teaching in future years and I can see myself using this a lot if I am in a certain type of school. Even if I am not I think it would be hugely helpful to use this at the beginning of every year for a week with each class just so you can get an idea of what works with them. I think the best part of this questionnaire is the fact that you have so many options and that these allow you to understand what is happening if you use them properly. As someone once said, knowledge is power. See youse next week. (ITE Online Dialogue: Week 7, classroom management questionnaire)

A different type of issue is raised by the next posting quoted. The participant here is in the process of making the explicit connection between the use of data collection instruments and the process of engaging in meaningful reflection:

> I have found that while the questionnaires aid reflection, they do not guarantee it. One must really engage with the process for it to be successful. It is too easy at times to fill in a questionaire and believe you have engaged with self evaluation when in fact all you have done is fill in a questionnaire. (CPD Online Dialogue: General Evaluation Discussion)

This position is echoed in one of the final ITE postings quoted below:

> I am really curious about the whole idea of reflection. Since I have started this programme I have been told that I have to reflect and to be honest I haven't had a clue what it meant for most of the time. I think as I come to the end of this self-evaluation project I am beginning to get an idea of what it might be. It might be easier to say what it isn't. Reflection isn'tt (sic) just filling out forms and forgetting about them. In fact I don't think it really has anything to do with filling out forms except that you get information there. From what I can see reflection is about thinking about what you do but it is pointless to do it without knowing wht (sic) you do. That is where I think the questionnaires come in. They let us know what we do and if we use them properly they should be able to let us know what to do. I think. (ITE Online Dialogue: overall reflection)

Overall then, the process of engaging with the data collection instruments in a meaningful manner has resulted in a greater level of understanding and insight for the majority of programme participants. The development of this understanding is an essential pre-requisite for the achievement of the final part of the model proposed, that of ownership.

Ownership

Taking ownership of the mechanisms for generating useful data about one's own practice is one of the key goals of any self-evaluation process. The act of taking ownership can, and indeed probably should, take place at two levels; those of the individual teacher and the broader evaluating community. The former is important as the structure of our education system ensures that this is ultimately the level at which the initial judgements as to the quality of practice are made. The latter is essential also because, as we have seen, all individual practice contexts are influenced by the broader community of practice in which they are located (Lave and Wenger, 1991). In the context of this study, the process of taking ownership involved the participants altering, augmenting and adding to the instruments designed.

A typical posting, such as the one below, relating to the alteration of an instrument tended to indicate what was done and why:

> For q3,q4 I have added 'what did you incorporate into your learning session to-day to benefit your students'. Because I work with 4 different classes and teach different subjects I need to write down to help me to remember what I did incorporate into the session to make it more beneficial. (CPD Online Dialogue: Using the classroom management questionnaire)

Another CPD participant made a similar point when speaking of the planning instrument:

> The planning questionnaire did prompt me to reflect on my practice in relation to planning. Not all of the questions were relevant to me and also some of them were very general. I feel that my reply to these questions (3,5,9,11 & 12) will be the same no matter how many times I complete them. For the next time I use them, I am planning to put them in a separate section and only use them when I feel that something new has happened. (CPD Online Dialogue: Using the planning questionnaire)

Perhaps the most significant incidence of a group of participants taking ownership of the data collection instruments can be seen in the case of the ITE cohort's development of a new daily evaluation questionnaire. Having worked through three previous data collection instruments, there was a feeling in the group that while much of the data that was being produced was interesting, they needed a form of questionnaire that allowed them an overview of what was happening in the course of their teaching day. Following an extensive in-class debate the participants decided to produce a new instrument that 'combined everything we thought was good about the previous questionnaires' (final evaluation report, ITE Student). Perhaps unsurprisingly in the light of the previously quoted discussion on question types, this questionnaire was made up entirely of open questions. The general reaction to the instrument was positive with participants going out of their way to point out what they thought was good about it. One participant zoned in on the format:

> I found the latest self-evaluation sheet very useful. If you feel one part of the class went particularly well or bad you have all the opportunities to write about it and it will be there for you to look at later. And since there is no ticking boxes you will know what actually happened in the class. (ITE Online Dialogue Using the Daily Evaluation Sheet)

Another in the same dialogue made a similar point:

> I liked the evaluation sheet it was broad but had the different sections and the second page for any general comments (ITE Online Dialogue Using the Daily Evaluation Sheet)

The next posting highlights the issue of the class generated nature of the sheet:

> I like the latest evaluation sheet. It's concise, easy and quick to fill out and the second page is perfect for making comments on any of the 5 areas. Also, I think it is really ours because we developed it as a class and not as groups (no offence to the groups) (ITE Online Dialogue Using the Daily Evaluation Sheet)

In summary, the design and use of the data collection instruments proved to be an enormously beneficial experience for most programme participants. There was as general welcome for not only how the instruments were designed but also for the final results of that design process. The cycle of implementation described resulted in participants developing a critically informed understanding of the strengths and weaknesses of each of the instruments as well as a methodology for making contextually appropriate alterations. At the end of this cycle, participants had a clearer understanding of not only how data was generated but also what sort of data was useful in their own professional settings. There was moreover clear evidence of participants beginning to display a sense of ownership over the process.

Stage Two: Engaging and Understanding

The second element of the analytic framework proposed was designed to assess the extent to which participant engagement with a structured self-evaluation process influenced their understanding of and commitment to the concept of self-evaluation. While it can been argued that the design and use of the data collection instruments was important to the participants' experience of self-evaluation, it is ultimately their attitude to the very idea of self-evaluation that will decide whether they ever repeat such a process in their professional lives. In this section we will attempt to assess participants' perceptions of the value of self-evaluation as well as examining the practical impact that engaging in the programme designed had on their professional practice.

Valuing Self-Evaluation—Ongoing Commitment or Short-Term Engagement?

One of the central challenges facing any innovative programme designed to influence the beliefs and practices of educational professionals is to ensure that the changes in that practice are maintained beyond the life of the intervention. The data generated in the final evaluative survey would seem to suggest that this programme has a high chance of having a long-term impact on the professional practice of participants. Both cohorts indicated that they would continue to evaluate their teaching and training in future years. In total one hundred percent of the CPD and over ninety two percent of the ITE agreed with this statement when it was put to them.

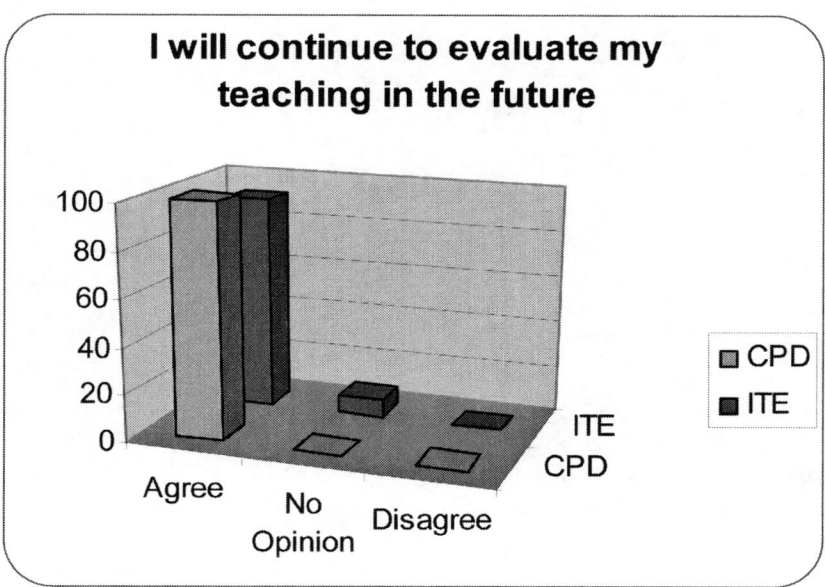

FIGURE 9.4: I WILL CONTINUE TO EVALUATE MY TEACHING IN THE FUTURE
(ITE N = 13 ; CPD N = 24)

Encouraging though these statistics may be, researchers should always be a little wary of accepting an end of programme declaration of future intentions completely at face value. While not seeking to question the intention of participants to continue evaluating their own work in future years, it is important to examine the data closely in order to understand why they have made this ongoing commitment.

For most programme participants, whether they were from the CPD or ITE cohorts, the process of engaging in self-evaluation was invariably linked with the process of improving their professional practice. Virtually every respondent to the final programme survey indicated that they felt that self-evaluation was an essential element of good teaching.

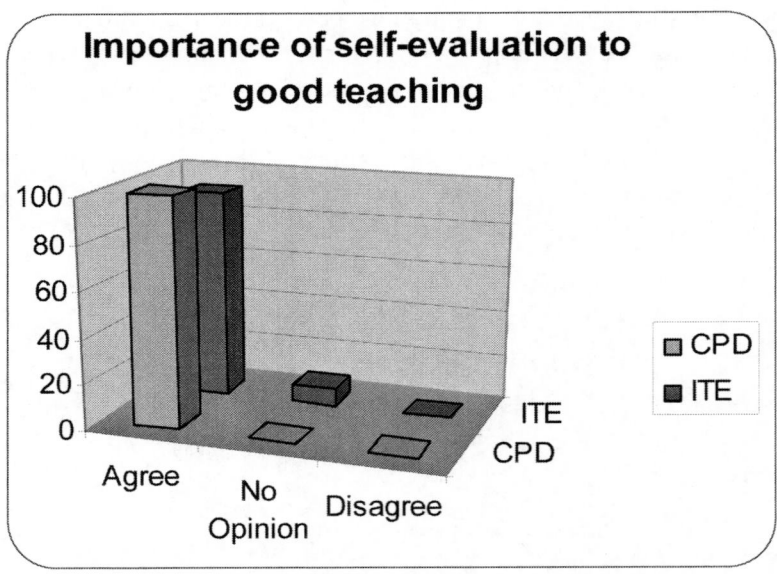

FIGURE 9.5: SELF EVALUATION IS ESSENTIAL TO GOOD TEACHING / TRAINING
(ITE N = 13 ; CPD N = 24)

This acceptance of the link between self-evaluation and improvement in teaching quality is confirmed by the qualitative data. To quote from the final report of one of the CPD participants:

At one stage I asked myself why I was doing all this and then it hit me, I was doing this to make my teaching better. (Respondent 9: Terminal Evaluation Survey)

Another, expressing some surprise at the idea, makes much the same point:

> I am astonished at how this (process) has opened my eyes to the value of self evaluation. It has helped me to refocus with fresh energy and motivation, highlighting areas of my teaching practice that needs addressing. (Respondent 1: Terminal Evaluation Survey)

An ITE participant echoes this insight in his final report. Addressing the reasons for his interest in self evaluation he states:

> I basically think that self evaluation is important because it helps you to improve your teaching and especially helps you improve as a teacher . . . For you to improve I feel you need to be able to see what worked and why it was successful? (ITE Respondent 7: Terminal Evaluation Report)

The MOODLE forum saw a number of participants from both cohorts agree with this general position. The point was summarised by one ITE participant in a posting where he stated:

> I found self-evaluation useful as it allowed me to examine my teaching and how to better it. It allowed me to find why something went wrong and also how to correct it. (ITE Online Dialogue: Daily Evaluation Sheet)

There is a clear theme running through these comments which links self evaluation with the ability to obtain clarity about the true quality of one's practice. This knowledge allows participants to make informed judgements as well as providing them with a sound basis from which to make changes in their practice. For some, as in the posting below, it is the discipline of recording this knowledge immediately after the class period that makes the information so valuable.

> I've learned that self evaluation is an invaluable tool in improving your teaching.It allows you to learn from both your mistakes and your successes by giving you real information about each of them. Because you are forced to record what happened soon after it happened you get a lot of really good information that you might have forgotten. (ITE Online Dialogue: Week 9)

For others, it is the relatively objective and original nature of the information that makes it so useful. Writing in the final evaluation survey, one CPD participant pointed out that:

> The value of this whole process to me is that over a series of weeks I was able to sit down and record what I do in a way that I had never done before. This was really useful but what was more useful was the fact that when I read over what I had written

down I was able to see patterns. It is funny that things I have been doing for years which I never thought of suddenly jumped out at me as being issues. Not major ones, just simple things like the fact that I always use groupwork in double classes. I am not saying that this is a bad thing but it is interesting to know. Because of the methodologies questionnaire I have started to try new things in my double classes that at least are making things different. (Respondent 3: Terminal Evaluation Survey)

This is an interesting comment as it demonstrates that quite often the impetus for change comes through a cumulative development of knowledge rather than one blinding flash of inspiration. Also, the type of change being instituted as a result of the analysis of the emerging information is relatively limited in scope. This is in keeping with the notion of incremental change that is suggested by champions of self-evaluation approaches such as MacBeath (1999). His argument is that small scale, organic change which results from insights generated by an individual or school community is far more likely to have a long term impact than revolutionary, radical and imposed change forced on an organisation by an outside agency or individual.

A second connected theme links engagement in the process of self-evaluation with a higher sense of awareness about the reasons for the participant's patterns of practice. One of the CPD participants explicitly acknowledged this sense of heightened awareness as being one of the main benefits of the process in her final report when she said:

I found this process to be extremely beneficial in developing my self awareness both personally and professionally. Completing the evaluation instruments raised my awareness that in turn enabled me to improve my performance. This research has proven to me the importance of the self in evaluation. (Respondent 11: Terminal Evaluation Survey)

At times this awareness could be uncomfortable and led individuals to uncover aspects of their teaching that they maybe would have preferred not to address. The CPD participant quoted below encapsulates this perspective:

Taking part in self-evaluation allowed me to see things about myself and my teaching that I had never thought of before. It opened up corners of my classroom that had been in the dark for quite a number of years. While this was a good thing in the end, there were times when I was doing it that I wondered why I was putting myself through it. (CPD Online Dialogue: General Evaluation Discussion)

Another CPD correspondent, writing in his final evaluative report, made a similar point:

The process of engaging in a self-evaluation course has impacted on my practice in ways that I would never have expected. Flaws and gaps that I have either been ignoring or hiding from myself became visible in my practice, the greatest one being a lack of awareness about why I do things in a particular way. (Respondent 22: Terminal Evaluation Survey)

One of the ITE respondents acknowledged the role of the self-evaluation process in broadening his horizons as a teacher. Here, awareness of practice was an essential pre-requisite to developing a professional identity and the beginnings of an understanding of what the role of teacher actually involved:

I feel that self evaluation was useful. When you first start out your (sic) so preoccupied with teaching you don't see anything else. That's your main focus. But gradually with the help of self evaluation you learn to look at other things, and it gets easier as you settle in. I do feel that it helped me to improve as a teacher and to understand better what it means to be a teacher. (ITE Online Dialogue: Daily Evaluation Sheet)

Another ITE participant taking part in the same dialogue quite eloquently makes a similar point. She suggests that the process of engaging in self-evaluation has led her to redefine herself as a learner as well as a teacher whose fundamental role is to improve her practice in order to ensure that her students succeed. Again, she makes explicit the link between knowledge, awareness and improvement:

Over the course of my teaching practice, I have come to realise that self evaluation is not only necessary but essential. The success of a class is crucially dependent on effective teacher self evaluation. I think that a good teacher will instinctively wish to reflect on their work, evaluate it and look for ways to improve it. A fundamental principal is that the teacher should see themselves as learners. I myself have learned something new after each lesson I have taught, whether it be about planning or classroom management. (ITE Online Dialogue: Daily Evaluation Sheet)

Of course this awareness did not always lead to dramatic discoveries. Indeed, another of the CPD participants made the point in their final report that:

Evaluation may not always result in startling findings. While they do fill in gaps in knowledge and correct misconceptions they more often than not serve to confirm impressions and affirm good practice. Yet as a result of self evaluation I think I can say that my contribution to CTSCC has changed significantly and that this change began with a simple alteration made to my planning after using the first questionnaire. (Respondent 14: Terminal Evaluation Survey)

The data generated from the final programme survey would suggest that this was the experience of the majority of the programme participants. When asked whether engaging with the self-evaluation process had had an impact on their teaching, almost ninety three percent of the ITE cohort and more than seventy two percent of the CPD group confirmed that it did (see Figure 9.6).

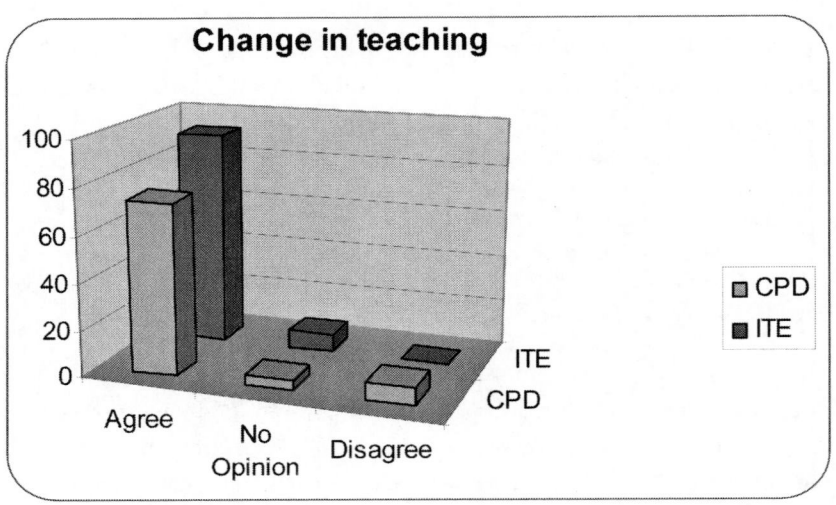

FIGURE 9.6: I CHANGED HOW I TAUGHT AS A RESULT OF
USING THE SELF EVALUATION INSTRUMENTS
(ITE N = 13 ; CPD N = 24)

Perhaps the best overall summary of the interaction between the different aspects of the self-evaluation process was provided by one of the ITE participants in his final MOODLE posting. In it, he was trying to encapsulate his growing understanding of the importance of self-evaluation to his own professional life and he summarised it as follows:

> As a new teacher i have found self evaluation to be very important and practical in becoming a better teacher. Been (sic) new to this profession my experience and knowledge is limited, but with self evaluation i (sic) have been able to improve my classroom management, class plans etc. With self evaluation i can review my performance in the class, what areas did i do well in and what areas do i need to improve in to suit the needs of my pupils and make the classroom an environment where people can learn. With self evaluation i have learnt that you can
>
> * identify the professional education you need to further develop your capacity to teach well
>
> *improve the educational experiences you provide for your students

* prepare for your performance review with your supervisor. So self evaluation is a beneficial and worth while aspect of teaching, with it one can only improve as a teacher. (ITE Online Dialogue: General Reflection)

In these postings there are clear echoes of the work of the OECD (2005) and its focus on the need for continuous professional development, MacBeath and McGlynn's (2002) emphasis on the need for all evaluation to be fundamentally concerned with the quality of teaching and learning and Nevo's identification of the role of dialogue as the key determinant of the success of evaluative systems (Nevo, 1995).

Broadening the Self-Evaluation Community— Valuing other Voices

The second major theme to emerge from participants' engagement with a structured self-evaluation programme was the extent to which this led them to explore the centrality of other individuals and communities to the process of investigating their own practice. For many participants, the discipline imposed by the requirement to assess the quality of their own work made them aware, perhaps for the first time, of how such judgements rarely take place in isolation. As a result of this there were a number of individual initiatives from participants in both the CPD and ITE groups which were designed to find ways of involving others in the self-evaluation process being developed. These initiatives tended to focus on designing methodologies that brought other members of the participants' school communities into the process and in particular, on how to find a mechanism for including the voices of students and other staff members. There were also attempts to explore how the new relationship between individual school communities and the emerging system of national evaluation was impacting on the participants' understanding of the programme process. We will start with an exploration of the reasons why participants chose to involve others in what was, at least in theory, a self-evaluation process.

In explaining why he chose to involve other stakeholders in his organisation in the evaluation process one of the CPD participants stated that,

it was essential to get as many views as possible to get an overall picture of the situation. I discovered how many of my colleagues affect how well I carry out my teaching practice. (CPD Online Dialogue:General Evaluation Discussion)

This notion of the potential impact of other colleagues' actions on the professional practice of individual course participants was echoed in another CPD final report. Here the participant stated that,

> I have always seen myself as part of a team and up to now would have thought that the best way for me to evaluate what I do is to ask other members of the team. My view has changed a little over the course of the programme and I can see the value in taking a long hard look at yourself first but I do still think that it is important to ask others what they think. (Respondent 23: Terminal Evaluation Survey)

For some, this engagement with other stakeholders with a view to drawing them into the process is an article of faith as well as a quality control mechanism:

> Once more I re-iterate the belief that involvement from all stakeholders is highly desirable if the strong forces generated by our own self evaluations that can lead to self deception are to be exposed and challenged. (CPD Online Dialogue: Using the classroom management instrument)

This theme is taken up by another CPD participant in their final report. In their opinion one of the major flaws of the self-evaluation process is that:

> It puts the onus on the teacher to judge themselves. This has the potential to cause problems around impartiality and bias, as it can be difficult to put oneself in the firing line and make objective judgments about ones own work. . (therefore) I believe that the self-evaluation process has the capacity to remain inward looking and had the potential to lack a holistic vision of the bigger picture unless others are involved in enriching the process with their views. (Respondent 7: Terminal Evaluation Survey)

From this viewpoint, the involvement of other perspectives enriches the process as well as removing some of the pressure from individuals to be overly critical of their own work.

A second important point is the acknowledgement that the process of getting a balanced perspective involves the teacher not only listening to colleagues but also to students. This was echoed by another ITE participant in the same dialogue who said:

> As i have also said before i think getting students to evaluate us is a great idea as they know how much they are learning or not learning. i know it can be a bit intimidating at first to ask them to make a comment about you, but if you set down the ground rules from the beginning it works really well, i feel that i had a totally different relationship with my 6th years after i asked their opinion. They were honest, gave me good ideas and

afterwards told me that they were really happy to be asked their opinion cos it had never happened before. (ITE Online Dialogue: General Reflection)

A number of the CPD participants also emphasised the vitally important role of the student voice in the evaluation process. One participant's contribution to the MOODLE forum concentrates again on the unique perspective on the quality of learning taking place that students can provide:

To promote this learning and fully engage in self-evaluation and reflection, I feel students learning must be assessed through input from them as to how they feel about the teacher, the school, and methodologies used and how they feel they learn best etc. (CPD Online Dialogue: Final week)

Another speaks in her final report of the relational nature of teaching and of how it would not only be disrespectful but also counter productive not to include the student perspective:

In my opinion any system of school evaluation that fails to take into account the legitimate and valid viewpoints of the students will be incomplete. I have always understood my classroom to have been a place where I created a learning relationship with my students. Like any relationship that works this has to be viewed as a two way reality. For this reason I listen to my students and value what they say to me. It doesn't mean that I always agree with them, but I trust them enough to tell me what they think the truth is about what they are learning. (Respondent 11: Terminal Evaluation Survey)

Of course, not every participant saw the value of including other voices. There were a number of comments from the ITE participants which indicated a sense of discomfort with the thought of engaging with a process that they felt might leave them vulnerable.

The comment below from the final series of MOODLE postings sums up this perspective,

although i (sic) agree with eb on the whole area of peer evaluation i would consider it more when i was fully qualified. i mean it is fantastic to hear about it, but as a student teacher i would need more time to get relaxed in a classroom situation before i'd like my peers to be studying my every move. once you feel part of the school, that the classroom is yours then maybe you have no problem with that practice. also not having them in means that if you make a mistake when you evaluate you can understand what happened without thinking your peer thinks you are an idiot. (ITE Online Dialogue: General Reflection)

This honest assessment of their own level of professional development draws attention to the sense of exposure that teachers can feel when they are asked to 'perform' in front of their colleagues or peers. The sense that external evaluation brings with it an element of discomfort and tension is undoubtedly a common one as is the fear of making a mistake in front of someone whom you know. Despite the student teachers' confidence that this discomfort will disappear as they become more experienced, there is a not insignificant body of evidence to suggest that for many teachers the process of opening themselves up to external scrutiny will always be a difficult process (MacBeath and McGlynn, 2002; MacBeath, 1999; Davies and Rudd, 2000).

Participants on the CPD programme indicated a different set of barriers to including different voices. A number of them reported on the resistance that they encountered when they broached the subject of introducing a form of peer evaluation in their own workplace. The reactions included by one participant in one of his MOODLE postings is instructive:

> When I suggested to the other teachers they might like to use the questionnaires to evaluate their own teaching they nearly had a heart attack they responded with questions such as would I give the results of their findings to management. I had to reassure them the evaluation would be for their own benefit. These are very good teachers but the fear of evaluation of their teaching methods was very strong. I will keep working with them to reduce the fear they have of evaluation. (CPD Online Dialogue: Final week)

Aside from the colourful comments this posting gives a real sense of the problems faced by anyone considering the extension of an evaluation system to include a peer review element. The fear that it induces is real and permeates many teachers' responses to evaluation as a whole and peer evaluation in particular.

A final area of external relationships which had a significant impact on self-evaluation in the project was the new national system of school evaluation. As we have seen elements of the new framework were chosen to structure much of the research. During the project, one of the practicum schools was chosen to undergo a Whole School Evaluation (WSE) while the student teacher was there. He spoke about it extensively in class, and in his last MOODLE posting describes the external evaluation process and his impressions of the impact that it had on the school:

> I also saw another version of evaluation when I was in the school and I was able to compare it to what we were doing. In my sixth week (I think) the school went through WSE. This was really interesting to me because it involved the teachers getting used to having someone looking at them. Because I was part of the school, the WSE team

looked at me too. I have to say that I found it really interesting. They were very nice and professional and gave me some good advice on teaching maths. They also seemed interested in what I was doing and looked at the evaluation sheets that we were using then and thought it was good. The rest of the school did really well too but you could see that teachers were nervous. The Principal spent ages getting documents together and some of the staff went sick in the days coming up to it. I don't think that anyone got a bad report because it is a really good school but it was an eye opener to see how difficult good teachers found the whole thing. (ITE Online Dialogue: General Reflection)

Despite being fragmentary in nature, this posting does make some interesting points. The first is that the WSE team observed the participant even though he was only a temporary member of staff. Secondly, he was able to make a small but real link between his own self-evaluation work and the WSE structure. Perhaps most importantly, given the comments in the previous section, he clearly identifies the sense of discomfort and even fear that the external visit engendered even among experienced teachers.

A second and more substantial analysis of the impact of a Whole School Evaluation (WSE) visit was provided by one of the CPD participants. As part of her final report she produced a detailed analysis of her understanding of the differences between the self-evaluation process that she was undergoing as part of her professional development and the externally mandated evaluation that she was being required to take a role in as part of her professional duties. The participant chose to summarise the differences in tabular form which is reproduced on the next page.

This is a fascinating and quite complex table which summarises with great originality the fundamental differences, that in the participants' view, exist between an external evaluation system and a process of self-evaluation. Perhaps the most significant differences occur at the effect and outcome levels. The overall analysis of the effect of both evaluation procedures seems to indicate that the self-evaluation process produces less anxiety and is more honest. However it does suffer from having less organisational impact. In terms of the overall outcome, there appears to be less clarity about which is the most beneficial. Both result in higher motivation, one at an organisational and one at personal level. While the externally facilitated evaluation process validates the work of the entire organisation the self-evaluation process acts very much as a learning platform that allows individuals to improve the standard of their professional practice.

Perhaps the most telling comparison is made in the final comment about 'commonly used phrases'. She suggests that where the external system requires professional educators to ask whether their work is good enough; the self-evaluation system affirms their current practice but challenges them to find better ways of doing it.

	External Evaluation	Self-evaluation
The purpose	To evaluate the work of the organisation	To identify areas for improvement in professional practice
The process	A 5 day process involving 6 external evaluators reviewing all practices	A four week process involving the practitioner
The Evaluators	Six professional evaluators	The practitioner who is culturally and politically immersed in the organisation
The Effect	Anxieties very high throughout all levels of the organisation. The organisations reputation would be damaged if the report was bad. This resulted in the organisation hiding/ disguising weak areas and embellishing others. Many projects previously unfinished were prioritised and brought to completion.	No anxiety and no impact at organisational level, but high level impact on a personal level. An honest inquiry into all areas of practice Took place in practice without any preparation time or changes before inquiry.
The Outcome	External validation of the work undertaken by the whole organisation. Celebrations and renewed commitment and motivation in the organisation. Commonly used phrase 'is my work good enough?'	Review of my practice and identification of areas for improvement. Renewed commitment to my professional practice. Commonly used phrase ' How can I do this better?

TABLE 9.2: THE DIFFERENCE BETWEEN EXTERNAL AND SELF-EVALUATION IN MY ORGANISATION

In a later part of her report, the author of the above argues that the ideal solution would be to:

Combine both processes, (as) the strengths of both will compliment (sic) each other and the weaknesses will be diminished.

In the context of the broader literature regarding the range of possible relationships between systems based on self-evaluation and those based on externally mandated evaluations, this comment is significant. To an extent it echoes the position of both the authors of the *LAOS* system and that of Miliband (2004) in that it suggests that external and internal evaluation need to interact in a way that ensures that they are complementary rather than competitive. However there is a strong hint of the criticisms made by MacBeath (2004) and Nevo (2002) about externally mandated systems. In particular her comments relating to external evaluators only getting to view what the school community thinks they might want to see echoes the debate surrounding the self-inspection and self-evaluation dichotomy.

Stage Three: Taking Ownership and Enhancing Practice

The third element of the analytic framework was designed to assess the extent to which participants gradually took ownership of the self-evaluation process and began to use it in their day to day work to enhance their professional practice. The following sections report on the research evidence which emerged in this regard. This evidence largely takes the form of a number of interventions designed and reported by programme participants. These were undertaken purely on individual initiative and went beyond the norm in terms of commitment and enthusiasm to the theory and practice of self-evaluation. Nonetheless these individual case studies are illustrative of the possibilities for professional development which a strong engagement with self-evaluation can bring about.

Case Study One: Informal Sharing with Colleagues

The first case study deals with the development of an informal evaluating relationship between an ITE participant and her mentor teacher. As will be seen from the material quoted below, this relationship seems to have been enormously enriching for both parties without ever really having been structured in any formal sense. The process was described as follows by the participant in a post programme interview. She began by describing how she had spent some time explaining the central ideas of the self-evaluation process to her colleague. She also shared a number of the group designed data collection instruments which prompted the following response,

> (he said that) he would do the whole thing of reflective practice himself. That every once in a while he would sit down and say, this is what I wanted to get done, this is what I got done, what can I change? And he has been teaching now for 45 years and

he was still doing this. So whenever I gave him, I think I gave him the teaching methodology and the combined evaluation sheet, he loved the teaching methodology one. He thought it was great. He actually sat down and said, I did this, I did this, and I did this. He said "look E, I covered all of these what did you cover in your class?" and it was a case of "oh be quiet M, you've been teaching for ages". . . . He was asking me what teaching methodology meant because he did his teacher training when he was 16 . . . So I was going down through the whole area of teaching methodologies and he was going, "oh right, I use an awful lot of them in the class but I never knew what they meant". So the whole area of the combined evaluation sheet he was able to answer some of them but the participant learning and the teaching and learning methodologies he needed some guidance on. But he found them really useful as well. He really enjoyed filling out the sheet and then the fact that he was going to be quoted later on MOODLE, he loved that as well. (ITE student interview)

At an interpersonal level it is fascinating to see how the use of the data collection instruments allowed her to develop a relationship with a colleague who was over forty years her senior. However, there are other important insights that can be gleaned from this episode as well. The first of these is the realisation on the part of the young teacher that highly experienced teachers actively engage in the process of reflecting on their professional practice even if this is done informally. This touches on the general point alluded to by Simons (2002) that most successful teachers engage in some form of self-evaluation whether they acknowledge it formally or not.

Secondly, there was the enthusiasm shown by the mentor teacher for the data collection instrument designed by the class group precisely because it enabled him to name his practice in a way that made sense to a new generation of teachers. Here we see a strong confirmation of the point made by Barzano (2002) who argued that one of the key tasks of any system of self-evaluation is to give practitioners a vocabulary with which to engage initially with each other and subsequently with external stakeholders.

The third and final insight that can be drawn from this short vignette is the mentor teacher's happiness at the prospect of his insights being shared with a wider community on the MOODLE website. Again the notion of the public nature of self-evaluation is brought to the fore. Writers from MacBeath (1996) to Nevo (2006) argue consistently that just because self-evaluation deals with individual or single organisation practice, it does not mean that it should be completed behind closed doors. There is an essential public aspect to self-evaluation that demands that some form of open sharing of the insights generated take place. In this example, the mentor teacher not only accepts that this needs to happen, he positively celebrates it!

Case Study Two: Spreading the Message

The second case study provides us with an example of how an individual with an interest in self-evaluation can have an impact on the professional practice of an entire organisation. In a process similar to that described by Barzano (2002), a participant from the CPD cohort became a champion for self-evaluation in his own organisation and encouraged colleagues to begin the process of assessing their own work using two specially designed data collection instruments. The participant indicates in his final report that the initial impetus for starting this process came from his participation in the training programme under discussion. In a posting to the MOODLE discussion forum he details the different stages of the process of sharing his self-evaluation focus with his colleagues as well as the impact that it has had on his professional practice:

> I will used an amended version of the four questionnaires in the future and have given a copy to the four trainers I work with. We will hopefully produce an amended version to use in training.
> Self-evaluation was not always top of my work agenda in the past. In using this self-evaluation instrument it had enabled me to given more focus to self-evalutaion (sic) and I have already begun to build this into my training routine. (CPD Online Dialogue: Using the Planning Instrument)

In a subsequent posting, he expanded on the specific details of how he encouraged others to take part in the process. He also speaks of some of the barriers that he faced,

> the use of the questionnaire with my colleagues was optional, a few have used it and gave me some feedback,. . . . . Yes i think the culture of my own organisation has gone through change of late, in saying that I really mean the department I work within. . . . . Our department is slowly becoming one of sharing of ideas etc. as you referred to, however, this is not without its problems, competition always raises its ugly head, which can at times be positive. The culture is very important to me in the process of self-evaluation, it needs to be supportive and encouraging, again something that is changing within my own organisation. (CPD Online Dialogue: Using the Planning Instrument)

The end result of this process was his production and distribution of two evaluation instruments which were to be used by teachers after each class. The participant reports that,

> to date these questionnaires have proved to be a beneficial evaluation instrument, which has lead to the process evaluating each module within the overall programme.

> At present this evaluation process is time consuming as the programme has 18 different class modules. (CPD Online Dialogue: Using the Planning Instrument)

In summary then, as a direct result of taking part in the programme under discussion in this study, this CPD participant has designed a similar intervention for his own workplace. This intervention seems, at this early stage at least, to have had a positive impact on his organisation as a whole and his colleagues appear to be interested in continuing to evaluate their own work for the medium term.

Case Study Three: Engaging with a self-evaluating school community

The third case study presented here deals with the experiences of an ITE participant who found himself teaching in a school which already had a culture of peer evaluation. He decided to integrate the materials that were developed by his colleagues in the programme with the culture of evaluation that he found in the organisation where he was working. This resulted in a genuine commitment on his part to the integration of a peer evaluation element into his future professional practice.

He began by describing the evaluation process that existed when he arrived in the school:

> They engage in peer evaluation where one teacher will sit in on another teacher's class. That's the form they have that's an example of one where they have one column for teacher activities and one for students in three minutes intervals. Basically you try to keep the teachers one as low as possible and the students activities as high as possible and sort of if you have all your students ones empty you're running into trouble, that's just the way they do it on a very basic level. (ITE student interview)

The central parts of the evaluation process as described are the peer review element and the use of what appears to be a very basic interaction analysis document. It is interesting to see that the staff equate good teaching with limited teacher activity.

The next stage involved the ITE participant distributing the data-collection instruments designed by his cohort for their use and consideration:

> So then I got them to use the questionnaires for themselves for self-evaluation and some of them found them more useful than others, but all of them agreed that it might be

a better idea to get peers to use them for you or to allow students evaluation of your lessons, they found that more helpful than self evaluation. (ITE student interview)

Despite seeing a value in the instruments designed, the teachers still valued the input of other professionals or even students over and above the information that came from the questionnaire. The interviewee gave the following explanation for this:

They just didn't think that they themselves could be objective enough looking at their own teaching they thought it would be better if someone else was to look at it for them. There so involved in the lesson they don't pick up on things that someone else would pick up on you know so they felt it better for some one else to do it for them rather than do it themselves. (ITE student interview)

Here again we have the issue of objectivity. Teachers are either unable or unwilling to tell the truth about their practice, even to themselves, and therefore need the discipline of having an 'objective' colleague in the room with them to tell them where they are going right and where they are going wrong. While there is a common sense aspect to this argument, it does seem to go against many of the central tenets of the reflective practice and practitioner research movement that have had a significant impact on the development of the self-evaluation approach. Ultimately it is impossible to know whether the argument is valid. Many teachers would argue passionately that they are capable of examining their own work in an honest and objective way while a number clearly feel that this is not possible.

The ITE participant was certainly convinced about the usefulness of the peer review element. As he explains,

I got one of them to sit in and I got one of them to use our questionnaires for me and I found the information I got more helpful for self-evaluation. You know they picked up on a lot of things I wouldn't have picked up on I found it pretty helpful. (ITE student interview)

Case Study Four: Involving the Student Voice

The fourth case study provides details of the design and implementation by an ITE participant of self-evaluation process also designed to capture the student voice. The participant was clear about his reasons for doing this. In his final report he stated that he felt that it was wrong that 'the most informed sources on the qualities of teachers tend to be ritually ignored, that is the pupils.

In order to put this to the test, he designed a questionnaire which sought their views on the quality of their educational experiences and, quite courageously, on the standard of the teaching they were receiving. The survey was carried out among first, second and fifth year pupils in order to get a good range of responses. The instrument that was distributed was designed by the participant and was simple and to the point (see Figure 9.7 below).

Teaching questionnaire

As part of a research assignment I am carrying out I would appreciate your help, as a secondary school student, in telling me what YOU think is important in a teacher. Below is a list of attributes (characteristics) of a typical teacher. Please rate each of these points as you see as being important for the benefit of your learning in class. 1 = most important, 2=2nd most important etc. (You may place the same number beside different points if you feel they are equally important to you in your learning)

- ▢   A teacher who gets on really well with the student __
- ▢   A teacher who can keep the class quiet __
- ▢   A teacher who can clearly explain information __
- ▢   A teacher who is strict __
- ▢   A teacher who gives a lot of homework __
- ▢   A teacher who gives productive home work __

xxxxxxxxxxxxxxxxxxxxxxxxxxxxxxxxxxxxxxxxxxxxxxxxxxxxxxxxxxxxxxx

If you think there are any points I have forgotten to include, please list them on the back of this page and rate them.

Thank you for your cooperation
(Do not write your name on this page !!!!!!)

FIGURE 9.7: TEACHING QUESTIONNAIRE

As part of the process of getting student information, the ITE participant analysed the data and fed it back to them (see Figure 9.8 below). This was considered to be quite unusual by the pupils but appears to have been greatly appreciated.

Results

Pupil Teaching Questionnaire

A teacher who gets on really well with students	44	76%
A teacher who can keep a class quiet	8	14%
A teacher who can clearly explain information	25	43%
A teacher who is strict	2	3%
A teacher who gives lots of homework	1	2%
A teacher who gives productive homework	10	17%
A teacher who does plenty of practical / experimental work	8	14%
A teacher who can vary the running of the class everyday	6	10%
A teacher who carries out continuous assessment regularly	3	5%
A teacher who never raises his / her voice	5	9%

Other notes by pupils:

"A teacher who doesn't give too much homework and therefore allows you to study"
"A teacher who is only strict to keep class quiet"
"Always is in a happy mood and a teacher who can give you help when you are stuck"

FIGURE 9.8: RESULTS OF TEACHING QUESTIONNAIRE

The participant indicates in his final report that this process greatly enhanced the quality of his relationship with his pupils. It also demonstrates that it is quite possible to gather useful information from students of all ages and to treat it with the same respect as information generated by other sources. This participant's experience suggests that there was no diminution of authority associated with asking their opinion. In fact the opposite was true. Students valued the opportunity to offer a viewpoint and respected the teacher who asked them. In keeping with MacBeath's (2003) insight, if asking pupils to comment is so easy and so useful, why do so many teachers shy away from it?

In summary, the process of engaging with a self-evaluation programme was seen by most participants as adding to the quality of their professional practice. On a personal level, it was seen as providing them with the knowledge and awareness needed to identify and improve specific areas of practice. On an organisational level, the process of engaging in a self-evaluation process led many participants to involve other stakeholders in the task of improving the quality of teaching and learning that took place in their organisation. Many of these attempts at broadening stakeholder involvement resulted in innovative and unique organic programmes of evaluation being designed and implemented at a range of levels in organisations. These models could be seen as providing templates for other individuals or organisations who are considering adopting a localised, practitioner-led and data-driven approach to judging the quality of the practice taking place in their own organisations.

Conclusion

In chapter eight a training programme designed to encourage self-evaluation among teachers was described. In this chapter an evaluation of the outcomes of this process is considered. As the teachers went through the training programme and implemented self-evaluation of their practice, the experience was researched by the evaluation team using a range of methodologies including questionnaires, interviews and particularly the analysis of online postings on the MOODLE virtual learning environment. Simply put, the purpose was to assess the extent to which the project participants gradually adopted a self-evaluation mindset and practice in their day to day practice. The point ultimately was to see whether the type of training in self-evaluation given in the project could lay the foundations to enable self-evaluation bit by bit to take root in schools.

The initial indications are positive. The researchers used a three dimensional analytic framework to structure the data. The first part of the findings examine participants' attitudes to the process of research instrument design as well as detailing a very interesting three stage cycle of instrument usage. The evidence here showed that participants grew in confidence as their research design and experience developed. The first stage saw most participants move through a period of initial engagement followed by the development at stage two of a greater practice-grounded understanding. In the final stage of the process, we saw many participants moving to a position where they took ownership of the instruments to the extent that they were willing to change and adapt them.

The final part of this chapter explored participant reaction to self-evaluation as a concept as well as assessing the extent to which it impacted on their practice. On the whole, there was a great deal of satisfaction with the process with the majority of both ITE and CPD participants indicating that they intended to continue to self-evaluate even after the programme had finished. Indeed, so taken were some participants by the process that they chose to share it with their work colleagues, and the final part of the chapter reports a number of interesting case studies that emerged from this process.

The authors are fully aware of the limitations of this research in that the positive feelings reported may well be transitory and follow up research which is planned may well find little ongoing use of self-evaluation among the research participants. Experience shows that many promising developments end up this way and only time will tell. However one key factor which does not apply in the case of most experimental projects may make a major difference regarding self-evaluation. This is the fact that there is, in the form of the new national system of school evaluation, a clear purpose and goal for teachers and schools to engage in self-evaluation–to enable them to as it were to speak for themselves in the context of external inspection.

CONCLUSION

Empowering Self-Evaluating Teachers and Schools

The Self-Evaluating Professional—
Charting the Way Forward

This work divides into three parts. Part one is concerned with the worldwide growth of an evaluative culture in recent decades. In many areas of life, but particularly in the public service and even more particularly in education, there has been an intense push to develop systems of accountability and increasing concerns with obtaining value for money. In the opening chapter the roots of this movement are explored. In the case of education these policy directions have been compounded by the immense importance which governments worldwide attribute to student achievement and effective schools. A successful education system is now widely seen as an essential component of economic success without which countries cannot hope to compete for the mobile capital which characterises the modern world economy.

In consequence, in virtually every country in the developed world, and increasingly in the developing world, the state has systematically sought to improve the quality of education and training, not only as in the past by increased expenditure, but also by attempting to increase output through systems of evaluation and surveillance. However it is also noted that these same developments are being increasingly challenged in society in general and in education in particular as the serious consequences of such policies gradually become apparent.

In chapter two the arguments, both philosophical and practical, in relation to the evaluation of schools and teachers are thrashed out. It is suggested that much of the policy direction described in the previous chapter is founded on two fundamental flaws. The first of these is that school evaluation systems, which by their nature must be founded on data and information acquired through social science research methodologies, can ever in fact produce clear, unambiguous and implementable results, policies or plans. This is simply because, as a great deal of work in the social sciences in the past thirty years has shown clearly, complex systems with wide and various goals such as education are hugely resistant to quantifiable measurement. The second fundamental flaw alleged against the neoliberalist approaches to evaluation and appraisal is that these policies downplay or totally ignore the serious side effects inherent in unduly interfering in the reasonable exercise of professional autonomy by such groups as teachers. It has become increasingly apparent that, in a nutshell, such policies when implemented in certain forms do more harm than any demonstrable benefits that may result.

In consequence, while governments in many countries are actively creating or re-structuring school and teacher evaluation systems, what is emerging in fact is surprisingly sophisticated and nuanced. In chapter three it is suggested that emerging evaluation systems in many countries represent a series of compromises which, while involving significant increases in the oversight of schools and teachers, yet are based fundamentally on the premise that these groupings should primarily evaluate themselves with a degree of external monitoring. This concept of self-evaluation, virtually unknown ten or fifteen years ago, has now become a major force in the discourse on school and teacher evaluation. In consequence most evaluation systems have now become a hybrid involving internal or self-evaluation by individual teachers and entire schools with a greater or lesser degree of external inspection. In part two of the book, Ireland is presented as a case in point.

Chapter four describes the nineteen ninety six to nineteen ninety nine pilot project during which a new system of school and teacher evaluation was tested by the DES in Ireland. The extremely cautious consultative and iterative nature of the developmental process is spelled out and the evaluation of that pilot which was published in late nineteen ninety nine is considered in some detail.

In chapter five the new national system of whole-school evaluation which eventually emerged from the pilot project is described. It is argued that the DES saw the implementation of a new approach to school evaluation and inspection as potentially deeply difficult and controversial. The system developed therefore placed a strong emphasis on schools and teachers evaluating their own performance but being subject to regular inspections by the national inspectorate of the DES. In many ways the hybrid of self-evaluation and external inspection which emerged was, it is argued, closely in line with similar compromise systems in other jurisdictions and was strongly influenced by such developments across Europe. However it is also pointed out that the evaluation framework threw up unmistakable areas of concern for the future. While on the positive side it was perhaps remarkable that the new system attracted so little outright opposition, it became clear that this was, to a significant degree, due to the non-pursuit of several key elements which were theoretically built into the scheme. These included the key fact that in practice neither schools nor teachers were expected to produce data or evidence to support the judgements which they made on their own performance. This, as the response of the Inspectorate to the pilot project makes clear, made it very difficult to come to any objective conclusions regarding the effectiveness or otherwise of particular teachers, subject departments or schools. Other flaws clearly highlighted in the evaluation report of WSE in nineteen ninety nine (DES, 1999a) included the very limited role accorded to key stakeholders including parents, pupils and the wider community, and the bland and superficial nature of the final evaluation reports produced. None of these flaws, it is argued, were dealt with in the new WSE framework entitled Looking at Our Schools which has become the basis of national school evaluation policy and practice. School evaluations under this framework began in two thousand and four.

Chapter six reports on case studies in twenty-four schools involving both school leaders and teachers. The schools chosen have all recently undergone whole school evaluation and the research was designed to evaluate responses to the system as it operated in practice. The outcome of this research is very mixed. On the one hand the WSE system has proved highly acceptable to both schools and teachers, is regarded as fair and is seen as an aid to improvement. It is also perceived to have direct and indirect benefits. Direct in the sense that it encourages collegial responsibility and cooperation and indirect in that certain practices, for example wider use of ICT and more regular teacher and department meetings, have resulted. The inspection teams are respected for their professionalism and for their sensitivity to the particular organisational realities that they encounter.

On the other hand the research also reconfirms serious weaknesses in the WSE scheme. As already indicated difficult issues such as an appropriate role for parents and pupils have not been addressed and the final evaluation reports, although now published, remain extremely bland and difficult to read for the non-expert. These shortcomings can perhaps reasonably be attributed to the fact that the system is in its infancy and that is perceived that great care must be exercised in order not to damage school and teacher morale or interfere with reasonable professional autonomy. However, the other fundamental flaw identified, namely that theoretically at least the framework is built on a self-evaluation capacity that largely does not exist, continues to undermine the effectiveness and credibility of the system. Developing a self-evaluative capacity in teachers and schools is certainly not something that could be achieved overnight. However it is argued that there is as yet no discernible effort by the DES in this direction.

In contrast it is interesting to note that projects to develop self-evaluation capacity in schools and teachers have become very common in recent years right across Europe and beyond. This is because as suggested earlier in this work virtually every emergent school evaluation system is predicated to a greater or lesser degree on the concept of self-evaluation. Of course what has become clear in virtually all of these cases is that the idea that such capacity exists is dubious at best and moreover that developing it is a difficult and complex process. Chapter seven describes several different approaches in a number of countries to ways in which schools and teachers can be helped to systematically research their own practices and produce rigorous and defensible evidence to support their professional judgements. Such systems vary from external agencies, whether state or other, gathering substantial data from schools and feeding it back in a format suitable for self-evaluation, to more modest projects involving groups of individual teachers or schools being trained in the philosophy of self-evaluation and in research methodologies.

Chapter eight describes such a project recently undertaken in Ireland. It was designed to produce, implement and test an experimental training programme for teachers around the concept and practice of self-evaluation. The project involved practitioners in developing self-evaluative research tools, testing these tools and reporting on their use in an online environment. The chapter describes the gradual development of a three-year programme involving teachers in initial teacher training and more experienced practitioners involved in continuing professional development. The project proceeded through successive stages involving introducing the participants to the concept of self-evaluation, placing them in the context of the newly emerging system of whole-school evaluation in Ireland and introducing them to research methodology. It sought specifically to facilitate the development of contextually appropriate self-evaluative research instruments, the systematic use of these instruments over time, the use of a virtual learning environment to create communities of practice and finally a rigorous evaluation of the extent to which the participants became both committed to and skilled in the art and science of self-evaluation.

In chapter nine the outcomes of this project are evaluated under three main headings. The first two of these deal with emerging capabilities in research design and implementation and teacher responses to their first experiences of using self-evaluation. The third phase was concerned with the participants moving beyond the original project structures and describes their innovations in the field of self-evaluation through the use of a number of case studies.

Project Outcomes and Recommendations

The outcomes of the project described in part three of this study were very positive in the sense that the teachers trained in self-evaluation techniques demonstrated a good understanding of the concept and a willingness to extend it into their own work. The research reported in chapter nine shows teachers seeing the value of developing and using research instruments to analyse their own professional practise. Over time, their skills in this regard grew steadily as did their self-reported feelings of engagement, ownership and implementation of self-evaluation. Moreover, as they grew used to it, teachers in the project developed a sophisticated understanding of the philosophy of self-evaluation, seeing it as a way not only to improve professional practice, but also as a means of collaborating with other stakeholders such as colleagues and pupils. They also saw it as a valuable and relevant way of responding the newly emerging national system of whole-school evaluation. In some cases, teachers involved in the project became very active advocates for self-evaluation in their schools and made extensive efforts to spread the idea among colleagues.

All of this, of course, does not mean that this project has discovered some foolproof way of developing active self-evaluators who will consistently monitor their own practice and convince their schools to adopt an extensive research-engaged focus. Many apparently successful projects, including many around practitioner and action research, have faded away when the impetus for them has been withdrawn. What may be different here is that the impetus in this case, namely the arrival of a school and teacher evaluation system which places emphasis on self-evaluation, is not likely to disappear. In fact, exactly the opposite, in that, as this work demonstrates, WSE may well fall into disrepute in the medium term if a more substantial evidence-based approach to support inspectorial judgements cannot be created. There must be a limited lifespan to any system of evaluation which is, in effect, evidence free, and thus it would appear to be in the interests of the DES to actively, as opposed to rhetorically, support the creation of research engaged schools and teachers.

In this context, the self-evaluation training module described in this book seems a good place to begin. The steps underpinning it, namely introducing the concept of self-evaluation, developing and using research instruments and engaging in collaborative debate, either face to face or through the medium of a virtual learning environment, have been shown to work very effectively. Such training could be built into the education of new teachers quite easily. Serving teachers are more difficult to reach, but a good model already exists in the training of teachers to support development planning in their schools. This could be replicated for the purposes of WSE. In fact, this research makes a strong case to integrate these two processes—whole-school evaluation and school development planning—more closely, and the training of teams to work on both simultaneously would be a good start. Of course, self evaluation in schools requires more than training. It also requires a rationale which teachers buy into and which this project seemed able to provide. It requires an immediate focus or purpose for self-evaluation and this is provided by WSE. Finally, it requires a communications platform or mechanism. For time and resource reasons, this can be problematic in schools. For example, regular teacher meetings other than normal staff meetings are difficult to sustain. However in this regard our project demonstrates the creative possibilities offered by a virtual learning environment.

In summary, it is certainly not beyond the bounds of possibility to engage teachers and schools in self-evaluation and to make schools more research-engaged institutions. Our research has left us in no doubt that schools in other countries, most noticeably England, have developed a capacity to collect, analyse and use data which is invaluable and goes far beyond the present capacity of schools in Ireland. It might be argued that this development was forced on English schools by the unwise early iterations of Ofsted. Nonetheless the range of self-evaluative research now being undertaken in English schools has revolutionised the data and evidence base on which planning, development, decisions and judgements can be based. It is, in our view, perfectly possible to replicate this positive outcome in Ireland without engaging in destructive conflict and without changing the essentially negotiated and collaborative nature of the WSE process as at present structured. Our work shows that teachers and schools come quickly to see the value of research-led practice, provided it is in a context of professional development devoid of threatening elements.

Finally, this work represents a key developmental experiment in the growing field of practitioner and school self-evaluation. The work shows that it is widely accepted virtually everywhere that, to paraphrase Professor John MacBeath, schools must speak for themselves. Virtually every education system, in seeking to make a reality of this proposal, is in the process of designing teacher and school evaluation systems predicated on the concept of self-evaluation. Part two of this work shows that Ireland, in common with so many other countries, is engaged in exactly this process. However from this research it is clear, as it also is in many other countries, that self-evaluation will not happen simply because it is mentioned in documents. There must be a concerted effort to inculcate the values and methodologies of self-evaluation through specific, targeted training programmes during initial teacher education programmes and continuing professional development. Part three of the work describes one such project. It shows beyond doubt that practitioners quickly come to see immense developmental potential and possibilities of empowerment through the process of investigating their own practice. This has also been shown to be true in other similar projects. However, research also shows, unfortunately that these processes are hard to sustain since isolation and lack of ongoing motivation seems to gradually erode early enthusiasm for reflection and self- study. A very promising way of reducing this isolation and providing ongoing motivation may well now be available in the form of virtual learning environments. This project showed that a VLE can reduce or eliminate most of the practical barriers (such as time and opportunity for practitioners to meet) to sustained collaborative practitioner-research. More importantly a VLE can provide an interesting and motivating environment within which working research relationships can develop and flourish.

REFERENCES

Airasian, P.W. and Gullickson, A.R. (1997) *Teacher Self-Evaluation Tool Kit* California: Corwin Press.

Anderson, G. L. (2002) Reflecting on Research for Doctoral Students in Education. *Educational Researcher*, 31 (7) pp 22–25.

Anderson, J. A. (2005) *Accountability in Education*, Education Policy Series, International Academy of Education. Washington, D.C.: International Institute for Educational Planning.

Anton, J. (2005) The 'Estonian Education System'. Paper given at the *Annual Meeting of the Syneva.NET Leonardo da Vinci Programme Project*, Taillin, 23 March.

Apple, M. (2001) *Educating the Right Way* London: Routledge.

Banks, G. (2005) 'Comparing School Systems' Across Australia. Paper given to the *Australia and New Zealand School of Government Conference*, Sydney, 28–29 September. [Online] Available from: *http://www.pc.gov.au/speeches/cs20050928/cs20050928.pdf*. [Accessed May 25th 2006].

Ball, S.J. (2001) Performativities and fabrications The Education Economy: Towards the Perforamtive Society. *IN*: Gleeson, D. and Husbands, C. (eds.) The Performing School (pp 195–206) London: Routledge Falmer

Barzano, G. (2002) School Self-evaluation Towards a European Dimension. *European Journal of Teacher Education*, 25 (1) pp 83–100.

Becta (2006) The Matrix [Online] Available from: http://www.becta.org.uk/leaders/display.cfm?section=11 [Accessed July 31st 2006].

Bjorklund, A., Clarke, M.A., Edin, P., Fredriksson, P. and Kruger, A. (2005) *The Market Comes to Education in Sweden*. New York: Russell Sage Foundation.

Black, C. and Delong, J. D. (eds.) (2002) *Passion in Professional Practice, Action Research in Grand Erie.* Ontario: Grand Erie District School Board.

Bottery, M. (2004) *The Challenges of Educational Leadership.* London: Paul Chapman Publishing.

Boyle, R. (1993) *Making Evaluation Relevant.* Dublin: Institute of Public Administration.

Boyle, R. (1997) Civil Service Reform in the Republic of Ireland. *Public Money and Management,* Jan-March, pp 49–53.

Boyle, R. (2002) A Two-Tiered Approach: Evaluation Practice in the Republic of Ireland. *IN:* Furubo, J. E., Rist, R. C. and Sandahl, R. (eds.) *International Atlas of Evaluation,* pp 261–272. Brunswick, NJ: Transaction Publishers.

Boyle, R. (2006) *Measuring Public Sector Productivity: Lessons from International Experience.* CPMR Discussion Paper 35. Dublin: Institute of Public Administration.

Brennan, M. (1996) *Multiple Professionalisms for Australian Teachers in an Information Age.* New York: American Educational Research Association.

Bringer, J., Halley Johnston, L. and Brackenridge, C. (2006) Using Computer-Assisted Qualitative Data Analysis Software to Develop a Grounded Theory Project. *Field Methods,* Vol. 18 (3) pp 245–266.

Bristol Children and Young People's Services (2005) *Guidance and advice on completing the School-evaluation form (SEF Part A)* [Online] Available from: http://www.bristol-cyps.org.uk/schools/improve/guide.html [Accessed July 31st 2006].

Brophy, J. (ed.) (2004) *Using Video in Teacher Education.* London: Kogan Page.

Brunsson, N. and Jacobsson, B. (2002) *A World of Standards.* Oxford: Oxford University Press.

Carr, W. and Kemmis, S. (1983) *Becoming Critical: Education, Knowledge and Action Research.* London: The Falmer Press.

Caufield, H. (2004) Health Policy and Provision: Public Management and its influence on regulation in England. *IN:* Tingle, J. and Wheet, K. (eds.) *Healthcare Policy: Legal and Professional Issues* London: Butterworth Heinemann.

CERI (1995) *Schools Under Scrutiny: Strategies for the Evaluation of School Performance.* Paris: OECD.

Chevalier, A., Dolton, P. and Levacic, R. (2004) 'School Equality and Effectiveness', Working Paper 04/10, Department of Economics. Dublin: University College Dublin.

Christie, D. (2003) Competencies, Benchmarks and Standards in Teaching. *IN:* Byrce, T. and Humes, W. (eds.) *Scottish Education,* pp 952–963. Edinburgh: Edinburgh University Press.

Clarke, J., Gewirtz, S. and McLaughlin, E. (2000) (eds.) *New Managerialism, New Welfare?* London: Sage.

Cochrane-Smith, M. (2005a). Introduction to the issue: The politics of teacher education. *Journal. of Teacher Education,* 56(3)pp179–180.

Cochrane-Smith, M. (2005b) 'The Competencies Approach to Teacher Professional Development'. Paper given at the *Standing Conference on Teacher Education North and South,* St Patrick's College, Dublin, 13 June.

Coolahan, J. (2005) 'The Operational Environment for Future Planning in Teacher Education: OECD and EU Initiatives'. Paper given at the *Standing Conference on Teacher Education North and South,* St Patrick's College, Dublin, 13 June.

Cronbach, L. J. (1975) Beyond the Two Disciplines of Scientific Psychology. *American Psychologist,* 30 pp 116–127.

Cullingford, C. (ed.) (1999) *An Inspector Calls: OFSTED and its effects on School Standards.* London: Kogan Page.

Darling-Hammond, L. (1996) The quiet revolution: rethinking teacher development. *Educational Leadership,* 53(6) pp 4–10.

Darling-Hammond, L. and Younges, P. (2002) Defining 'Highly Qualified Teachers': What does 'Scientifically-Based Research' Actually Tell Us? *Educational Researcher,* 31(9) pp 13–25.

De Lissovoy, N. and McLaren, P. (2003) Educational Accountability and the Violence of Capital: A Marxist Reading. *Journal of Educational Policy,* 18(2) pp 131–143.

Denzin, N.K. & Lincoln, Y.S. (Eds.) (2000) Handbook of Qualitative Research London: Sage Publications.

Department of Education and Science, Ireland (1999a) *Whole School Evaluation.* Dublin: DES.

Department of Education and Science, Ireland (1999b) *School Development Planning Guidelines.* Dublin: DES.

Department of Education and Science, Ireland (2000a) *Evaluating Quality in School Education at Second Level.* Dublin: DES.

Department of Education and Science, Ireland (2000b) *Whole School Evaluation: Draft Criteria for the Evaluation of Schools.* Dublin: DES.

Department of Education and Science, Ireland (2002c) *Procedure for Review of Inspections on Schools and Teachers under Section 13(9) of the Education Act 1998.* Dublin: DES.

Department of Education and Science, Ireland (2003a) *Looking at Our School, an aid to self-evaluation in primary schools.* Dublin: DES.

Department of Education and Science, Ireland (2003b) *Looking at Our School, an aid to self-evaluation in second level schools.* Dublin: DES.

Department of Education and Science, Ireland (2003 c) *Professional Code of Practice on Evaluation and Reporting for the Inspectorate.* Dublin: DES.

Department of Education and Science, Ireland (2004) *A Guide to Subject Inspection at Second Level.* Dublin: DES.

Department of Education and Science, Ireland (2005) *Customer Survey.* Dublin: DES.

Department of Education and Science, Ireland (2006a) *A Guide to Whole School Evaluation in Post-Primary Schools.* Dublin: DES.

Department of Education and Science, Ireland (2006b) *A Guide to Whole School Evaluation in Primary Schools.* Dublin: DES.

Department of Education and Science, Ireland (2006c) *Publication of School Inspection Reports, Guidelines.* Dublin: DES.

Department of Education and Science, Ireland (2006d) *An Evaluation of Planning in Thirty Primary Schools.* Dublin: DES.

Department of Education and Science. (Homepage). [Online]. Available from: http://www.education.ie [Accessed May 12th 2006].

Developing European Schools into Learning Organisations (DESLO) (Homepage)[Online]. Available from: http://www.progettodeslo.it/ [Accessed August 16th 2006].

Devine, D. and Swan, D. (1997) *The International School Effectiveness Project: the Irish Study.* Dublin: University College Dublin.

Diaz Barriga, A. (2003) Curriculum Research: Evaluation and Outlook in Mexico. *IN:* Pinar, W.F. (ed.) *International Handbook of Curriculum Research,* pp 443–456. New Jersey: Lawrence Erlbaum.

Earley, P. (ed.) (1998) *School Improvement After Inspection?* London: PCP Publishing.

Eisner, E. (1991) *The Enlightened Eye*. New York: Macmillan.

Eisner, E. (1999) The Uses and Limits of Performance Assessment'.*Phi Delta Kappan*, 80,pp 658–60.

Elliott, J. (1991) *Action Research for Educational Change*. Buckingham: Open University Press.

Elliott, J. (1995) Self Evaluation and Teacher Competence. *Irish Educational Studies*, 14,pp 1–12.

Elliott, J. (1998) *The Curriculum Experiment: Meeting the Challenge of Social Change*. Milton Keynes: Open University Press.

Elliott, J. (2004) 'Making Evidence-Based Practice Educational'. *IN*: Thomas,G. and Pring,R. (eds.) *Evidence-Based Practice in Education*. pp 164–186. Maidenhead: Open University Press.

Elmore, R. F. and Fuhrman, S. H. (2001) Research Finds the False Assumption of Accountability. *Educational Digest*, 67 pp 1–9.

European Commission (1997) *Evaluating Quality in Schools, a Practical Guide to Self Evaluation*. Brussels: European Commission.

European Commission (2003) *Berlin Communiqué–Realising the European Higher Education Area*. A Communiqué of the Conference of Ministers responsible for Higher Education, 19 September.

European Commission (2004) *Evaluation of Schools Providing Compulsory Education in Europe*. Brussels: European Commission.

The European Parliament and The Council of the European Union (2001) Recommendation of the European Parliament and of the Council of 12 February 2001 on European cooperation in quality evaluation in school education [Online] Available from: http://europa.eu.int/smartapi/cgi/sga_doc?smartapi!celexapi!prod!CELEXnumdoc&lg=EN& numdoc=32001H0166&model=guichett [Accessed July 31, 2006].

Eurydice (2004) *Evaluation of Schools providing Compulsory Education in Europe*. Brussels: European Commission.

Evening Herald (22 June, 2006: 1)

Fitz-Gibbon, C. T. (1995) OFSTED, SCHMOFSTED. *IN*: Brighouse,T. and Moon,B. (eds.) *School Inspection*, pp 98–104. London: Pitman Publishing.

Fitz-Gibbon, C. T. (1996) *Monitoring Education Indicators, Quality and Effectiveness*. London: Cassell.

Fitz-Gibbon, C. T. (1998) Can OFSTED Stay Afloat? *Managing Schools*, 6 pp 22–26.

Fitz-Gibbon, C. T. (1999) OFSTED is inaccurate and damaging: how did we let it happen? *Forum*, 41(1) pp 14–17.

Fitz-Gibbon, C. T. (2000) 'Value-added for those who despair: Research Methods Matter' *Vernon Wall lecture for the annual meeting of the Education Section of the British Psychological Society* Saturday 4th November 2000 [Online] Available from http://www.cemcentre.org/Documents/ CEM/publications/downloads/CEMWeb015%20Vernon%20Wall%20Lecture%2026%20Fe b%202001%20C%20T%20Fitz-Gibbon.pdf [Accessed on November 20th 2006]

Fitz-Gibbon, C. T. (2001) The Future of Inspection, *Education Review*,14(2) pp 83–85.

Flynn, C (2006) 'The attractiveness of School Leaders Role' Paper presented at the *Leadership Development for Schools Consultative Seminar*. Dublin, October 10th .

Fullan, M. (1993) *Change Forces: Probing the Depths of Educational Reform*. London: Falmer.

Fullan, M. (2006) *Quality Leadership- Quality Learning, proof beyond reasonable doubt*. Dublin: Irish Primary Principals Network.

Gaden, G. (1983) The case for specialization. *Irish Educational Studies*, 3 pp47–60.

Gallagher, D. J. (2004) Educational Research, Philosophical Orthodoxy and Unfulfilled Promises: The Quandry of Traditional Research in US Special Education. *IN*: Thomas,G. and Pring,R. (eds.) *Evidence-Based Practice in Education*. pp119–132. Maidenhead: Open University Press.

Giddins, A. (2004) *Sociology*, 4ᵗʰ Ed. London: Policy Press.

Gorard, S. with Taylor, C. (2004) *Combining Methods in Educational and Social Research*. Berkshire OUP/McGraw Hill.

Government of Ireland (1998) *Education Act*. Dublin: Stationery Office.

Halnan,A.C., Darby, J. and Conole, G.(2006) *South East Grid for Learning : Learning Platform Project Report School of Education, Southampton University*. [Online] Available from: www.segfl.org.uk/library/1141913118/soton_learning_platform_project_report.doc [Accessed July 31st 2006]

Hammersly, M. (2004) Some questions about evidenced-based practice in education. *IN*: Thomas, G. and Pring, R. (eds.) *Evidence-based practice in Education*. pp 133–149. Maidenhead: Open University Press.

Hannan, D., Smyth, E., McCullagh, J., O'Leary, R. and McMahon, D. (1996) *Co-Education and Gender Equality, Exam Performance, Stress and Personal Development*. Dublin: Economic and Social Research Institute.

Hansson, F. (2006) Organizational Use of Evaluations: Governance and Control in Research Evaluation. *Evaluation*, 12(2) pp 159–178.

Harasim, L. (1993). Networlds: Networks as social space. *IN*: Harasim, L. (ed.) *Global Networks: Computers and international communication*. Cambridge: MIT Press.

Hargreaves, A. (1994) *Changing Teachers, Changing Times: Teachers' Work and Culture in the Postmodern Age*. London: Cassell.

Hargreaves, A. (2006) 'Leadership and Community.' Paper given at the *Annual Conference of the Irish Inspectorate*, Galway January 12th.

Hargreaves, D. (1997) In Defence of Research for Evidence-Based Teaching. A Rejoinder to Martin Hammersly. *British Educational Research Journal*, 23 (4) pp 410–433.

Hargreaves, D. (1999) Revitalising Educational Research: Lessons from the past and proposals for the future. *Cambridge Journal of Education*, 29 (2), pp 106–120.

Hargreaves, D. and Hopkins, D. (1993) School Effectiveness, School Improvement and Development Planning *IN*: Preedy,M. (ed.) *Managing the Effective School*, pp 229–41. London: Open University in association with Paul Chapman.

Haug, P. and Schwandt, T. (2003) *Evaluating Educational Reforms, Scandinavian Perspectives*. Connecticut: Information Age Publishing.

HayGroup (Homepage). [Online] Available from: http://www.haygroup.co.uk/HGS/Online_Learning/index.asp?GoTo=HGS [Accessed 30 August 2006].

Heywood Metz, M. and Page. R. N. (2002) The Uses of Practitioner Research and Status Issues in Educational Research–Reply to Gary Anderson. *Educational Researcher*, 31 (7) pp 26–8.

Hofman, R.H., Dukstra, N.J. and Adriaan Hofman, W.H. (2005) School Self-evaluation instruments: An assessment framework. *International Journal of Leadership in Education*, 8(3),pp253–272

Hopkins, D., Ainscow, M. and West, M. (1994) *School Improvement in an Era of Change*. London: Cassell.

Hopkins, D. and Lagerweij, N. (1996), 'The school improvement knowledge base'. *IN*: Reynolds, D., Bollen, R., Creemers, B., Hopkins, D., Stoll, L. and Lagerweij, N. (eds.) *Making Good Schools: Linking School Effectiveness and School Improvement*, pp. 59–93. London: Routledge.

Irish Times (23 June, 2006: 8)

ISOC Socrates Project Database (Homepage)[Online]. Available from: http://www.isoc.siu.no/ isocii.nsf [Accessed July 31st 2006].

Johannesson, I. S., Lindblad, S. and Simola, H. (2002) An Inevitable Progress? Educational Restructuring in Finland, Iceland and Sweden at the Turn of the Millenium. *Scandinavian Journal of Educational Research*, 46 (3) pp 325–338.

Joyce, B. and Showers, B. (2002) *Student Achievement Through Staff Development: Fundamentals for School Renewal*. Alexandra, VA: Association for Supervision and Curriculum Development.

Kincheloe, J. L. (2004) *Teachers as Researchers*. London: Routledge Taylor and Francis Group.

Kushner, S. (2000) *Personalizing Evaluation*. London: Sage.

Lave, J. and Wenger, E. (1991) *Situated Learning. Legitimate peripheral participation*. Cambridge: University of Cambridge Press

Leithwood, K., Aitken, R. and Janizi, D. (2001) *Making Schools Smarter: a System for Monitoring School and District Progress*. Thousand Oaks, CA: Corwin Press.

Leithwood, K., Seashore-Lewis K., Anderson, S. and Wahlstrom, K. (2004) *How Leadership Influences Student Learning*. New York: Wallace Foundation.

Lenihan, H., Hart, M. and Roper, S. (2005) Developing an Evaluative Framework for Industrial Policy in Ireland: Fulfilling the Audit Trail, or An Aid to Policy Development. *Economic and Social Research Institute Quarterly Economic Commentary*. Summer, pp 69–85.

Lisi, P., Neeve, G. and Davidsdottir, S. (2005). 'Empowering Leadership Practices in the Implementation of School Self-Evaluation in Iceland.' Paper given at the *INTERLEARN* 2005 conference, Helsinki, Finland, 1 December.

Livingston, K. and McCall, J. (2005) Evaluation: Judgemental or Developmental?. *European Journal of Teacher Education*, 28 (2) June, pp 165–178.

Lortie, D. (1975) *Schoolteacher: A Sociological Study*. Chicago: University of Chicago Press.

Lynch K. and O'Riordan, C. (1996) *Social Class, Inequality and Higher Education: Barriers to Equality of Access and Participation among School Leavers*. Dublin: University College Dublin.

MacBeath, J (1999) *Schools Must Speak for Themselves : The case for School Self-Evaluation* London:Routledge-Falmer.

MacBeath, J. (2003) *The Self-Evaluation File*. Glasgow: Learning Files Scotland.

MacBeath, J. (2004) International Comparisons. *Education Journal*, 76 pp21 [Online] Available from: http://www.educationpublishing.com/index.html [Accessed 30th June 2006].

MacBeath, J. (2005) *Self-Evaluation: Models, Tools and Examples of Practice* [Online] Available from: http://www.ncsl.org.uk/media/93C/D5/self-evaluation-models-tools-and-examples-of-practice.pdf [Accessed July 31 2006].

MacBeath, J. (2006) New Relationships for Old Inspection and self evaluation in England and Hong Kong. *International Studies in Educational Administration*, 34(2) pp2–18.

MacBeath, J., Boyd, B., Rand, J and Bell, S. (1996) Schools Speak for themselves [Online]

Available from: http://www.teachers.org.uk/resources/pdf/schools.pdf [Accessed July 31st 2006].

MacBeath, J., Meuret, D., Schratz, M. and Jakobssen, L.B. (1999) *Pilot Project On Quality Evaluation: Final Report*. Brussels: European Commission.

MacBeath, J with Schratz, M., Meuret, D. and Jakobssen, L. (2000) *Self-Evaluation in European Schools: A Story of Change*. London: Routledge-Falmer.

MacBeath, J. and McGlynn, A. (2002) *Self-Evaluation, What's in it for schools?* London:Routledge-Falmer.

MacIntyre, A. (1981) *After Virtue: A Study in Moral Theory*. London: Duckworth

MacMillan, Katie & Koenig, Thomas (2004). The Wow Factor: Preconceptions and Expectations for Data Analysis Software in Qualitative Research. *Social Science Computer Review*, 22(2) pp179–186.

Matus, C., & McCarthy,C. (2003) The triumph of multiplicity and the carnival of difference, curriculum dilemmas in the age of postcolonialism and globalization. *IN*: Pinar, W.F. (ed) *International Handbook of Curriculum Research*. pp73–82. Mahwah, NJ: Lawrence Erlbaum and Associates.

McAvoy, D. (2004) The Future of Inspection, *Education Journal*, 76 :19 [Online] Available from: http://www.educationpublishing.com/index.html [Accessed June 30th 2006]

McDonald, B. (1996) How Education Became Nobody's Business. *Cambridge Journal of Education*, 28(2) pp 241–249.

McIntyre,D., McCleod, G. and Griffiths, R. (1977) *Investigations of Microteaching*. London: Croom Helm.

McNamara, G. and O'Hara, J. (2001) Process and Product Issues in the Evaluation of School Development Planning. *Evaluation*, 7(3) pp 99–109.

McNamara,G., O'Hara,J and Ni Ainglis, B. (2002). Whole School Evaluation and School Development Planning: an Analysis of recent Initiatives in Ireland. *Educational Management Administration And Leadership*, 25 (2) pp201–211.

McNamara, G. and O'Hara J. (2004) Trusting the Teacher: Evaluating Educational Innovation. *Evaluation*, 10 (4) pp 463–474.

McNamara, G. and Kenny,A. (2006) 'Quality Evaluation: Policy, theory and practice in the education sector.' Paper given at the *Joint International Conference of the European Evaluation Society and the UK Evaluation Society* October 2006

McNiff, J. (with J. Whitehead) (2002a) *Action Research in Practice*. London: Routledge Falmer.

McNiff, J. (2002b) 'Evaluating Information and Communications Technology: New ways of evaluating new ways of knowing.' Paper presented to the *Special Interest Group, Research on Evaluation, at the American Educational Research Association Annual Meeting*, New Orleans, April 1–5. [Online] Available from: www.jeanmcniff.com [Accessed 23rd October 2006].

Meuret, D. and Morlaix, S. (2003) Conditions of Success of a School's Self-Evaluation: Some Lessons of an European Experience. *School Effectiveness and School Improvement*, 14(1), pp 53–71.

Milliband, D. (2004) 'Personalised Learning: Building a New Relationship with Schools' Speech delivered to *North of England Education Conference*, Belfast, 8th January 2004 [Online] Available from: http://publications.teachernet.gov.uk/eOrderingDownload/personalised-learning.pdf [Accessed 30 October 2006].

Moos, L. (2003) *Educational Leadership: Understanding and Developing Practice*. Copenhagen: Danmarks Paedagogiske Verlag.

Mortimore, P., Sammons, P., Stoll, L. and Elob, R. (1988) *School Matters: the Junior Years*. London: Open Books.

National College for School Leadership (NCSL) (Homepage)[Online]. Available from: http://www.ncsl.org.uk/ [Accessed July 31st 2006].

Neave, G. (1998) The evaluative state reconsidered. *European Journal of Education*, 33(3) pp. 265–284.

Neil, P., McEwan, A., Carlisle, K. and Knipe, D. (2001) The self-evaluating school- a case study of a special school. *British Journal of Special Education*, 28 (4) pp 174–181

Nevo, D. (1995) *School-Based Evaluation: A Dialogue for School Improvement*. Oxford: Pergamon.

Nevo, D. (2002). *School-Based Evaluation: An International Perspective*. Oxford: Elsevier Science.

Nevo, D. (2006) Evaluation in Education IN: Shaw, I. Greene, J. and Mark,M. (eds.) *The SAGE Handbook of Evaluation*. London:Sage

Norton Grubb, W. (1999) Improvement or Control–a U.S. View of English Inspection. *IN*: Cullingford, C. (ed.) *An Inspector Calls*. pp 70–86. London: Kogan Page.

NVIVO 7 (Homepage) [Online] Available from: http://www.qsrinternational.com/products/pro-ductoverview/NVivo_7.htm [Accessed 20th July 2006].

O'Brien, D. (2006) The End of Ideology. *Irish Times*, 31 July: 12.

O'Dalaigh, C. (2000) School Development Planning: A Department of Education and Science Perspective. *IN*: Furlong,C. and Monaghan,L. (eds.) *School Culture and Ethos: Cracking the Code*. pp 141–51. Dublin: Marino Institute of Education.

OECD (2005) *Teachers Matter: Attracting, Developing and Retaining Effective Teachers*. Paris: OECD

Ofsted (1998) *Proposals for a Differential System of School Inspection*. London: HMSO.

Ofsted (2000) *The Handbook for the Inspection of Schools*. London: OFSTED.

Ofsted (2004) *A New Relationship with Schools* [Online] Available from: http://www.ofsted.gov.uk/publications/index.cfm?fuseaction=pubs.summary&id=3666 [Accessed July 31st 2006].

Ofsted (2005) Self-evaluation and the Self-Evaluation form in OFSTED Direct Issue 2 [Online] Available from: http://www.ofsted.gov.uk/ofsteddirect/index.cfm?fuseaction=displayarticle&type=4&articleid=28&issueno=2 [Accessed July 31, 2006].

Ofsted (2006) Self Evaluation form for Secondary Schools (With and Without Sixth Forms) Middle Schools (Deemed Secondary) [Online] Available from: http://www.ofsted.gov.uk/assets/Internet_Content/Shared_Content/Files/sef_secondary.pdf [Accessed 30 August 2006].

O'Hara, J. and McNamara, G. (1999) Evaluation: Business or Vocation?. *Evaluation*, 5(4) pp 497–503.

O'Neill, N. (2002) *A Question of Trust*. Cambridge: Cambridge University Trust.

O'Toole, F. (2000) Looking at the Teachers' Strike. *Education and Living*, 10 October: 2–3. Dublin: Irish Times.

Pearson, L. C. Moomaw, W. (2005) The Relationship between Teacher Autonomy and Stress, Work Satisfaction, Empowerment, and Professionalism. *Educational Research Quarterly*, 29 (1) pp37–53.

Peters, R.S. (1973) *Authority, Responsibility and Education*. London: Allyn and Unwin.

Pinar, W.F. (ed.) (2003) *International Handbook of Curriculum Research*. New Jersey: Lawrence Erlbaum.

Power, M. (1997) *The Audit Society: Rituals of Verification*. Oxford: Oxford University Press.

Pring, R. (2004) Conclusion: Evidence-Based Policy and Practice. *IN*: Thomas,G. and Pring, R. (eds.) *Evidence-Based Practice in Education*. pp 201–213. Maidenhead: Open University Press.

Rafaeli, S. Ravid, G. Soroka, V. (2004) 'De-lurking in virtual communities: a social communication network approach to measuring the effects of social and cultural capital' Paper Presented at *System Sciences, 2004*. Proceedings of the 37th Annual Hawaii International Conference 5–8 Jan. 2004 [Online] Available from: http://ieeexplore.ieee.org/xpl/freeabs_all.jsp?arnumber=1265478 [Accessed August 23rd 2006].

Reece, M. and Lockee, B. (2005) Improving Training Outcomes through Blended Learning. *Journal of Asynchronous Learning Networks*. 9 (4), pp 1–11 [Online] Available from: http://www.sloan-c.org/publications/jaln/v9n4/v9n4_reece.asp [Accessed June 20th 2006].

Rosenholtz, S. (1989) *Teachers' Workplace: The Social Organisation of Schools*. New York: Longman.

Rothery, A. (2004) 'VLEs and Blended Learning.' A discussion paper based on TLIG meetings held during 2004 Universities and Colleges Information Systems Association Teaching, Learning and Information Group [Online] Available from: www.ucisa.ac.uk/groups/tlig/docs/BlendedLearningDiscussion.pdf [Accessed October 3rd 2006]

Ruane, F. (2004) Creating a Culture of Evaluation–Getting From Rhetoric to Possibility. Paper given at *The Irish Evaluation Network, Inaugural Annual Conference*, Dublin City University, 24 September.

Rudd, P. and Davies, D. (2000) 'Evaluating School Self Evaluation'. Paper given at the *British Educational Research Association Conference*, Cardiff University, 7–10 Sept [Online] Available from: http://www.leeds.ac.uk/educol/documents/00001641.htm [Accessed May 11th 2006].

Sachs, J. (2003) *The Activist Teaching Profession*. Buckingham: Oxford University Press.

Saunders, L. (1999) Who or What Is School Self-Evaluation For? *School Effectiveness and School Improvement*, 10(4),pp 414–421.

Sanders, J. R. and Greaney, V. (1986) Self-Evaluation of the Irish primary school. *Oideas*, 29,pp 41–51.

Scheerens, J. (2002). School Self-Evaluation: Origins, Definition, Approaches, Methods and Implementation *IN*: Nevo, D. *School-Based Evaluation: An International Perspective*. pp 35–73. Oxford: Elsevier Science.

Scheerens, J.,van Amlelsvoort, H. and Sonohoe, C. (1999) Aspects of the Organizational and Political Context of School Evaluation in Four European Countries. *Studies in Educational Evaluation*, 25,pp 79–108.

Scheerens, J. and Bosker R. (1997) *The Foundation of Educational Effectiveness*. Oxford: Pergamon.

Schmoker, M. (1999) *Results: the Key to Continuous School Improvement*. Alexandra, VA: School for Supervision and Curriculum Development.

Schollaert, R. (ed.) (2000) *Effective Staff Development, an Evaluation Manual*. Leuven: Garant.

Schollaert, R. (ed.) (2002) *In Search of the Treasure Within, Towards Schools as Learning Organisations*. Leuven: Garant.

School Centre.net (Homepage). [Online] Available from: http://www.skillsfactory.co.uk/school-centre_net/default.asp?css=1 [Accessed 30 August 2006].

Schon, D. A. (1983) *The Reflective Practitioner. How Professionals Think in Action*. New York: Basic Books.

Schon, D. A. (1987) *Educating the Reflective Practitioner*. CA: Jossey Bass.

Schon, D. A. (1995) The New Scholarship Requires a New Epistemology. *Change*. (27)6, pp27–34.

Schwartz, C. and Struhkamp, G. (2004) 'Does Evaluation Build or Destroy Trust?' Paper given at the 6*th* *Conference of the European Evaluation Society*. Berlin, 30 September-2 October.

Seale, C. (2005) 'Using Computers to Analyse Qualitative Data'. *IN:* Silverman, D. *Doing Qualitative Research*, 2*nd* ed. pp. 188–206. London: Sage.

Shadish, W. R., Chagon-Muscoso and Sanchez, J. (2005) Evidence-Based Decision Making: Earmarking Systematic Reviews of Program Evaluation Results in Europe. *Evaluation*, 11(3), pp 95–109.

Silverman, D. (ed.) 2004) *Qualitative Research Theory, Method and Practice*. London: Sage.

Silverman, D (2005) *Doing Qualitative Research*. London: Sage

Simons, H. (2002) School Self-Evaluation in a Democracy. *IN:* Nevo, D. (ed.) *School-Based Evaluation: An International Perspective*. pp 17–34. Oxford: Elsevier Science.

Simons, H. (2004) Utilizing Evaluation Evidence to Enhance Professional Practice. *Evaluation*, 10(4) pp 410–429.

Slattery, P. (2003) Hermeneutics, Subjectivity and Aesthetics: Internationalising the Interpretative Process in US Curriculum Research. *IN:* Pinar, W.F. (ed.) *International Handbook of Curriculum Research*, pp 651–666. New Jersey: Lawrence Erlbaum.

Slavin, R.E. (2002) Evidence-Based Education Policies: Transforming Educational Practice and Research. *Educational Researcher*.31(7), pp 15–21.

Smith, D. G. (2003) 'Curriculum and Teaching Face Globalisation?' *IN:* W. F. Pinar (ed.) *International Handbook of Curriculum Research*. pp 35–52. New Jersey, Lawrence Erlbaum.

Smyth E. (1999) *Do Schools Differ?* Dublin: Economic and Social Research Institute.

Söderberg, S. (2004) 'School Evaluation in Sweden.' Paper presented at the 6*th* *Conference of the European Evaluation Society*. Berlin, 30 September to 2 October.

Special Edition, British Educational Research Journal, Sept. 2001.

SPSS (Homepage) 'Supporting Excellence in Education' [Online] Available from: http://www.spss.com/ [Accessed 20*th* July 2006].

Stenhouse, L. (1975) *An Introduction to Curriculum Research and Development*. London: Heinemann Educational Books.

Stern, E. (2002) 'Making Evaluation Useful and Usable.' Presentation to the *Irish Evaluation Network*, Dublin, 10 November.

Stevenson, H. (2006) 'The Research Engaged School.' Paper given at annual *British Educational Leadership Management and Administration Society Conference* Aston University Conference October 7*th*-8*th.*

Stoll, L. and Fink, D. (1996) *Changing Our Schools*. Buckingham: Open University Press.

Sugrue, C. (1997) *Complexities of Teaching: Child-Centered Perspectives*. London: Falmer.

Sugrue, C. (1999) Primary Principals' Perspectives on Whole-School Evaluation. *Irish Journal of Education*, 10 (2), pp 15–31.

Sugrue, C. (ed.) (2004) *Curriculum and Ideology: Irish Experiences, International Perspectives*. Dublin: Liffey Press.

Swaffield, S. and MacBeath, J. (2005) School self-evaluation and the roles of a critical friend. *Cambridge Journal of Education*, 35(2), pp 239–252.

Teddie, C. and Springfield, S. (1993) *Schools Make a Difference: Lessons Learned from a Ten-Year Study of School Effectiveness*. New York: Teachers College Press.

Thomas, G. and Pring, R. (eds.) (2004) *Evidence-Based Practice in Education*. Maidenhead: Open University Press.

Thrupp, M. and Wilmot, R. (2003) *Education Management in Managerialist Times*. Maidenhead: Open University Press.

Tymms, P. (1999) *Baseline Assessment and Monitoring in Primary Schools*. London: David Fulton.

Tymms, P. and Coe, R. (2003) Celebration of the Success of Distributed Research with Schools: the CEM Centre Durham. *British Educational Research Journal*, 29 (5) pp 639–653.

Tymms, P. and Dean, C. (2004) *Value Added in the Primary School League Tables, A Report for the National Association of Head Teachers*. Durham: CEM Centre, University of Durham

Vaughan, N., & Garrison, D. R. (2005) Creating cognitive presence in a blended faculty development community. *Internet and Higher Education*, 8(1) pp 1–12

Weiss, C. (1998) *Evaluation: Methods for Studying Programmes and Policies*, 2nd ed. Englewood Cliffs, NJ: Prentice Hall.

Weitzman, E A. (2000) Software and Qualitative Research. *IN*: Norman K. Denzin, & Yvonna S. Lincoln (eds.), *Handbook of Qualitative Research*. pp.803–820. London: Sage Publications

White, J. (ed.) (2004) *Rethinking the School Curriculum, Values, Aims and Purposes*. London: Routledge Falmer.

Whitty, G. (2002) *Making Sense of Education Policy*. London: Paul Chapman Publishing.

Whitty, G., Power, S. and Halpin, D. (1998) *Devolution and Choice in Education*. Buckingham: Open University Press.

Winch, C. (2001), Towards a Non-Punitive School Inspection Regime. *Journal of Philosophy of Education*. 35 (4) pp 684–694.

Wolf, L. and Craig, D. (2004) Tiptoe Through the Plateaus: Personal Reflections on Interviews with Andy Hargreaves and Molly Quinn. *Journal of Curriculum and Pedagogy*, Vol. 1 (1) pp 131–153.

Woodhead, C. (2002) *Class War*. London: Little Brown.

Zepeda, S. (2003) *Instructional Leadership for School Improvement*. Larchmont, NY: Eye on Education.

INDEX

Irish Studies

Edited by Robert Mahony

The popularity of Irish Studies among both students and scholars has grown very markedly in the 1980s and 1990s, extending well beyond Ireland. This series is designed to serve and foster that interest. Currently featuring works in Irish history and literature, this interdisciplinary series will broaden its scholarly range in the future to include political and cultural studies generally.

For further information, or the submission of manuscripts, please contact:

> Peter Lang Publishing
> Acquisitions Department
> 29 Broadway, 18th floor
> New York, New York 10006

To order other books in this series, please contact our Customer Service Department:

> (800) 770-LANG (within the U.S.)
> (212) 647-7707

Or browse online by series:

> www.peterlang.com